Balance of Payments Adjustment

Balance of Payments Adjustment

Macro Facets of International Finance Revisited

EDITED BY

Augustine C. Arize
Theologos Homer Bonitsis
Ioannis N. Kallianiotis
Krishna M. Kasibhatla
John Malindretos

Contributions in Economics and
Economic History, Number 203

GREENWOOD PRESS
Westport, Connecticut • London

Library of Congress Cataloging-in-Publication Data

Balance of payments adjustment : macro facets of international
  finance revisited / edited by Augustine C. Arize . . . [et al.].
      p.   cm.—(Contributions in economics and economic history,
  ISSN 0084–9235 ; no. 203)
    Includes bibliographical references and index.
    ISBN 0–313–30826–8 (alk. paper)
    1. Balance of payments. 2. Keynesian economics. 3. Chicago
  school of economics. I. Arize, Augustine C. II. Series.
  HG3882.K49   2000
  382'.17—dc21   98–15330

British Library Cataloguing in Publication Data is available.

Library of Congress Catalog Card Number: 98–15330
ISBN: 0–313–30826–8
ISSN: 0084–9235

First published in 2000

Greenwood Press, 88 Post Road West, Westport, CT 06881
An imprint of Greenwood Publishing Group, Inc.
www.greenwood.com

Printed in the United States of America

The paper used in this book complies with the
Permanent Paper Standard issued by the National
Information Standards Organization (Z39.48–1984).

P

Contents

Tables and Figures

TABLES

FIGURES

Introduction

The traditional approach to international adjustment was developed in this century by theorists such as Alexander (1952), Keynes (1929), Machlup (1943), Meade (1951), Robinson (1947) and others. Because of the euphoria that resulted after World War II as a consequence of the policy recommendations of J. M. Keynes, the traditional approach was called Keynesian. However, even though many of its elements are Keynesian, the approach also differs from Keynes's framework in certain important aspects, as discussed by Malindretos (1984).

By the late 1970s a few analysts, like Frenkel, Johnson and Mundell, had established an alternative to the traditional theory, which they named the Monetary approach to the balance of payments. They expostulate that the Monetary approach is, in fact, a theory that has existed since the time of David Hume. They feel that their theory is a replacement of the Traditional approach, which they view as an insufficient theory.

This book undertakes an elaborate analysis of the two approaches to international adjustment. We divide the book into five parts. Part I looks at the two theories from a theoretical viewpoint. Chapter 1, by Ghosh and Duteil, discusses the adjustment mechanism of the Traditional approach in the case of fixed exchange rates and describes both the comparative statics and the dynamics of that adjustment. Chapter 2, by Tsanacas, Kasibhatla and Malindretos, examines the Monetary approach to international adjustment. The authors first examine the assumptions of this view: that there is full employment, the law of one price holds true, money forces essentially determine the balance of payments and general equilibrium exists. Next, the authors analyze how these axioms determine the results of the theory. The third issue on which they expound involves several qualifications of the view and the way in which they intertwine in the core theory.

Part II addresses the empirical evidence for the two theories. Chapter 3, by Englander, Johnson and Malindretos, discusses empirical evidence for the traditional approach to the capital account and points out that the basic determinants are the relative amounts of wealth, stocks of money, income and alterations of capital barriers among the nations. In Chapter 4, Arize, Grivoyannis, Kallianiotis and Lawson survey the empirical evidence for adjustment in the Traditional approach. They expound on the different types of models that exist: single equation, simultaneous equation and world trade. Generally, the authors find that the Marshall–Lerner condition holds as far as the price elasticities of imports and exports are concerned. Next, the authors postulate that there are mainly two factors influencing the accounts: international competitiveness and relative incomes between the deficit and surplus nations. The critical questions for those two factors are the sizes and signs of their elasticities of demand, the stability of their coefficients and, finally, the quickness of response of the trade balance to changes in the two. The sign of international competitiveness is appropriate (i.e., it relates positively to the trade balance alteration). The size of the price elasticity of demand varies, sometimes substantially, from study to study, but the consensus is that trade is sensitive to price alterations and that the sum of the absolute values of the price elasticity of demand of exports and imports exceeds 1. The evidence on the stability of the price elasticity of demand is somewhat ambivalent, but the preponderance indicates that there is instability. As far as the speed of adjustment goes, the evidence is that trade responds to international competitiveness but with a lag, which can be as long as a few years. The second factor influencing trade flows is the relative incomes between the deficit nation and foreign nations. The majority of the evidence indicates that the income elasticity of demand for the focus nation is positive. Moreover, the great majority of the studies show that the income import elasticity of demand alters intertemporally. Finally, the evidence supports a quick response of trade to income changes; in fact, it is quicker than the response to changes in international competitiveness.

Chapter 5, on the empirical evidence for the Monetary approach, gives an array of models. Essentially, however, all the models specify that international reserves are a function of the domestic component of high-powered money, the price level, the interest rate and the income level of the nation. The domestic component elasticity of international reserves should be about negative unity. That is, ideally, for every 1 percentage creation of high-powered money domestically, 1 percentage should flow abroad through the international accounts. The income elasticity of international reserves should also have a value of $+1$. The interest elasticity of international reserves should be between 0 and 1 and should be negative. The reason, according to the Monetary approach, is that any increase (decrease) in the domestic interest rates cause investors domestically and abroad to desire to hold fewer (more) money balances and correspondingly more (fewer) interest-earning securities. They can do so by exporting (importing) money and importing (exporting) interest-earning securities. Finally, the Monetary approach states that the price elasticity of international reserves is positive and less than unity. Thus, if, domestically, price levels rise (fall), international reserves will increase (decrease).

The authors contend that even though there are many tests that, basically, give rather impressive support to the predictions of the Monetary approach, there are econometric problems with those tests. First, there is a simultaneity of equations bias. That is, the regressand of international reserves is determined by the regressors of income, prices, interest rates and domestic reserves, but these regressors are also influenced by international reserves. Another econometric flaw is that there are missing variables in the specification of the diverse models, including foreign interest rates, prices, incomes and reserves as well as other real variables, which can and do affect the balance of payments of a nation. The third econometric problem is that the Monetary approach assumes exogeneity of the reserves and money supplies of a country, when in fact endogeneity is probably the case for these factors.

Part III refers to criticisms of both approaches to international adjustment. Chapter 6, by Bonitsis and Malindretos, criticizes the Traditional approach, arguing that several of its axioms are unrealistic. These are the belief in perfectly competitive input and output markets, the acceptance of all countries as non-reserve, the exclusion of a few international accounts in the process of external adjustment, the basic irrelevance of monetary variables, irrelevance of the disposition of discretionary international account policies, the inapplicability of the root causes of a balance of payments disturbance, the basic irrelevance of the supply side and the acceptance of general equilibrium.

In Chapter 7, Gray criticizes the Monetary approach to international adjustment and compares the two approaches on certain issues. Gray postulates that the Monetary approach cannot deal with real shocks since it presupposes that they do not exist (or matter). A second flaw of the Monetary approach is the non-incorporation of alterations in the international net worth of a nation. Additionally, a test of the Monetary view in examining whether a devaluation influences the trade balance proved it to be basically incorrect. The reasons are that there is insufficient time allowed to have the effect of the devaluation felt and, furthermore, that no other effects, whether policy or non-policy, are included in the empirical statement. Furthermore, both theories need to adjust in order to explain international adjustment. This is owed to the fact that the institutional context has altered in the last two decades. That context now includes the liberalization of trade and capital flows, the integration of capital markets (especially those of the OECD nations) and the currency substitution attained by international financial and nonfinancial companies. Finally, Gray argues that there is a danger of financial collapse in cases where there is no mechanism or policy for adjustment to huge international account disequilibria.

Part IV pursues a theoretical comparison of the two views of the balance of payments. Chapter 8, by Johnson, Kasibhatla and Malindretos, compares the two approaches to the balance of payments and basically elaborates on the assumptions of the two, concluding that if those assumptions were the same, the two theories would be very similar. Second, the two views emphasize different variables, which provides an additional reason for their divergent predictions. The authors postulate that the differences of the two views are helpful in deriving more encompassing conclusions and should not be considered a negative factor.

The four chapters in Part V are tests to determine the better theory between the two. Three chapters use the same technique: the polynomial distributed lag model. This model tests two basic issues. First, it tests whether real variables or monetary ones have a faster impact on the international accounts. If real (monetary) variables have a faster impact, then the Keynesian (Monetary) theory is vindicated. The second issue the authors test is the faster influence of the trade balance versus the official settlements balance. Specifically, if the trade balance adjusts more (less) quickly to alterations of the regressors than the official settlements balance, the Keynesian (Monetary) theory is given more support. In Chapter 9, Rivera-Solis, Kasibhatla and Malindretos give evidence that in the case of Kenya, the two views are given equal support. Similarly, in Chapter 10, Kasibhatla, Malindretos and Kutasovic give evidence that in the case of Korea, the two approaches are equally vindicated. However, in Chapter 11, Bonitsis and Malindretos show that the Monetary view is more supported in the German case. In Chapter 12, Arize examines the effects of exchange-rate volatility on export flows.

Part VI addresses the determination of exchange rates according to competing theoretical approaches. Chapter 13, by Arize, Grivoyannis, Kallianiotis and Englander, expounds on the sundry theories that are grouped under the names Traditional and Monetary. The theories are the purchasing power parity, international Fisher effect, balance of payments view, portfolio balance view, interest rate parity and speculative views. The only one of these that is in the Monetary vein is the theory of purchasing power parity. The rest of the views are in the Traditional mode.

Chapter 14, by Ghosh, Mulugetta and Tessema, continues the analysis and compares the two approaches by defining the balance of payments, the Fleming–Mundell and the portfolio balance models as "traditional" and contrasts them to the Monetary model. The authors conclude that both models could hold true at different points of time.

Finally, Part VII examines the empirical evidence on exchange rate determination. In Chapter 15, Giannaros gives econometric evidence that there is no superior theory of exchange rate determination. The results seem to be influenced by the time period studied, whether the study refers to the short run or the long run, the particular set of currencies used to express the exchange rate and also whether the specification uses a single equation or simultaneous equations. Chapter 16, by Francis, Hasan and Lothian, examines Canada by using a cointegration test and gives evidence that there is support for the Monetary approach and the law of one price.

REFERENCES

Alexander, Sidney S. "Effects of a Devaluation on a Trade Balance." *International Monetary Fund Staff Papers*, 2 (1952): 263–278.

Keynes, J. M. "The German Transfer Problem." *Economic Journal*, 39 (March 1929): 1–7.

Machlup, F. *International Trade and the National Income Multiplier*. Philadelphia: Blakiston, 1943.

Malindretos, John. "The Traditional and Monetary Approaches to the Balance of Payments: A Theoretical Comparison." *American Business Review*, 2 (June 1984): 31–42.

Meade, James E. *The Theory of International Economic Policy. Volume 1: The Balance of Payments*. London: Oxford University Press, 1951.

Robinson, Joan. "The Foreign Exchanges." In *Essays in the Theory of Employment*. 2nd ed. Oxford: Blackwell, 1947. Reprinted in *Collected Economic Papers IV*. Cambridge, Mass.: MIT Press, 1973.

Part I

A Theoretical Review of the Keynesian and Monetary Approaches to the Balance of Payments

Chapter 1

Full Employment, Balance of Payments and Adjustments in Unified (Fixed) Exchange Rate Regimes

Dilip K. Ghosh and Gilles Duteil

INTRODUCTION

Disequilibrium in the external balance of a country develops due to disparities in export revenues and import expenditures, on the one hand, and owing to the inequality in capital inflows and outflows, on the other hand. Since the economy of any country is a fully integrated network of internal and external accounts, imbalance in one area is likely to influence other areas through all the tubes and tunnels that define the flow structure. Policy makers and regulators of an economy therefore try to correct any imbalance with the least cost and loss of time. In this chapter, an attempt is made to examine the balance of payments disequilibrium and the available policy menu that has been or can be used to correct it. The analytical framework is built around the unified (fixed) exchange rate regimes we have witnessed since the existence of the classic conditions under the Gold Standard and through modern times.

GOLD STANDARD AND ADJUSTMENT

Under the Gold Standard, the money supply of a country was strictly proportional to the stock of gold the country owned. The more gold a country had, the greater was its total stock of money, and vice versa. The rate of exchange was virtually fixed, as a natural corollary. That is, the value of a British pound sterling in terms of another nation's currency, such as U.S. dollars, was invariant. If 1 troy ounce of fine gold was worth £10 in the United Kingdom and $20 in the United States, then the price of 1 British pound sterling was equal to 2 U.S. dollars, by virtue of the law of one price.

Let us analyze the adjustment mechanism in conditions of balance of payments imbalances of any two countries, say the U.K. and U.S., in their bilateral exchange structure under the Gold Standard. Assume that the U.K. was in deficit and the U.S. was in surplus in their balance of payments accounts. What could (or did) happen at that point? The built-in automatic adjustment mechanism, popularly known as the *specie flow price mechanism*, restored equilibrium in that fixed exchange regime. The steps of adjustments are presented here by the flow chart in Table 1.1.

As indicated in the table, the deficit country lost its gold stock and the surplus country gained gold stock, which in turn induced a decrease in the money supply for the deficit country and, conversely, an increase in the money supply in the surplus country. That was the adjustment mechanism under the classical paradigm of the Gold Standard. A critical reexamination of this adjustment mechanism reveals that under conditions of full employment, the Gold Standard performed well to correct the external imbalance. However, in situations of underemployment, the specie flow price mechanism could not really be considered a reliable vehicle for adjustment. The Keynesian economic setting then called for policy prescriptions on this score, and various analyses came into being as a consequence. Meade (1951), Johnson (1963, 1966a, 1966b), Mundell (1960, 1962), Sohmen (1967, 1968), and Jones (1968), among many others, have guided us in our search for a policy menu that can lead to the warranted adjustments for a suffering economy.[1]

KEYNESIAN STRUCTURE AND ADJUSTMENTS: COMPARATIVE STATICS

In this chapter, we present the analytical structures that show how an economy under conditions of disequilibrium moves to its external and internal balance points. To do so, we first present the macroeconomic structure à la Keynes, which is defined by the following relations:

$$Y = C + I + G + X - M, \tag{1}$$

$$B = X - M + K_i - K_o. \tag{2}$$

where Y, C, I, G, X, M, K_i, K_o, and B represent national (aggregate) income, consumption expenditure, private investment outlay, government (public) expenditure, exports, imports, capital inflows, and capital outflows, and balance of payments, respectively. Let $C + I + G$ be denoted by E^D (domestic expenditure); $X - M$ by T (trade balance); and $K_i - K_o$ by K (net capital inflows). One may then reexpress (1) and (2) as follows:

$$Y = E^D + T, \tag{1*}$$

$$B = T + K. \tag{2*}$$

Table 1.1
Specie Flow Price Mechanism

U.K. (deficit country) $X \leq M$ and/or $K_i \leq K_o$	U.S. (surplus country) $X \geq M$ and/or $K_i \geq K_o$
1. Gold outflow from U.K. into U.S.	1. Gold inflow into U.S. from U.K.
2. Decrease in money supply in U.K.	2. Increase in money supply in U.S.
3a. Price deflation in U.K.; b. Rise in interest rate in U.K.	3a. Price inflation in U.S. b. Drop in interest rate in U.S.
4a. Increase in U.K.'s exports and decrease in U.K.'s imports; b. Increase in capital inflow into U.K. and decrease in capital outflow from U.K.	4a. Decrease in U.S. exports and increase in U.S. imports; b. Decrease in capital inflow into U.S. and increase in capital outflow from U.S.
5. U.K.'s current and capital accounts improve;	5. U.S. current and capital accounts deteriorate;

6. This sequence continues, and finally equilibrium is restored.

Notes: X = export; M = import; K_i = capital inflow; K_o = capital outflow.

It is traditionally postulated in the Keynesian literature that exports (X) are not influenced by the home country's national income, and rather are a function of a foreign country's gross national product (GNP), but imports (M) are induced by domestic income level (Y); in other words, T depends on Y. In this chapter, we postulate (without any loss of accuracy) the following:

$$T = T(E^D) \text{ where } T_{E^D} < 0. \tag{3}$$

In fact, in view of the standard assumption that the marginal propensity to consume lies between 0 and 1, we should then maintain the following restriction: $-1 < T_E^D < 0$. Next, it can be assumed that net capital inflows depend on the general economic activities (captured effectively by Y) and domestic interest rate (r).[2] That is,

$$K = K(Y, r). \tag{4}$$

It is normally expected that net capital inflows into a country increase when the general economic activities in the country, *ceteris paribus*, are measurably in high gear and/or the interest rate rises; in other words, $K_y > 0$ and $K_r > 0$.

By incorporating equations (3) and (4) into (1*) and (2*), we derive the following expressions:

$$dY = (1 + T_{E^D}) dE^D, \tag{5}$$

$$dB = \{(1 + T_{ED})K_Y + T_{ED})\} \, dE^D + K_r dr. \qquad (6)$$

Note that in (6), since $(1 + T_E^D) > 0$ and $T_E^D < 0$, a small value of K_Y can make the term $\{(1 + T_E^D)K_Y + T_E^D\}$ negative, while a large K_Y can make it positive. More formally, if:

$$K_Y < -\{T_{ED}/(1 + T_{ED})\}, \qquad (7a)$$

then the coefficient of dE^D in (6) becomes negative; but if:

$$K_Y > -\{T_{ED}/(1 + T_{ED})\}, \qquad (7b)$$

then the coefficient of dE^D in (6) becomes positive.

Figure 1.1 depicts the economic picture of the domestic economy and adjustment mechanism under the available policy menu. In these diagrams, the horizontal and vertical axes measure domestic spending and interest rate, respectively. The vertical line Y^F represents the full employment–level national income (which means $dY = 0$), and the B^B curve defines the balance of payments equilibrium (that is, $dB = 0$). Obviously, the zone left of the vertical line Y^F expresses the situation where the economy has less than a full employment–level national income and the area above the B^B curve represents conditions of balance of payments surplus (and below, of deficit). The overall equilibrium for the economy must be defined by the intersection (Z) of the vertical line Y^F and the upward-rising B^B curve in part (a) of Figure 1.1 (and the downward-sloping B^B curve in part [b]). Consider now that the economy is not at this point on the overall equilibrium point. Let it be located at, say, either point U or point V in these diagrams. Point U means that the economy is in an underemployment situation but a balance of payments balance prevails. Point V refers to disequilibrium in both the external and internal balances. In the case of the situation portrayed in part (a) of Figure 1.1, one may immediately see that domestic spending has to rise, but a rise in domestic spending alone can trigger a deficit in the balance of payments. Thus, there is a need to increase the interest rate *pari passu*. If V happens to be northwest of Z, then interest rates must be lowered. If the economy is depicted by part (b) of the figure and the initial point is either U or V, domestic spending must rise and the interest rate must fall in order to drive the economy toward its equilibrium point, Z.

The next question, then, is how to change the values of E^D and r appropriately. First, we rewrite domestic expenditure as follows:

$$E^D = E(Y, r) + G, \qquad (8)$$

and bring out the equilibrium in the monetary sector as follows:

$$M = L(E^D, r). \qquad (9)$$

Figure 1.1
Dynamic Adjustments: E^D − r Space

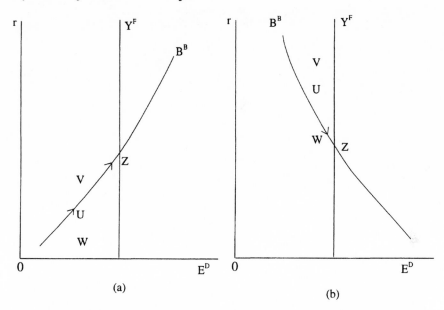

(a)　　　　　　　　　　　　　　　　(b)

Here M stands for money supply and L denotes liquidity preference. Without affecting the Keynesian transaction demand for money as a function of national income, Jones (1968) introduced this specification of liquidity preference. One should have no problem in recognizing the following signs of the partial derivatives:

$E_Y > 0$, or $1 > E_Y > 0$, $E_i < 0$, $L_{ED} > 0$, and $L_i < 0$.

Following the total differentiation of (8) and (9) and the substitution of dY from (5) into the total differential expression of (8), we obtain the following relation:

$$\{1 - (1 + T_{ED})E_Y\}dE^D + E_r dr = dG \tag{10}$$

$$L_{ED}dE^D + L_r dr = dM, \text{ whereupon} \tag{11}$$

$$dE^D = \{dG + (E_r/L_r)dM\}/R, \tag{12}$$

$$dr = \{-(L_{ED}/L_r)dG + \{[1 - (1 + T_{ED})E_Y]/L_r\}dM\}/R \tag{13}$$

where $R = [1 - (1 + T_E^D) E_Y + (E_r/L_r)L_E^D] > 0$. In this case, the reciprocal of R is, obviously, the open-economy multiplier. In the G-M (government

Figure 1.2
Dynamic Adjustments: G – M Space

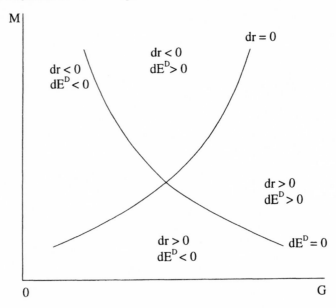

expenditure-monetary) policy space in Figure 1.2, the curves $dr = 0$ and $dE^D = 0$ are, respectively, positively and negatively sloped. That is,

$$\frac{dM}{dG} \mid_{dr \,=\, 0} > 0, \text{ and } \frac{dM}{dG} \mid_{d_{E^D} \,=\, 0} < 0.$$

Obviously, the right side (or, alternatively, the lower region) of the $dr = 0$ schedule signifies that $dr > 0$ (an increase in interest rate), and the right side (or, alternatively, the upper area) of $dE^D = 0$ schedule means $dE^D > 0$ (that is, an increase in domestic expenditure). If the economy is at point U in Figure 1.1, domestic expenditure must go up to move the economy toward full-employment income. That means that the economy must move to the area right of the curve $dE^D = 0$ curve in Figure 1.2. That is not sufficient, however, for the maintenance of the other objective—keeping the balance of payments of equilibrium intact. For this purpose, policy makers must make sure that along with the increase in domestic spending, the interest rate either *rises*, in the case of (a) in Figure 1.1, for which $K_Y < - \{T_E^D)/(1 + T_E^D)\}$, or *falls*, the case of part (b) appropriately so that the overall equilibrium point, Z, is attained. For expositional ease, consider part (a) of Figure 1.1 first. If the economy is at U, then one can see from (12) and (13) that an increase in G *alone* (that is, money supply is held constant) will cause an increase in domestic spending (E^D)—which is needed as the policy goal. If the increase in the interest rate is either too much or too little, obviously the balance of payments balance will be disturbed and the economy will stray from the B^B curve. If the economy moves up in the left of the B^B curve, a balance of payments surplus will be created for the economy on its way to full-employment income; if the economy moves up to the right of the B^B curve, a balance of payments deficit will be created for the economy on its way to full-employment income. If $dG > 0$ has moved the economy to the left of B^B curve, monetary expansion ($dM > 0$) must accompany the fiscal expansion to bring the interest rate down appropriately. If the increase in government spending has put the economy to the right of the B^B curve, then a contractionary monetary policy ($dM < 0$) is required for the warranted move to attaining external and internal balances simultaneously. The comparison of the slope of the B^B curve, defined by $dr/dE^D \mid_{dB = 0} = -\{K_r/[(1 + T_E^D)K_Y + T_E^D]\}$, and the slope of fiscal expansion, defined by $dr/dE^D \mid_{dM = 0} = -L_D^E/L_r$ (derived from [12] and [13] will help policy makers decide what mix of fiscal and monetary policy to implement. If initially the economy is at U and $dr/dE^D \mid dM = 0$ exceeds (falls short of) $dr/dE^D \mid dB = 0$, money supply should be increased (if it fall short, money supply should be decreased). If, however, the economy initially is at a point like W, it may be necessary to increase, decrease, or hold constant the money supply, depending on the speed and position of W in relation to Z. The analytical prescriptions for driving the economy portrayed by part (b) of Figure 1.1 can now be easily derived. These results, which were originated in Jones (1968), can be taken to various possible scenarios with more involved specifications of the macrostructures of an open economy. Of course, some policy menus may further hinge on the speed of adjustments via monetary and fiscal operations. Our analysis thus far has been grounded on comparative statics, a framework within which speed cannot be highlighted, and therefore it may be instructive to bring out a dynamic structure in an open economy.

KEYNESIAN STRUCTURE AND ADJUSTMENTS: DYNAMICS

In this section, we present a basic structure that defines the dynamics of adjustments by way of rewriting the Keynesian aggregates that we introduced and discussed in the previous section. Here we closely follow Mundell (e.g., 1960, 1962), who has articulated the policy assignment and thus thrown into clear relief when and how monetary and fiscal policies should be implemented to bring about balance of payments equilibrium along with full employment. His analyses rest on the dynamics of adjustments on the policy space, and the adjustment mechanism is captured by the excess functions in the balance of payments and the internal balance. Let us bring out the equations of balance—internal balance, as already defined by (1), and external balance, already given by (2):

$$Y = C + I + G + X - M, \text{ or, alternatively,} \tag{1}$$

$$I^* - S + X - M = 0, \text{ where } I^* = I + G. \tag{1'}$$

Here (1)—or, alternatively, (1*)—describes the condition of internal equilibrium (or internal balance). One may easily restate this condition as follows:

$$A = I^* - S + X - M, \text{ when } A = A(h, r) = 0. \tag{1**}$$

The condition of equilibrium in the external balance (that is, in the foreign exchange market) is restated as follows:

$$B = X - M + K_i - K_0, \text{ when } B = B(h, r) = 0. \tag{2**}$$

From (1**), we obtain the following:

$$A_h dh + A_r dr = 0, \text{ and} \tag{1.1}$$

$$B_h dh + B_r dr = 0. \tag{2.1}$$

Mundell interpreted h as domestic budget surplus in his 1962 work and terms of trade (that is, ratio of domestic and foreign price levels) in his 1960 article. Let us take h as representing budget surplus first. From (1.1), we find:

$$dr/dh \mid_{dA = 0} = -(A_h/A_r) < 0, \tag{1.2}$$

since $A_h < 0$, and $A_r < 0$. Similarly, from (2.1), we get the the following expression:

$$dr/dh \mid_{dB = 0} = -(B_h/B_r) < 0, \tag{2.2}$$

since $B_h < 0$, and $B_r < 0$. The BB schedule, whose slope is given by (2.2), is flatter than the AA schedule, whose slope is defined by (1.2), provided capital flows are interest sensitive. Figure 1.3 exhibits these schedules of internal and external balance.

In Figure 1.3, the horizontal and vertical axes represent, respectively, budget surplus (h) and interest rate (r). Along the AA schedule we have internal balance and along the BB schedule, external balance. Obviously, below the AA schedule we get inflationary situations, and above this schedule, deflationary pressures. Similarly, along the BB curve we have a condition of external balance. The area below this curve portrays balance of payments deficits, and the area above this curve depicts balance of payments surpluses. At this point, suppose the economy is at point m, which means that it is at internal equilibrium but is in deficit in its balance of payments. Policy makers in this situation may attempt to correct

Figure 1.3
Dynamic Adjustments: h − r Space

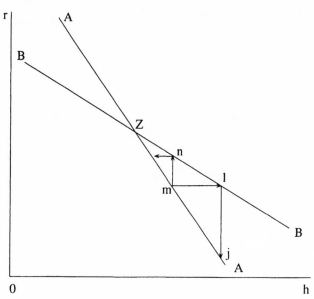

the disequilibrium by either raising the interest rate, by mn, or raising budget surplus, by ml. If the interest rate is increased, the economy moves to point n, which brings about external balance but generates deflationary pressure. In the next round, then, policy makers inject a reduction in budget surplus, thus restoring the internal equilibrium but causing a smaller amount of deficit in the balance of payments accounts. A series of interest hikes followed by drops in the budget surplus can thus eventually move the economy to its overall equilibrium at Z. If, however, at the initial disequilibrium point m, policy makers had raised budget surplus by ml to correct the external imbalance, the economy would have moved to point l, wiping out external imbalance but creating a large degree of deflation. To correct that internal deflation, the required decrease in interest rate by lj would have thrown external equilibrium off-balance by a much larger degree. The whole sequence in this case would have been centrifugal—taking overall equilibrium further and further away from equilibrium.

Next, consider the situations where h in (1.1) and (2.1) is construed as the terms of trade. Under this interpretation of h, one gets the following from (1.1) and (2.1):

$$A_h dh + A_r dr = 0, \text{ and} \qquad (1.3)$$

$$B_h dh + B_r dr = 0. \qquad (2.3)$$

Figure 1.4
Dynamic Adjustments: Terms of Trade and Interest Rate Space

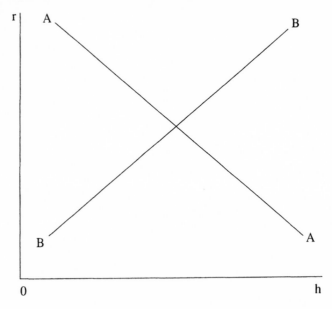

Here, as before, A_i ($i = h, r$) < 0, $B_h < 0$, and $B_r > 0$. The internal and external balances are portrayed by the AA and BB schedules in Figure 1.4. Obviously, in this figure, the slope of the AA schedule is negative, $dr/dh \mid_{dA} = 0 = -(A_h/A_r) < 0$, and the slope of BB schedule is positive, $dr/dh \mid_{dB} = 0 = -(B_h/B_r) < 0$). Consider the dynamics of the terms of trade (h) and interest rate (r), as follows:

$$dh/dt = sA(h, r), s > 0 \qquad (1.4)$$

$$dr/dt = -vB(h, r), v > 0 \qquad (2.4)$$

where s and v are the speeds of adjustments for internal balance and external balance when deviations from respective equilibriums have already appeared for some reason or other. Equation (1.4) states that terms of trade rises in proportion to the deviation (excess demand) in the domestic economy for goods and services. Equation (2.4) similarly specifies that interest rate falls in proportion to the difference between foreign exchange payments and receipts. A Taylor expansion of (1.4) and (2.4) then yields:

$$dh/dt = sA_h(h - h^*) + sA_r(r - r^*), \qquad (1.5)$$

$$dr/dt = -vB_h(h - h^*) - vB_r(r - r^*). \qquad (2.6)$$

Here, h* and r* denote the equilibrium values of h and r, respectively. The system of equations, defined by (1.4) and (2.4), yields the following eigenvalues:

$$q_1 = 1/2.[(sA_h - vB_r) + \{(sA_h - vB_r)^2 + 4sv(A_hB_r - A_rB_h)\}^{1/2},$$
$$q_2 = 1/2.[(sA_h - vB_r) + \{(sA_h - vB_r)^2 + 4sv(A_hB_r - A_rB_h)\}^{1/2}.$$

From the signs on the partial derivatives, $A_h < 0$, $A_r < 0$, $B_h < 0$, and $B_r > 0$, it is evidently clear that the eigenvalues are negative when real, or have negative real parts when they are complex. That signifies that the system approaches equilibrium either asymptotically or cyclically. If $\{(sA_h - vB_r)^2 - 4sv(A_hB_r - A_rB_h)\} > 0$, equilibrium is attained asymptotically; but if $\{(sA_h - vB_r)^2 - 4sv(A_hB_r - A_rB_h)\} < 0$, equilibrium is attained cyclically. If B_r is very large (which signifies that capital is highly interest sensitive, or mobile), $\{(sA_h - vB_r)^2 - 4sv(A_hB_r - A_rB_h)\} < 0$. Alternatively, if $B_r = 0$ and $s/v > 4(A_r/A_h)$, we still will have $\{(sA_h - vB_r)^2 - 4sv(A_hB_r - A_rB_h)\} > 0$, and hence, the asymptotitic convergence to equilibrium.

More complicated adjustment mechanisms and more sophisticated macroeconomic structures can be envisaged, and more complicated analytical results can be derived. In this chapter, we have offered a basic analysis with a unifying approach to an open economic picture where policy makers are seeking guidelines for achieving full employment with price stability and balance of payments equilibrium. The analysis is thus simple and significantly sound.

NOTES

This chapter was completed while the first author was visiting CETFI—Université d'Aix-Marseille III, Aix en Provence, France and Groupe ESC Marseille, France. The authors would like to acknowledge their indebtedness to CETFI—Université d'Aix-Marseille III France for financial support for the research, and express their sincere appreciation to Professor Claude Bensoussan for providing the best possible working environment, and to Professor John Malindretos for inviting us to complete this chapter. It must be noted that this piece heavily draws on the work of Jones (1968) and Mundell (1960, 1962) for their clarifying paradigms for this research.

1. For further details on the literature, some of the other studies listed in the references should be examined.

2. Since foreign national income and interest rate are not within the control of the domestic policy makers, we consider them as given parameters.

REFERENCES

Fleming, J. M. "Domestic Financial Policies under Fixed and Floating Exchange Rates." *International Monetary Fund Staff Papers*, 9 (1962): 369–379.
Johnson, Harry G. "Equilibrium under Fixed Exchange Rates." *American Economic Review*, 53 (May 1963): 112–119.
Johnson, Harry G. "The Objectives of Economic Policy and the Mix of Fiscal and

Monetary Policy under Fixed Exchange Rates." In *Maintaining and Restoring Balance in International Payments*, ed. Fritz Machlup et al. Princeton, N.J.: Princeton University Press, 1966a, pp. 1–198.

Johnson, Harry G. "Some Aspects of the Theory of Economic Policy in a World of Capital Mobility." In *Essays in Honour of Marco Fanno*, ed. T. Bagiotti. Padua, Italy: Cadam, 1966b, pp. 228–245.

Jones, Ronald W. "Monetary and Fiscal Policy for an Economy with Fixed Exchange Rates." *Journal of Political Economy*, 76, no. 4 (July–August 1968): 921–943.

Keynes, J. M. *The General Theory of Employment, Interest, and Money*. London: Macmillan, 1936.

McKinnon, R. I. *Money in International Exchange*. New York: Oxford University Press, 1979.

Meade, J. E. *The Balance of Payments*. Vol. 1 of *The Theory of International Economic Policy*. London: Oxford University Press, 1951, rpt. 1970.

Mundell, Robert A. "The Monetary Dynamics of International Adjustment under Fixed and Flexible Exchange Rates." *Quarterly Journal of Economics*, 74, no. 2 (May 1960): 667–681.

Mundell, Robert A. "The Appropriate Use of Monetary and Fiscal Policy for Internal and External Stability." *International Monetary Fund Staff Papers*, 9, no. 1 (March 1962): 532–548.

Niehans, Jurg. "Monetary and Fiscal Policies in Open Economies under Fixed Exchange Rates: An Optimizing Approach." *Journal of Political Economy*, 76 (1968): 281–297.

Sohmen, Egon. "Fiscal and Monetary Policies under Alternative Exchange-Rate Systems." *Quarterly Journal of Economics*, 81, no. 3 (August 1967): 515–523.

Sohmen, Egon. "The Assignment Problem." In *Monetary Problems of the International Economy*, ed. R. A. Mundell and A. Swoboda. Chicago: University of Chicago Press, 1968.

Swoboda, A. K. "Monetary Policy under Fixed Exchange Rates: Effectiveness, the Speed of Adjustment and Proper Use." *Economica*, 40 (May 1973): 136–154.

Chapter 2

A Survey of the Monetary Approach to International Finance

Demetri Tsanacas, Krishna M. Kasibhatla
and John Malindretos

INTRODUCTION

The role of money in the balance of payments adjustment process has been cast aside by the so-called Traditional approaches to balance of payments adjustments. These approaches, whether labeled the "elasticities approach," "income multiplier approach," "absorption approach," or "internal-external balance approach," have concentrated exclusively on real variables and ignored the monetary variables. Significant elements such as capital flows, government transfers and debt servicing have been treated as residuals to the trade accounts.

The Monetary approach to the balance of payments, which was developed over the years at the University of Chicago by economists like R. A. Mundell, H. G. Johnson, A. B. Laffer and J. A. Frenkel and advanced by the work of International Monetary Fund (IMF) economists, seeks to restore the role of money and money balances in the adjustment process. The balance of payments is viewed as essentially a monetary phenomenon, and the imbalances are rooted in the relationship between the demand and the supply of money.

Some of the economists mentioned here have suggested that the Monetary approach is indeed the intellectual grandchild of the "specie flow" mechanism developed by David Hume in the last century. Monetary flows are cornerstones to both theories. Moreover, both treat external imbalances as self-correcting, but they differ in the way monetary flows are thought to correct external disequilibria. The specie flow mechanism seeks adjustment through relative changes in commodity prices, while the Monetary approach seeks adjustment through a stable demand for money. The Monetary approach thus revolves around the basic premise that over the long run, there is a stable demand for money as a stock. Surpluses or deficits in the balance of payments reflect stock disequilibria between the demand and the supply of money. The specific composition of these inflows/outflows is secondary to the monetary theory. The disequilibria are thus temporary and self-correcting over time, providing the monetary authority remains neutral. Policy prediction and policy implications are different under the Monetary approach than those that will prevail under the Traditional approach.

The current analysis will thoroughly examine the assumptions of the Monetary approach, introduce qualifications to the simple assumption to make the Monetary approach more realistic and conclude with a summary of the results.

THE MONETARY APPROACH

The Monetary approach to international finance relies on four basic assumptions:

1. full employment
2. purchasing power parity in the law of one price
3. aggregate demand and aggregate supply, and thus the balance of payments, are determined by the money supply and demand
4. general equilibrium exists in all markets

FULL EMPLOYMENT

The Monetary approach assumes that the economy is, in the long run, at full-employment equilibrium (in the classical economist's view of employment). Any deviation from the natural level of unemployment will be a short-term, self-correcting situation. According to the monetarists, full employment is ubiquitous for three reasons:

1. the existence of general equilibrium and its corollary, that all markets clear
2. perfect substitution in consumption in both the product and capital markets, including money
3. wage and price flexibility in both the product and capital markets

The presence of general equilibrium and the infinite cross-elasticity of substitution will equilibrate the demand and supply in all markets including the labor market. Excess supply in one market causes intertemporal adjustments in others, thus restoring equilibrium in all markets. Even if the first two reasons do not hold true, the wage and price flexibility are sufficient to induce the economy to return to full employment equilibrium.

PURCHASING POWER PARITY

The assumption of purchasing power parity (PPP), also called the law of one price, treats the world as consisting of a single, integrated market for all traded goods and for capital. There are two versions of this assumption: movement toward PPP and changes in relative prices among countries. In the first version, given sufficient time for adjustment (and abstracting from transportation costs), all internationally traded goods will have the same price. Under the second version, relative price changes among competing countries is not possible; either the price of a devaluing nation will rise or foreign prices will decline until prices are fully equalized internationally. Specifically, competitive forces will quickly and directly eliminate changes in relative prices stemming from exchange rate changes by offsetting changes in domestic prices.

Under the Traditional approach, a nation can change its competitiveness through relative price adjustments following a devaluation. The results will be a change in the direction of trade: exports will rise, imports will fall, and the trade balance will improve. The law of one price does not allow for changes in relative prices, rejects the elasticities approach, and renders inoperative the various policies aimed at changes in relative prices. The Monetary approach ascertains that nominal variables affect only nominal variables and real variables affect only real variables. Thus, nominal variables such as prices and exchange rates cannot impact on real variables such as relative price and the trade balance.

There are distinct differences between the Traditional approach and the Monetary approach in predictions and in policy implications, especially as they relate to exchange rate change and commercial policy.

Exchange Rate Changes

The Monetary approach argues that changes in the exchange rate do not affect the trade balance or any other real variable, but they impact the balance of payments through possible effects on the demand for, and the supply of, the money balance and the resulting changes in domestic prices.

Devaluation

A devaluation of a nation's currency raises the domestic prices, exportables, importables, and, to a lesser degree, the trade of nontradables (product substitution). This general price rise increases the demand for monetary balances, which, if not satisfied from domestic sources, will be satisfied through money inflows from abroad, resulting in a balance of payment surplus. Devaluation reduces real domestic money balances and forces residents to seek to restore monetary equilibrium through the international markets, resulting in an effect that is only transitory.

Appreciation

A currency appreciation achieved by lowering domestic prices reduces the demand for monetary balances, generates an excess supply of money and leads to a transitory balance of payments deficit as residents seek to restore monetary equilibrium through the international credit and commodity market. The Monetary approach views exchange rate changes as incapable of generating lasting changes in the balance of payment and also as unnecessary, since external disequilibria are self-correcting over time. Furthermore, exchange rate changes merely affect the price level and have no effect on real economic variables. A more specific discussion follows.

The Terms of Trade (TOT). According to the Monetary approach, the terms of trade do not change simply because there are no changes in relative prices. Exchange rate changes affect the domestic prices of traded goods relative to those of nontraded goods, thus shifting resources to traded goods industries and shifting demand toward nontraded goods. Changes in the production and consumption mixes will help increase exports and reduce imports.

Distribution Effects. It is assumed that a devaluation does not have any effect on the distribution of income. If it did, though, and the marginal propensities to consume among the population were different, a devaluation would affect the trade balance since it would affect real variables.

Real Wealth. Real Wealth, if it changes, can change real variables and the trade balance. A devaluation can change real wealth by changing real balances. The whole point hinges on whether money balances are considered real wealth. If they are, a devaluation will change them, since it will raise prices; thus, it will have real wealth effects. If money is not net wealth, as ascertained by the Monetary approach, then exchange rate changes do not affect net wealth and do not impact on the trade balance.

Real Spending. It is possible that the propensity to consume could be altered through devaluation. The resulting change in real absorption would affect the trade balance.

Expectations. The Traditional approach argues that a change in the exchange rate could lead to two sets of expectations: changes in income distribution and in terms of trade and devaluation. Under the former expectation, even if there is no change in the distribution of income, the perception that the distribution has changed could lead to a change in the consumption patterns and impact on the trade balance. Under the latter, it is possible for the nation to feel more wealthy in real terms, following a devaluation. In this case, it could consume more and induce a negative change in its trade balance, even if there were no changes in the terms of trade. The reverse would also hold true.

Commercial Policy

The effects of import restrictions on the balance of payments are analyzed by the monetarists similarly to their analysis of devaluation. Restrictions that increase the domestic price of imports through substitutability increase the prices of domestically produced goods. The result will be an increase in the demand for money, which, if not satisfied through domestic sources, will lead to a transitory balance of payments surplus until monetary equilibrium is restored. *More analytically*:

Tariff. A tariff is an import tax that could raise the domestic price of a foreign good and could lead to production and consumption adjustments in the importing nation. Its impact can be analyzed from both an unemployment and a full employment perspective.

Under employment, the Monetary approach points out two possible effects, price effect and income effect, both of which will be manifested through real balances. The higher prices will force the residents of the importing nation to increase their demand for nominal money balances in order to maintain the same level of real balances. The adjustment will take place through money inflows from abroad, leading to an improvement in the balance of payments. The higher prices of imports could also stimulate domestic production as domestic producers expand and/or start production, thus increasing the level of domestic incomes and the demand for real balances. The higher demand for real balances will lead to an inflow of money from abroad and an improvement in the balance of payments.

The Monetary approach argues that under conditions of full employment, the imposition of a tariff cannot improve the trade balance because a reduced absorption of imports, by definition, means an absorption of exports. The balance of payments will improve, specifically, through the proceeds generated through the tariff. Higher tariff proceeds increase the domestic income and the desire to hold more money, which improves the balance of payments. It should be pointed out that the replacement of an optional tariff with a suboptional one, which would decrease the proceeds collected, would lead to a deterioration of the balance of payments.

Quota. A quota is a quantitative restriction on imports that could lead to increases in the price of imports and domestic production. As in the case of tariffs, quotas generate price and income effects that could increase the demand for money and, subsequently, improve the balance of payments.

Non-Tariff Barriers (NTBs). The various NTBs could raise prices and/or the income level domestically and have a positive influence on the balance of payments through increases in the demand for money. The inflows of foreign money would eliminate the excess demand for money.

Export Tax. Whether an export tax leads to an improvement or a deterioration in the balance of payments depends on the price elasticity of the demand for exports. If the export elasticity of demand (E_{Dx}) is less than 1 minus the marginal propensity to import (MPM), the balance of payments will improve for two reasons: (a) as the price of exports increase, other prices will also rise, leading to an excess demand for money; (b) the rising income levels lead to an increase in the demand for money. These two effects imply an inflow of foreign money to restore equilibrium and an improvement in the balance of payments. If, on the other hand, $E_{Dx} > 1 - MPM$, the balance of payments will deteriorate as local residents seek to eliminate the excess supply of money that will be brought about through the price and income effects.

Export Subsidy. The impact of an export subsidy on the balance of payments will depend on the price elasticity of demand for exports. If $E_{Dx} > 1 - MPM$, the balance of payments will improve as higher prices and higher incomes domestically generate an excess demand for money, which is satisfied through monetary inflows from abroad. The opposite will be true if $E_{Dx} < 1 - MPM$.

THE MONETARY NATURE OF THE BALANCE OF PAYMENTS AND ITS ESSENTIALITY

The third assumption is the fundamental assumption of the Monetary approach, which states that the demand for money is a stable function and that the relationship between the money supply and the money demand is the linchpin of the international accounts. Any disturbance in that relationship creates a disturbance in the current account, the capital account, and the balance of payments. The assumption can be subdivided into three corollaries:

1. the money supply of a country becomes endogenous if the exchange rate is pegged;
2. the balance of payments is determined by the demand for money and the supply of money;
3. the money demand and the money supply are stock variables, not flow variables.

The essentiality of the relationship between the demand and supply of money means that the implications of the Monetary approach hold regardless of whether the first two assumptions are true. That is, even in the absence of full employment and purchasing power parity, the basic precepts of the Monetary approach hold true.

The equation of exchange is (1) $MV = PQ$ or (2) $MV = PT$. The demand for money (M^D) can be obtained by substituting y for Q and defining:

$M^D = k$ Py (3) where
M^D = desired nominal money balances
k   = desired ratio of nominal money balances to nominal national income
y   = real output
P   = domestic price level
yP = GNP

The money supply (M^s) is a constant multiple (m) of the monetary base and consists of a domestic credit component created by the monetary authority (D) and an international component (R). Thus, (4) $M^s = m[D + R]$. The demand for money can be satisfied either from domestic or international sources. Any change in the domestic component of the money supply by the monetary authority will distort the equilibrium balance and lead to adjustments by the residents of that nation, which will affect the balance of payments. Full employment and purchasing power parity are not necessary conditions for these adjustments as long as the third assumption and its corollaries are true. Under the Monetary approach, disequilibria in the balance of payments are monetary phenomena and disturbances in the international accounts originate in the money market.

The Demand for Money

Equation (3), $M^d = kPy$, indicates that the money demand is a positive, stable function of the price level and of real income. More realistically, it also depends on interest rate expectations and other real effects.

Price Levels

Under a constant velocity, an increase in the price level will increase the demand for money as the public seeks to maintain the same real balances as before the increase, leading to money inflows from abroad and an improvement in the balance of payments. A price decrease will have the opposite effect as the public unloads its excess supply of money.

Income

Increases in real income lead to increases in the demand for money and an improvement in the balance of payments. Decreases in real income have the opposite effect. Income, however, relates negatively to the trade balance as stipulated by the Traditional approach. If the balance of payments improves and the trade balance deteriorates following a growth in income, it means that the improvement in the capital account will more than offset the deterioration of the trade balance.

Interest Rate

The interest rate and the demand for money are negatively related. As the interest rate rises, the quantity of money that is demanded falls, which results in an excess supply of money. Adjustments in the excess supply of money lead to a deterioration in the balance of payments. If, however, the rate of interest falls, the quantity of money demanded will increase and the balance of payments will improve. This result is completely contradictory to the results stipulated in the Traditional approach concerning how changes in the interest rate affect the balance of payments.

Expectations

Inflationary expectations induce the public to hold lower money balances, while deflationary expectations induce them to hold higher balances. In the first instance, the balance of payments will deteriorate; in the second, it will improve.

Real Effects

Changes in demand, absorption or output will affect the balance of payments through their impact on the demand for real balances arising from changes in the prices of tradable goods and in their production.

The Supply of Money

Equation (4), $M^s = m [D+R]$, represents the supply of money. Any increase in the domestic component (D) with an unchanged M^d will generate a deficit. Any decrease in D under the same M^d will generate a surplus. In general, any change in the domestic component of the money is ultimately offset by an equal and opposite change in the international reserve component through the balance of payments. The monetary authority could attempt to "offset" or "sterilize" the flows of funds, but in the absence of any government involvement, the imbalances between the demand for money and the money stock will be temporary and self-correcting. The self-correction is based on the stable demand function for money as a stock rather than a flow. When the desired stock is achieved, the flows of foreign funds stop, as does the balance of payments adjustment. It needs to be pointed out that the money supply is stock, whereas annual changes in money supply are flows that are added to, or subtracted from, that stock.

Under a flow concept formulation, continuous surpluses can occur under conditions of continuous increase in the demand for money over rises in the domestic component (D) of the money supply. A continuous increase in the level of income in excess of the rate of increase in domestic credit will result in disequilibria in the money market and persistent surpluses in the balance of payments. In a flow formulation, continuous deficits can occur through recurrent increases in the growth rate of the domestic money supply component (D) in excess of the growth in real income.

GENERAL EQUILIBRIUM

Equilibrium is defined as a state where there is no inherent tendency for change. General equilibrium in this case is the simultaneous clearing of all goods and services markets, money markets and factor markets. Equilibrium is brought about through price and quantity adjustments that eliminate either excess demand or supply. The general equilibrium assumption is a critical assumption to the Monetary approach because it permeates the other three assumptions, and indeed, without general equilibrium, the other three would not hold true. Specifically, the essentiality of the money market presupposes the assumption of general equilibrium. A closer examination of the integration of the general equilibrium assumption with each of the other assumptions is thus warranted.

General Equilibrium and Full Employment

General equilibrium means equilibrium in all markets including the labor market, and therefore, full employment. Walras's law states that all markets clear. An excess supply of labor will be eliminated intertemporally through quantity integration and/or price integration. Under quantity integration, the interrelationship between the markets and the substitutability of the commodity being traded would imply that an excess supply of money, securities or goods/services would result from an excess supply of labor. As the excess supplies of money, securities or goods flow into the labor market, they restore equilibrium. Under price integration, the excess supply of labor means a decrease in its price, an increase in the quantity of labor demanded, and a reduction in unemployment.

General Equilibrium and Purchasing Power Parity

General equilibrium applies also to the PPP axiom. If country A has a higher price than country B, it will only be temporary since the resulting quantity effects would eliminate the price difference. Specifically, the quantity effects in A would mean a higher volume of production, while in B, there will be additional export volume to A. Both these factors will lead to a reduction in the price level in country A. Simultaneously, the indigenous consumers would reduce their consumption, which would reduce the prices in A. These adjustments revolve around the general equilibrium assumption—that all markets clear and that there is a high degree of price and quantity integration which eliminates excesses in the markets.

General Equilibrium and the Essentiality of the Money Market

The essentiality of the money market is much more influenced by the general equilibrium assumption than by the other two assumptions. The money market is, for the Monetary approach, the essential commodity market, around which all others adjust. Any disturbance in the money market will lead to disturbances in the other markets. Disequilibria in the money market are corrected through adjustments in portfolio holdings of securities and/or goods and services. Disequilibria in the money market could also be eliminated intertemporally through a price mechanism. Let us argue that there are no quantity adjustments possible in the presence of an excess supply of money. The price of money will fall, increasing the quantity being demanded, and the excess supply will be reduced to zero. If excess demand for money exists, the interest rate will rise to bring about equilibrium.

The relationship between general equilibrium and the essentiality of the money market is indeed the core of the Monetary approach. Walras's law, that all markets clear, together with price and quantity integration, would lead temporary disequilibria to become permanent long-run equilibria. The culprits of the balance of payments disturbances are usually the money market and the money account.

THE MONETARY APPROACH TO INTERNATIONAL FINANCE: SOME QUALIFICATIONS

The chapter so far has expounded the basic theory of the Monetary approach. In the following section, qualifications to Monetary approach will be offered which will, somewhat, alter the basic theory. These qualifications are as follows:

1. Country Size and Effect of Balance of Payments Policies
2. Speed of Adjustment of Monetary Policy Changes and Devaluation
3. Stock versus Flow Equilibrium
4. Real Variables versus Monetary Variable Effects
5. Nondistinction between the Statuses of the Three Different Accounts
6. Extent of Tradability of Commodities
7. Reserve Currency Country Status
8. Currency Substitutions
9. Exchange Rate Flexibility
10. Currency Inconvertibility

Country Size

Country size is crucial to the assumption of endogeneity of the money supply. An expansion in a country's money supply is distributed proportionately in all countries. Thus, a larger country will acquire more money in absolute units. The smaller the country, the less its control over its money supply, and thus, the smaller the gains from monetary policy, irrespective of the policy's initiator. The large country, however, retains most of the expansion of the money stock and also retains an element of exogeneity over its money supply. These results hold under dynamic assumptions for expectations of monetary policy, equilibrium, growth, and inflation.

A currency devaluation will raise domestic prices or cause foreign prices to decline until all prices are fully equalized internationally. The price adjustments affect the demand for money, and thus the balance of payments. Two questions are relevant at this point: (a) Are the price adjustments symmetrical? (b) What is the impact of devaluation on the increase in the price level? Mundell and Laffer argued that the price responses are not symmetrical, thus leading to what they call a "ratchet effect." With respect to size, devaluations in small countries lead to increases in the price level equal to the percentage of devaluation; in larger countries, the price level increase will be close to zero. The balance of payments will improve according to the percentage increase in the price level.

Speed of Adjustment

A currency devaluation raises the domestic price level and reduces real balances. The pursuant adjustment via the foreign markets will lead to an improvement in the official reserves transactions balance (ORTB). The impact of the devaluation on ORTB depends on the percentage change of the price level, the speed of the price level adjustment and the public's perception about the true value of these real balance holdings.

The larger the percent change of the price level, the greater the effect on the real balances and the greater the influence on the ORTB. Second, the faster the impact on the price level, the faster will be the impact on the ORTB. Third, the greater the feeling of loss in real balances experienced by the population following the devaluation, the greater would be the effect on the international account. Moreover, in all cases, the reverse holds true as well. The size of the nation and the degree of substitutability of domestic for foreign goods are important elements in the determination of the impact on the price level, and the Monetary approach presupposes a very high degree of substitution.

The speed of adjustment in the money market following a disturbance in the equilibrium position depends on capital mobility and the existence of nontraded goods. The higher the degree of capital mobility, the faster the speed of adjustment in the balance of payments. The presence of nontraded goods reduces the speed of adjustment.

Stock versus Flow Concepts

The Monetary approach analyzes the balance of payments under a stock perspective, in contrast to the Traditional approach, which utilizes a flow perspective. Surpluses and deficits are, for the monetarists, temporary and self-correcting. Continuous surpluses/deficits in the balance of payments are the result of differences in the growth rate of real income and the growth rate of the domestic component of the money supply.

For the monetarists, disturbances are either in stock or in the portfolio. Portfolio disturbances innately deal with the money market. Equilibrium is defined as portfolio equilibrium. The balance of payments equilibrium will be disturbed if variables that disturb the equilibrium in the money market are disturbed. The balance of payments will always balance by definition but will not always be in equilibrium. Nonetheless, the very forces that disturb the equilibrium will work to restore it. The Monetary approach describes neither the dynamic process that the economy must undergo to reach the new equilibrium nor the elapsed time necessary to reach that equilibrium. It is concerned with the final, long-run equilibrium position.

The stock versus flow framework presents problems in the formulation of policy between the Monetary and the Traditional approaches. Consider a devaluation. Under the Traditional approach, the trade balance will improve every year in the future due to the increased competitiveness of the domestic producers, with the exception of an adjustment path described by the ''J'' curve. The Monetary approach rejects this scenario and argues, instead, that the effect of the devaluation will be temporary. The higher import prices increase the price level in the devaluing country and create an excess demand for money to restore real balances. This excess demand for money is satisfied through the export of additional goods and/or securities, leading to an equilibrium in the trade balance. Following this adjustment, prices return to their original level—PPP holds, and the source of the disturbance disappears. Disturbances are, for the Monetary approach, self-correcting; while for the Traditional approach, because of the flow format, they can perpetually disturb and disequilibrate the balance of payments.

Similar adjustments will prevail in the presence of an import tax, export subsidy, or export tax. Under the proper conditions, the balance of payments will show temporary improvements before returning to equilibrium.

Changes in the level of income will alter the stock equilibrium of the focus country and lead to balance of payments disequilibria. A disturbance will create a one-time disequilibrium, which will be corrected through the importation of money. Disturbances can be real or monetary, but the adjustment will take place in the monetary variables to correct the balance of payments. Michael Mussa (1976) cites the case of Saudi Arabia which had experienced substantial improvements in its terms of trade after the oil price increases in 1972. According to Mussa the improvement in the balance of payments was the result of governmental policy which, with the improved revenue, required the government to print much less money to finance its expenditures than would otherwise have been needed. This tight monetary policy was the key to the balance of payments surplus. This is an example of a real variable (Terms of Trade—T/T) working through a nominal variable (monetary policy) to affect the balance of payments. The right monetary policy remained in effect year after year as the T/T improved through subsequent oil price increases. This is an example of a flow phenomenon. A similar example was offered in the continuous surpluses of Germany in the 1960s and 1970s. The continuous rate of increase in income, in excess of the rate of growth in domestic credit, caused continuous excess demand for money; that is, disequilibria in the money market caused a continuous inflow of foreign funds.

Technological improvements in a country's exports would be transmitted through the money account. The technological gains will improve the productivity of the workforce and its income while stimulating exports. The first gain will raise the demand for money, while the second gain will enhance the government's ability to collect revenue, negating the need to increase the domestic component of the money supply. The results will be a temporary improvement in the balance of payments until equilibrium in the money markets is restored. The only way that the technological lead will improve the balance of payments on a continuous basis is if there is continuous improvement in technology each year.

Real versus Monetary Variables

The Monetary approach, unlike the Traditional approach, clearly delineates between real and monetary variables and asserts the fundamentality and superiority of monetary variables over real variables. Monetary variables, like the money supply, the exchange rate, the interest rate, and the nominal price level, are superior to the relative price level and real income. Superiority in this case is defined by the monetarists as the ability of variables to act as initiators of disturbances and transmission channels. Monetary variables are both initiators and transmittors, while real variables are neither. In addition to monetary variables and real variables, there are monetary and real accounts. The trade balance is a real account, while the official reserves transactions balance (ORTB) is a monetary account.

In the context of general equilibrium and the essentiality of the money market, any disturbance whatsoever will affect the money market. We have shown how an improvement in the T/T (a real disturbance) alters the money supply (monetary variable) and induces residents to import money from abroad, thus improving the balance of payments. Assume that the interest rate falls in a focus nation, perhaps because of deflationary expectations. The demand for money will then increase and, given the willingness of the monetary authority to expand the money stock, the residents of the focus nation will import money from the rest of the world and, in return, surrender goods, services and/or securities. The actions of the residents will cause the ORTB, the TB and the capital account (KA) to improve. In this case, the interest rate (monetary variable) will influence the money market and the international accounts.

Nondistinction of the Different International Accounts

The Monetary approach, unlike the Traditional approach, does not differentiate among the various accounts or attempt to explain their individual behavior. Accounts such as goods and services, long-term capital, and short-term capital are lumped together into one, "above-the-line" category. The official reserve transaction balance is the "below-the-line" category, and it represents, for the monetarists, the preeminent account. Therefore, it has been described as analyzing the problem "from the bottom up." An ORTB surplus may be associated with either surpluses in either the capital or the current accounts, and the reverse also holds true.

Tradability of Different Commodities

The assertion of the Traditional approach that changes in competitiveness are long-lasting and that they alter the patterns of international trade is strengthened by the assumption that certain goods are not traded internationally. These goods, as well as certain tradable goods, command different prices internationally. The Monetary approach, on the other hand, asserts that all goods are tradable and that perfect international arbitrage would ensure that one price would prevail in all countries for each commodity. This would be achieved through the infinite cross-elasticity of substitution across countries.

Reserve Currency Country

The conclusions would be somewhat altered if an international financial system that includes a reserve currency country is introduced. In this situation, a set of assumptions is crucial to any explanation.

1. The nonreserve country holds zero currency of the reserve country.
2. Reserves are held as interest-earning securities.
3. The acquisition of reserves by the monetary authority of the nonreserve country is achieved through the borrowing or selling of securities in the reserve currency country.
4. The domestic currency changes by the central bank of the nonreserve country comprise a net addition to the money supply of the country.

If the nonreserve currency country pursues an expansionary monetary policy, the money supplies of both countries will remain the same. If, on the other hand, the reserve currency country pursues a loose monetary policy, the money supply of both countries will change. The reason for these conclusions is that the nonreserve country should maintain exchange rate parity with the reserve country, yet the reserve country does not need parity. The conclusions will change if the currency of the reserve country is pegged to a commodity like gold.

Currency Substitutions

It is possible that residents of a country hold more than one currency in their portfolio and that they alter these holdings based on the changing opportunity costs of each currency. In this situation, currency substitution is taking place. The substitution will most likely take place following a change in monetary policy or a currency devaluation.

Monetary Policy

Increase in the domestic money supply, whether recurrent or nonrecurrent, will change the domestic price level and lead to an outflow of excess money overseas. The possibility of increases in foreign as well as domestic prices will dampen the outflow to restore monetary equilibrium. Three basic conclusions are possible:

1. Even if central banks do not fix the value of these currencies, currency substitution will imply capital movements, and thus monetary interdependence.
2. Inflation is an integrated phenomenon in an integrated world, and price increases are transmitted internationally.
3. The presence of currency substitution will distort the balance of payments adjustments, which could partially explain the large statistical discrepancies in balance of payment statistics.

Currency Devaluation

The composition of the portfolio to include foreign as well as domestic currency will be reevaluated following a currency devaluation. The effect will be lower losses in real balances because of the increased value of the other currencies. The improvement in the balance of payments will then be much lower.

Alternative Exchange Rate Regimes

In addition to the fixed exchange rate regime, there are two other regimes: flexible (or freely floating) and managed (or "dirty float").

Flexible

Flexible exchange rates maintain continuous equilibrium in the balance of payments. The exchange rate, which is defined as the price of one currency in terms of another, is determined by the relationship between the price level of the two countries, which in turn depends on the relationship between the desired and actual stocks of money in each country. Consequently, the price of a currency is viewed as a relationship between a desire to hold stocks of assets denominated in that currency and the available quantity of these assets. In this formulation, money is an asset. Its demand is stable, and its price is determined by the comparison of the supply and demand for money. Since the demand for money depends on real income, interest rates, expectations, and so on, such factors will also affect the exchange rate. The implication is that the exchange rate is determined by all the accounts: current, capital and money. Changes in the money supply will affect the exchange rate and the balance of payments since changes in reserves (ΔR), the foreign part of the money supply, are held at zero. This is achieved through domestic price adjustments and money stock valuations. It should be pointed out that under fixed exchange rates these valuations are gradual, resulting in gradual adjustments in the balance of payments; while under flexible rates they are instantaneous.

Dirty Float

The adjustment process in the case of quasi-fixed, quasi-flexible exchange rates is gradual and self-correcting. The implications of the Monetary approach are very important, especially as they pertain to the coordination of international policy to affect the exchange rate. The Traditional approach calls for the coordinating effort of central banks in intervening in foreign exchange markets, and not for the coordination of their monetary policy. However, such intervention will be nullified by the private sector and therefore will be ineffective, requiring additional intervention. A sustained, permanent, and consistent monetary policy, as called for by the Monetary approach, will generate better, more sustainable results.

Inconvertibility of the Currency

The Monetary approach will generate results even in the presence of exchange controls. With respect to the exchange rate, the money market is the fundamental factor in the black market, and the transmission takes no more than two years. Further capital controls do not affect the overall capital account since these are imposed on the outflows of capital and not on the inflows, which will decrease and offset the smaller capital outflows.

CONCLUSION

This chapter has argued the merits of the Monetary approach to international finance, a theory whose roots are to be found in the specie flow mechanism. This approach highlights the role of money and monetary variables that have been cast aside by the Traditional approach to international finance.

The Monetary approach relies heavily on the four assumptions of a general equilibrium, full employment, purchasing power parity, and the essentiality of money. These assumptions have been expanded and modified here, and qualifications were offered.

The Monetary approach differentiates extensively between real and monetary variables, stocks and flows, country sizes and speed of adjustment following monetary policy action and currency devaluation.

Adjustments under the Monetary approach take place through the money markets and the portfolio adjustments of residents following a disturbance. The ORTB is the key balance, and both the capital account and the current account are of secondary importance. The introduction of currency substitution introduces an element of monetary interdependency, while the separation between reserve and nonreserve currency countries differentiates between the potency of monetary actions by various countries.

The Monetary approach is a significant contribution to the theories of international finance in its analytical framework, its predictions, and its policy implications. The approach deals with long-term adjustments and monetary disturbances. Thus, any tests to support or refute the theory should be based on long-term data. Perhaps a reconciliation of the Monetary approach with the Traditional approach would improve the current explanation of the balance of payments and enhance the policy implications. This survey has offered a substantial base for such a reconciliation.

REFERENCES

Artus, Jacques R. "The Behavior of Export Prices for Manufactures." In *The Effects of Exchange Rate Adjustments*, ed. Peter B. Clark, Dennis E. Logue and Richard J. Sweeney. Proceedings of a conference sponsored by OASIA Research, Department of the Treasury, 1974. Washington, D.C.: U.S. Department of the Treasury, 1977, pp. 319–338.

Boyer, Russel S. "Sterilization and the Monetary Approach to Balance of Payments Analysis." *Journal of Monetary Economics*, 5 (April 1979): 295–300.

Davidson, Paul. "Money and General Equilibrium." *Economie Appliqué*, 30, no. 4 (1977): 541–563.

Dornbusch, Rudiger. "Currency Depreciation, Hoarding and Relative Prices." *Journal of Political Economy*, 4 (July/August 1973): 893–915.

Dornbusch, Rudiger. "Devaluation, Money and Nontraded Goods." *American Economic Review*, 62, no. 5 (December 1973): 871–883.

Frenkel, Jacob A. "A Dynamic Analysis of the Balance of Payments in a Model of Accumulation." In *The Monetary Approach to the Balance of Payments*, ed. J. A. Frenkel and H. G. Johnson. Toronto: University of Toronto Press, 1976, pp. 109–146.

Frenkel, Jacob A., and Harry G. Johnson. "The Monetary Approach to the Balance of Payments: Essential Concepts and Historical Origins." In *The Monetary Approach to the Balance of Payments*, ed. J. A. Frenkel and H. G. Johnson. Toronto: University of Toronto Press, 1976, pp. 23–24.

Friedman, Milton. "The Role of Monetary Policy." *American Economic Review*, 58, no. 1 (March 1958): 1–17.

Gray, H. Peter. *An Aggregate Theory of International Payments Adjustment*. London: Macmillan, 1974, ch. 2.

Gray, H. Peter. "The Monetary Approach to International Payments Theory: A Critique." Unpublished manuscript, Douglass College, Department of Economics, Rutgers University, 1976.

Grubel, Herbert G. "Internationally Diversified Portfolios: Welfare Gains and Capital Flows." *American Economic Review*, 58, part 1 (December 1968): 1299–1314.

Johnson, Harry G. "The Monetary Approach to Balance of Payments Theory." In *Further Essays in Monetary Theory*, ed. H. G. Johnson. London: George Allen and Unwin, 1972.

Johnson, Harry G. "Towards a General Theory of the Balance of Payments." In *International Trade and Economic Growth*. London: George Allen and Unwin, 1980, pp. 153–168.

Keynes, J. M. *The General Theory of Employment, Interest, and Money*. London: Macmillan, 1936.

Laffer, Arthur B. "Exchange Rates, the Terms of Trade and the Trade Balance." In *The Effects of Exchange Rate Adjustments*, ed. Peter B. Clark, Dennis E. Logue and Richard J. Sweeney. Proceedings of a conference sponsored by OASIA Research, Department of the Treasury, 1974. Washington, D.C.: Department of the Treasury, 1977.

Laffer, Arthur B. "The Phenomenon of Worldwide Inflation: A Study in International Market Integration." In *The Phenomenon of Worldwide Inflation*, ed. David I. Meiselman and Arthur B. Laffer. Washington, D.C.: American Enterprise Institute for Public Policy Research, 1975, pp. 27–52.

Laffer, Arthur B., and Marc A. Miles. *International Economics in an Integrated World*. Glenview Ill.: Scott, Foresman, 1982.

Malindretos, John. "A Theoretical and Empirical Comparison of the Two Theories of International Finance: The Case of a Medium Sized, Reserve Currency Country." In *Advances in Quantitative Analysis of Finance and Accounting*, vol. 1, part B, ed. Chen-Few Lee. Greenwich, Conn: JAI Press, 1991.

Metzler, Allan H. "The Demand for Money: The Evidence from the Time Series." *Journal of Political Economy*, 71 (June 1963): 287–297.

Miles, Marc A. "Currency Substitution, Flexible Exchange Rates, and Monetary Independence." *American Economic Review*, 68 (June 1978): 428–436.

Miles, Marc A. *Devaluation, the Trade Balance and the Balance of Payments*. New York: Marcel Dekker, 1978.

Mundell, Robert A. "Inflation and Real Interest." *Journal of Political Economy*, 71 (June 1963): 280–283.

Mundell, Robert A. "A Reply: Capital Mobility and Size." *Canadian Journal of Economics and Political Science*, 30 (August 1964): 421–431.

Mussa, Michael. "A Monetary Approach to Balance of Payments Analysis." *Journal of Money, Credit and Banking*, 6 (August 1974): 99.

Mussa, Michael. "Tariffs and the Balance of Payments: A Monetary Approach." In *The Monetary Approach to the Balance of Payments*, ed. J. A. Frenkel and H. G. Johnson. Toronto: University of Toronto Press, 1976, 187–221.

Robinson, Joan. "The Foreign Exchanges." In *Essays in the Theory of Employment*. 2nd ed. Oxford: Blackwell, 1947. Reprinted in *Collected Economic Papers IV*. Cambridge, Mass: MIT Press, 1973.

Sommariva, Andrea, and Giuseppe Tullio. "International Gold Flows in Gold Standard Germany: A Test of the Monetary Approach to the Balance of Payments 1880–1911." *Journal of Money, Credit and Banking*, 20 (February 1988): 132–140.

Swoboda, Alexander K. "Monetary Policy under Fixed Exchange Rates: Effectiveness, the Speed of Adjustment and Proper Use." *Economica*, 40 (May 1973). Reprinted in Frenkel and Johnson, eds., *The Monetary Approach to the Balance of Payments*. Toronto: University of Toronto Press, 1976, 237–261.

Whitman, Marina V. N. "Global Monetarism and the Monetary Approach to the Balance of Payments." *Brookings Papers on Economic Activity*, no. 3 (1975): 491–555.

Part II

An Empirical Review of the Keynesian and Monetary Theories to the Balance of Payments

Chapter 3

Empirical Evidence for the Traditional Approach to the Capital Account

Valerie Englander, Melvin Johnson and John Malindretos

In one way or another, the Traditional approach models deal with the trade balance (TB) or the current account. This happens because without the qualifications that we make in the chapter in its criticism, the Traditional approach excludes the other components of the international accounts except for the current account. The balance of payments (BOP) goes up along with the current account. In the 1960s and through the 1970s, this view changed after studies on the factors determining capital account flows appeared.

The following consists of the reasons for the disinterest of empiricists in the capital account (KA):

1. The KA was not important in the late 1940s or in the 1950s in terms of size because all kinds of capital controls were imposed.

2. In general, real variables held primacy of place in the 1940s and 1950s. The trade balance (TB) was deemed worthwhile because it was the "real" account. The KA was not considered a real account, and thus it was not considered as important.

3. The nature of the KA is such that speculation can create tremendous instability therein and make attempts to estimate its determinants extremely difficult or simply wrong.

With the exception of the 1960s, most of the traditional econometric work has been on the TB. Kenen, in the 1960s, showed how capital flows are affected by the difference of levels of interest rates among countries (1963). The portfolio distribution model, which was developed by Tobin (1958), says that changes in the rates of return would change the allocation of capital. This will then affect the flow of capital by changes in interest rates. Tobin foreshadowed the Monetary approach (MA) to the BOP by stating that the capital account would be temporarily affected by an interest rate differential, and that in order to have a continuous change in the KA, a continuous change in the interest rates is needed. The same idea was echoed by Jan Tinbergen (1964).

Since William Branson (1968) defined capital flows as claims, he indicated that changes in the U.S. interest rates would affect U.S. financial capital flows inversely. Foreign interest rates are directly related to U.S. claims. Therefore, when interest rates abroad rise, U.S. residents send their money abroad, which gives rise to the claims U.S. residents obtain. Trade flows constitute another important element. When the United States exports, it usually provides credit to the foreign importers, which in turn gives rise to claims against foreigners. The opposite happens with imports, and the movement of claims here is negative (Branson, 1968).

Branson (1968) researched how output changes affect financial capital flows and found that the growth of U.S. GNP increases the claims of the United States, while the growth of foreign GNP reduces them. The inference is that securities are a normal good for the United States, and that as its wealth (GNP) rises, so does the demand for financial assets, such as claims.

However, if foreign GNP rises, claims of the focus nation decrease due to foreigners increasing their claims while becoming richer. One could say that if U.S. income grows at the same rate as foreign income, there should really be no change in U.S. claims. Branson concludes that international capital flows will occur because tastes are different, which means that domestic supply will not equal domestic demand.

Ralph Bryant and Patrick Hendershott (1972) examined capital flows for Japan. They used as independent variables the interest rates of the United States and Japan and found that borrowing by Japan is inversely related to U.S. interest rates and directly related to Japanese interest rates. They also used import flow figures, which they divided by Japanese net wealth, and which proved to be positively related to Japanese borrowing. Bryant and Hendershott used other variables to incorporate capital restrictions from the U.S. and Japanese sides into their model and found that as capital controls were eliminated, borrowing by Japan rose. Finally, the amount of capital controls imposed by the United States is inversely related to the amount of capital flows of Japanese constituents (Bryant and Hendershott, 1972).

Bryant and Hendershott (1972) looked at Japan's capital flows during 1959–1967 and defined capital accounts as the borrowing done by Japanese banks. As independent variables, they used the same variables as in their nonlagged approach estimations of KA. However, some of these variables are used in both nonlagged and lagged estimations in order to find the short-run and long-run elasticities. All the capital control variables have the same signs as in the nonlagged approach, which means they are inversely related to the capital flows. Therefore, as capital liberalization takes place, borrowing intensifies (Bryant and Hendershott, 1972).

Bryant and Hendershott (1972) used the difference between the Japanese and U.S. interest rates and found that the long-run responses are sometimes higher and sometimes lower than the short-run responses. However, even though the signs are correct every time, they find fault with the magnitude of the coefficients of the short run (nonlagged) import coefficient in that the capital flow is sometimes higher than the change of the import.

William H. Branson and Raymond D. Hill undertook an elaborate analysis of determinants of the KA for the United States and a few other OECD nations (Branson and Hill, 1971) and found that both domestic and foreign interest rates are important in affecting capital flows. The other important factors are the wealth variables domestically and abroad, the TB, the velocity of money, and a credit-rationing variable. In most instances, the signs of the coefficient of the independent variables were as expected. The domestic interest rate has a positive effect, while the foreign interest rate has a negative one. The wealth effects of the domestic and the foreign countries according to theory could have any sign; this is substantiated by the empirical analysis. The TB is negatively related to the flows of money because trade is financed by credit. Therefore, when net exports rise, flows of money to the focus country fall and claims of money rise. (However, if net exports fall, claims fall and flows of money into the focus country rise.) The velocity of money is a monetary indicator. If it rises, indicating a tightening of credit, its effects should be similar to an interest rate increase, and thus, money will flow into the focus country. The credit-rationing index is the final factor to consider. When it rises, money flows into the country. The basic policy of the monetary authority of the focus country is determined by the domestic interest rate, the credit-rationing index, and the velocity of money. However, this definition of the KA is not the usual one; rather, it refers to the inflow and outflow of money as related to the exchange of securities.

Niehans (1965) correlated the TB and the capital account by relating the TB deficit of Switzerland to that country's interest rate and found that the TB negatively influenced the interest rate. He stated that if there is a surplus in the TB, money will flow into the country. If income decreases and causes the improvement in the TB, we can see what effect it will have on the interest rate—it will fall due to the inflow of money and reduction in income level.

So far we have studied the KA and asked how trade flows may affect it. However, it is possible that the TB is dependent on the capital account. Roger A. Sedjo (1971) showed that the trade balance relates to capital flows by demonstrating that the Canadian trade balance depends on the capital flows of Canada and the United States. Capital flows are said to be the sum of the total of government and private long-term capital movements. These consist of such things as private sector unilateral transfers, long-term private investment and, on the government side, long-term capital repayments and nonmilitary unilateral transfers. Income from investments is excluded. Sedjo concluded that the elasticity of the TB with respect to changes in capital inflows of Canada is negative, which means that when the net securities of Canadians decrease, Canada obtains an increase in the amount of its exports divided by its imports. Sedjo also concluded that the Canadian TB elasticity is negative. The obvious reason for this is that Canadian exports relative to imports rise when the net position of U.S. residents, in terms of securities, decreases. If the United States and Canada were the only countries involved, this would be unlikely, since it would mean that the Canadian TB improves at times when the United States receives more capital and loses some of its securities holdings. However, we should keep in mind that there are many other countries whose actions could offset the relationship of U.S. capital inflows and Canadian TB and give it a negative direction.

REFERENCES

Branson, William H. *Financial Capital Flows in the U.S. Balance of Payments*. Amsterdam: North Holland Publishing Company, 1968, chs. 5, 6.

Branson, William H., and Raymond D. Hill. *Capital Movements in the OECD Area: An Econometric Analysis*. Paris: Organization for Economic Cooperation and Development, 1971.

Bryant, Ralph C., and Patrick H. Hendershott. "Empirical Analysis of Capital Flows: Some Consequences of Alternative Specifications." In *International Mobility and Movement of Capital*, ed. Fritz Machlup et al. New York: Columbia University Press, 1972, pp. 211–213.

Kenen, Peter B. "Short Term Capital Movements and the U.S. Balance of Payments." In *The United States Balance of Payments*. Hearings before the Joint Economic Committee, 88th Cong., 1st Sess., 1963.

Niehans, Jurg. "Interest Rates and the Balance of Payments: An Analysis of the Swiss Experience." In *Trade Growth and the Balance of Payments*, ed. R. E. Baldwin et al. Chicago: Rand McNally, 1965.

Sedjo, Rojer A. "Price Trends, Economic Growth and the Canadian Balance of Trade: A Three Country Model." *Journal of Political Economy*, 79 (May–June 1971): 569–613.

Tinbergen, Jan. *Economic Policy: Principles and Design*. Amsterdam: North Holland Publishing Company, 1964.

Tobin, James. "Liquidity Preference as Behavior towards Risk." *Review of Economic Studies*, 25, no. 1 (February 1958): 65–86.

Tobin James. "Economic Progress and the International Monetary System." *Proceedings of the Academy of Political Science* (May 1963): 84–85.

Chapter 4

The Traditional Theory to the Current Account: An Empirical Examination

Augustine C. Arize, Elias C. Grivoyannis,
Ioannis N. Kallianiotis and Stanley J. Lawson

THE BASIC MODEL

The Traditional view is effectively a view of the balance of payments (BOP), which is the current account (CA) and, even more specifically, the trade balance (TB). The Traditional approach (TA) basically attempts to describe the explanatory variables of the current account.

The TA proposes the following equation for the TB (Leamer and Stern, 1970).

$$(\Delta TB/TB) = \{(\Delta X/X) - \Delta M/M)\}_t = b_0 + b_1\{(\Delta Y_d/Y_d) - (\Delta Y_j/Y_j)\}_t \quad (1)$$
$$+ b_2\{(\Delta P_x/P_x) - (\Delta P_m/P_m)\}_t + \{\Delta ER/ER\}_t$$

where:

Δ = change
TB = trade balance
X = exports
M = imports
b_0 = constant of the regression equation
b_1 = coefficient of income
b_2 = coefficient of price
b_3 = coefficient of the exchange rate
Y_d = domestic income level
Y_j = world income level
P_x = price level of exports
P_m = price level of imports
ER = the exchange rate between the focus currency and the world currencies

The export price level relates negatively to the TB, and the import price level relates to it positively. However, if the price level of the particular nation rises faster than that of the foreign nation, the TB will deteriorate, and the reverse is also true. As a result, in the first case competitiveness worsens, and in the second, it improves. The ER reinforces the price effect: if the nation's currency revalues, the TB will decline, and if it devalues, the TB will improve.

Next, the reason why the focus country relates negatively to the TB is that if the income of the focus nation goes up, absorption does the same and so the TB worsens. However, if the world expands more rapidly than the focus economy, the TB will go up and the foreign income level will relate positively to the TB. In all these cases, the reverse also holds true.

Looking back at our examination, we can conclude that the following three factors determine the trade balance of a nation:

1. The price of one country's products relative to the world price.
2. The value of exchange of the focus currency relative to foreign currencies.
3. The relative incomes of the focus and foreign economies.

The first two factors can be called the price effect or competitiveness, since they can be combined into a single idea. The competitiveness or price effect, along with the relative income level, are the two final factors determining the international accounts of nations.

MODIFICATION OF THE CORE MODEL

The detail of the former model is not needed; therefore, we can make the following changes.

Simplifications

The price and exchange rate explanatory variables can be combined into one variable, which can be called price effect or competitiveness. We can keep the two different prices (domestic and foreign) and can also include an additional price variable, the price of the commodities consumed in the focus nation. We do this because we feel that the domestic goods compete with the exports of a nation and also to analyze the price level of the nations' goods relative to the price level of its exports.

Presupposition of Imperfect Substitution

Another assumption that we make is that there is imperfect substitution in domestic versus foreign goods. For example, under perfect competition, there is either complete supply by domestic producers or complete supply by foreign producers. When discussing imports or exports, perfect competition means infinite price elasticities of demand. The assumption is that there is no constraint on production; therefore, the price elasticities of supply with respect to exports and imports is infinite (or close to infinity), thus causing constant costs to exist. However, if we do not face infinite supply elasticities, cost will rise and then domination by either the focus or nonfocus country will not occur—even if there is perfect competition in the demand for their goods.

Later, in the section titled, "International Competitiveness," we consider the speed of adjustment due to the importance of the concept lags in our research.

TYPES OF EMPIRICAL MODELS ACCORDING TO THE KEYNESIAN THEORY

Different kinds of models have been proposed in the literature. The following is an analysis of each.

Single Equation Models

Empirical studies done after World War II show that prices did not appropriately affect trade flows. It was thought that since the Marshall-Lerner condition for TB improvement (i.e., the sum of the price elasticities of demand were not greater than one) did not hold, that ER changes were not important in correcting disequilibrium in the BOP, indicating elasticity pessimism. However, other studies also done at this time by Ball and Marwah (1962), Junz and Rhomberg (1973) and Houthakker and Magee (1969) indicate "elasticity optimism" (Magee, 1975).

Houthakker and Magee (1969) reported price elasticities of demand for imports between $+.23$ and -1.46 and export price elasticities of 0 to -2.27. The researchers also calculated the long-term elasticities between the long term and short term. Their research found an overall difference, which was greatest in finished manufacturers, where the price elasticities of demand for imports are $-.45$ and -4.05 for the short and long terms, respectively. The long-term elasticities were usually larger than the term-run elasticities, implying that the adjustment of habits is a more important phenomenon than inventory behavior. When consumers experience a rise in price, they do not react by buying more in the short term and less in the long term; instead, they react by buying more in the long term. As far as international trade goes, consumers are not predominantly affected by a desire to accumulate or decumulate inventory, but by the ability to conform to a given price change through time.

It is safe to say that this is not the case domestically. Houthakker and Taylor (1970) found that occasionally inventory behavior is more important than the adjustment of habits, and they calculated the short-term elasticities of consumption goods to exceed long-term elasticities in the case of the country domestically.

Dornbusch and Krugman (1976) examined the response of trade to change in relative prices for nine countries and found that during the period 1963–1975, nine out of eleven countries were affected in their export shares of manufactured goods by the price changes in the direction that we would expect (i.e., negative price elasticities of demand). For Germany and France, the values vary from $-.10$ to -3.38, with most elasticities between -1 and -3. The price elasticity figures for Germany and the United Kingdom have the expected sign but lack statistical significance.

Tracy Murray and Peter T. Ginman (1976) criticized Houthakker and Magee (1969) and argued that they failed to include other prices in their specification of trade equation such as prices for domestic tradables and nontradables. In contrast, Murray and Ginman argued that their study, which examined Canada and United States, indicated a higher price elasticity and a much lower income elasticity of demand (Murray and Ginman, 1976).

A study estimating price and income elasticities of demand for imports was done by Goldstein, Khan and Officer (1978) and embodies the price of non-traded goods and total traded goods in addition to the imports' price. They use the trend level of real income and the ratio of current real income to the trend. The price elasticities of demand that they found are very similar to the results found by Houthakker and Magee (1969). However, Goldstein and colleagues found much higher cyclical income elasticities of demand for most of the ten industrial nations that they studied. They also found that the price of nontradable goods does not appear to be a significant determinant of the demand for imports in most industrial countries (Goldstein, Khan and Officer, 1978).

Simultaneous Equations

The single equation models that we have been using experience a problem of specification. The simultaneous equation model seems to be prominent, since price and quantities are usually determined by both supply and demand. Magee uses these simultaneous equations to correct for bias and inconsistency and has thus increased elasticities for total exports and finished manufacturers. Many of the demand elasticities rise when he calculates them using instrumental variables (Magee, 1975). The model used is:

$$QM_j^d = f^1(Y_j, PM_j^d, P_j) \tag{2}$$
$$QM_i^s = f^2(PX_i^s, P_i)$$
$$QM_j^d = Qx_i^s$$
$$PM_j^d = FX_{ij}(1 + T_j)PX_i^s$$

where:

QM_j^d = imports demand in country j
Y_j = income in country j

PM^d_j = price of imports in country j
P_j = price of goods whose production occurs in country j
QX^s_i = quantity of exports supplied by country i
PX^s_i = price of exports of country i
P_i = price of goods produced in i
FX_{ij} = units of j's currency over units of i's currency
T_j = the proportional tariff rate in country j

Peter Hooper (1972) incorporated a tariff variable in his modeling and conducted a study where he included a tariff and some nonprice-rationing variables in examining U.S. trade with individual countries. He obtained higher import and export elasticities and found high U.S. import elasticities relatively to export elasticities, which he ascribed to his use of simultaneous equations and his inclusion of additional variables. Some of his price elasticities exceed ten in absolute value, and some income elasticities exceed the value of six. Some of his coefficients of determination values are too low, and as he himself conceded, the data used suffered from severe problems of aggregation (1972).

A similar equation was developed to examine the export behavior of eight industrial countries by Goldstein and Khan (1978). Their explanatory variables are (1) relative prices of domestic exports and world export goods, and (2) domestic capacity. In terms of income elasticities, the two results are similar; however, their price elasticities are usually higher than Houthakker and Magee's (1969). The cases of France, Japan, West Germany and Belgium are not comparable because France has a positive price elasticity in Houthakker and Magee (1969) and Belgium has positive elasticities in Goldstein and Khan (1978). Both agree about the very low and very high income elasticities of the United States and Japan and give evidence of the quick adjustment to change in explanatory variables. They also find supply elasticities for industrial nations, especially Japan (Houthakker and Magee, 1969).

Khan uses a simultaneous equation approach to discover elasticities of exports and imports of less-developed countries (LDCs) and found them to be rather high especially for imports, and comparable to those of the more developed countries (MDCs). The Marshall-Lerner condition is upheld (Khan, 1974).

Balassa (1979), on the other hand, rejected the idea that the export income elasticities are different among industrial nations, especially between Japan and the United States. Balassa calculated income elasticities for eighteen years and broke them up into two groups. He used the constant-market share model and concluded the following. First, in the time frames of 1953–1962 and 1963–1971, income elasticity varied for each of the thirteen researched nations. The income elasticity rose for each nation, with the percentage rise in Japan's case being around 74 percent. He also indicated that the export income elasticities were very similar. He calculated both the U.K. and U.S. income elasticities as greater than those of Japan. His policy statement is a supply-side one. He advocates that the United States should attempt to grow faster, because then it will be able to export more and have an export-led growth, which will also assist in avoiding deteriorating trade balances. Balassa stated that the very high income elasticities found in the previous studies are partially owed to the noninclusion of a nonprice variable like productivity. He also argued that price elasticity of demand is not positive according to the supply elasticity in the disequilibrium model and should be attributed to the abandonment of nonprice variables and the productivity gains of Japan during the period.

World Trade Models

The Armington (1969) and the Adams and Junz (1971) models are two empirical models that look at how each country affects the other. The Armington model is a world trade model where one country's export is another country's import and each depends on the other, so that total world imports equal total world exports.

The model can be written as:

$$X_{ij}/M_{ij} = b_{ij}{}^{G_j}/(P_{ij}/Pj)Gj$$

where:

G_j = the elasticity of substitution for the jth buyer
X_{ij} = the supply of the ith supplier to the jth buyer
M_j = the purchase of the jth demander
P_{ij} = the price of the ith supplier to the jth buyer
P_j = the price of the jth buyer
b_{ij} = distribution parameter

The Armington model assumes a constant elasticity of substitution (CES) and elasticity of demand. In order to calculate the direct and cross-price elasticity of demand, we can do the following: First, purchasers in country j have two prices, the traded and the nontraded, plus some nominal income in their possession. They will then indicate their purchase of traded goods. There will be a distribution of purchasing among the *i*th suppliers; the purchasers buy imports from the suppliers; and the suppliers sell imports to the purchasers.

From the Armington model, Branson (1972) developed direct price elasticities for the world's exports and imports, as combined in a world matrix of trade flows. Branson calculated the price elasticities of demand to be greater than 1 for almost all his countries. Branson assumed that the own-price elasticity of demand for commodity I by purchaser j is unity, which means that a given fraction of income is spent on tradable goods, and hence that changes in price of other goods do not affect the demand for tradables (1972). Branson also assumed that the elasticity of substitution was equal to 3. The benefits of using the Armington theoretical model are, Branson argued, (a) the acquisition of the values of the elasticities are reasonable; and (b) there is consistency among countries.

These advantages are accomplished by the world trade model (Adams and Junz, 1971), which shows that (a) the total of the trade balance effects is zero; and (b) the effects should have a connection with the market share of trade internationally. Even when the supply elasticity is not infinite, the elasticity of demand with respect to price changes is high (Adams and Junz, 1971).

Even though the Adams and Junz (1971) model of world trade gives high total trade value elasticities of demand, it is not as high as the Armington (1969) model. The combined trade value elasticities are nothing more than the price elasticity of demand of a country with respect to the entire world; hence the name *total trade value*.

Price Effects

As far as price is concerned, there are three important areas to consider: (1) size and sign of the price elasticity of demand; (2) stability of the coefficient of the price elasticity of demand; and (3) speed of adjustment of quantity responses to changes in price.

ANALYSIS OF DETERMINANTS OF THE TRADE BALANCE

In examining equation (1), we can divide our discussion into two main parts. The first part involves the fundamental determinants of the trade balance and is composed of the relative price levels and the exchange rate of the focus nation versus the world. The combination of the two factors is called international competitiveness. The second fundamental determinant of the trade balance is the relative income level of the focus country relative to the rest of the world.

INTERNATIONAL COMPETITIVENESS

The first critical determinants of the trade balance is international competitiveness, defined as:

$$C = \frac{P_f}{P_d} * ER$$

where:

P_f = foreign price level
P_d = domestic price level
ER = the exchange rate, defined as the focus nation's currency units
     divided by the rest of the world's currency units

We have observed several models of international trade as they relate to price effects and have discussed their size and sign. However, some questions arise with regard to competitiveness. For example, there have been many studies yet no definite answer, on, for example, the price elasticity of demand for total imports, for a category of imports for a certain country, or for a group of countries. From this observation stems concern for the whole issue of competitiveness.

The aspects of concern as far as international competitiveness goes are the following: (1) size and sign of the price elasticity of demand, (2) stability of the coefficient of price elasticity of demand, and (3) speed of adjustment of quantity responses to changes in competitiveness.

Size and Sign of Elasticity of Demand

Orcutt's Five Points, or Downward Bias (Orcutt, 1975)

Orcutt argues that the elasticity pessimism that occurred after World War II was due to five reasons:

Simultaneous Equation Bias. Simultaneous equations increase the magnitude of the price elasticities. Without simultaneous equations there will be downward bias (Magee, 1975).

Observation Errors. The price elasticity of demand will be biased toward zero if the errors in the dependent variable do not correlate with errors in the independent variables. Since the quantity variable relates negatively to the price variable, the errors will most likely be negative between the dependent variable (quantity) and the independent variable (price). In that case, the price elasticity bias will be close to -1 (Kemp, 1962b).

Timing. Even though Orcutt believes that elasticities do not include the long term, this is not always true. If consumers build up their stocks of goods when prices change, they will react more to the short than the long term, and therefore the elasticities will be biased upward (Houthakker and Taylor, 1970).

Quantum Effects. This point states that larger changes in prices have greater effects on elasticities than smaller changes. However, this is not always the case (Branson, 1972). Magee argues that the following two reasons may go against the quantum effect (Magee, 1975).

1. Prices do not quickly change after a change in the exchange rate.
2. There is underestimation of the length of the lags and so the full impact is not felt by trade during the period of analysis.

Nonetheless, Orcutt may be wrong as far as the quantum effect is concerned. The reasons are two, Magee explained. First, the price elasticity of demand for traded goods is an elusive concept as there are many different price elasticities of demand for different groups of commodities rather than for all traded goods;

and second, devaluations do not improve the trade balances (Laffer, 1973). Thus, price changes, whether small or large, do not affect trade flows. Therefore, the quantum effect could not possibly exist.

Aggregation Problem (Zellner and Montmarquette, 1971). It is not appropriate to simply multiply the total elasticity with the change in price if the aggregated price elasticity is an average of the weighted, disaggregated price elasticities. When the following conditions hold true, the aggregated approach will give the correct results:

1. The changes in price in a disaggregated fashion are not correlated with the multiplication of the elasticities and weights of the components.
2. Changes in prices are the same among the different components.

There will be a bias in the total change of quantity if the changes in prices relate to the elasticities of the components in an inverse fashion, which will cause the aggregate elasticity to be biased upward. However, if the changes in price relate to the elasticities of the components by having the same direction of intensity with them, then the aggregate elasticity will be biased downward (Magee, 1975). The downward bias in the analysis pertained to the aggregation of different goods, but the aggregation bias could be an intertemporal difficultly as well (Grenfeld and Griliches, 1960).

Upward Bias or Contra Orcutt

So far we have referred to the price elasticities of demand as biased downward, but there may be other effects that cause the price elasticities of demand to be biased upward. These are the following:

Cross-Price Effects (White, 1970). If we have differing elasticities of substitution in different markets and the results are derived from data in a disaggregated manner, then a certain exchange rate change could cause an upward biased in the responsiveness of quantity.

Structural Effects (MacDougall, 1952). It is also possible to overestimate the aggregate elasticity of substitution for the various components in some markets, as in the following cases:

1. A devaluation makes price changes equal in each market.
2. The size of the markets is the same.
3. The elasticity of substitution is the same for all markets.
4. The export values for all the competitors are the same.

Observation Errors (Kemp, 1962b). There will be overestimation if the price elasticities are less than 1 (in absolute value) due to the fact that errors in the price indices used to divide the values of exports and imports in order to calculate their quantities.

Aggregate Prices in Submarkets (White, 1970). If we assume that we have obtained the aggregate price index of the focus country's exports to the world, one of two cases may result.

1. The export values are deflated by the aggregate price index, which contains errors. If the price elasticities of demand for traded goods are less than 1 (in absolute terms), since the price index contains observation errors, it will cause the elasticities to be overestimated.
2. The price index (aggregate) does not contain errors in observation, which deflates export values.

The changes of price for low-elasticity countries will probably be high in comparison to the price changes of high-elasticity countries, even if the component price indices have the same direction as the aggregate price index. The aggregate price index will vary in its changes from either of its components in the low- and high-elasticity countries. Because the aggregate price index changes by more than the price index of the component low elasticity of demand countries, there will be an overestimation of the price elasticity. However, there will be underestimation of the elasticities of high-elasticity countries since there the price index changes by less than the aggregate price index.

Nonprice Effects (Magee, 1975). Changes in any of the nonprice variables will affect trade, and if they are not explicitly incorporated into the equation, they will make price variables receive all the blame for the changes in trade. This will overestimate the price elasticities.

Positive Component Elasticities and Lags (Magee, 1975). An overestimation of the elasticities is made when analysts throw out any price elasticities that are positive. Another problem is that we often use unit values to calculate price elasticities, which lowers the length of lags for price changes to affect quantities. This causes empirically tested models to overestimate the correct price elasticities of traded goods.

Stability of the Coefficient of Price Elasticity of Demand

There are two types of traded goods, perfect substitutes and imperfect substitutes.

Perfect Substitutes (Magee, 1975)

The relationship of the import price elasticity of demand, domestic demand, and supply elasticities is:

$$e_{mp} = (D/M)\ e_{dp} - (S/M)e_{sp} \tag{3}$$

where:

e_{mp} = price elasticity of demand for imports

D   = demand for domestic goods (importables)
S   = supply of domestic goods (importables)
M   = imports
e_{dp} = price elasticity of demand for domestic goods
e_{sp} = price elasticity of supply for domestic goods

The quantity of imports is a function of the following variables:

$$QM_j = F(Y_j, PM_j, P_j)$$
$$F_y > 0, F_{PM} < 0, F_p > 0$$

where:

QM$_j$ = quantity of imports in region j
Y$_j$ = income of region j
PM$_j$ = price of imports in region j
P$_j$ = price of goods in region j

Three points can be made. First, the elasticity of income has a shorter lag than the elasticity of price. Second, the price elasticity of demand for imports will be more unstable than the elasticity of demand or supply for domestic goods. Finally, it is usually assumed that there is no money illusion; therefore, in equation (1) the sum of elasticities of real imports is zero. Due to the strong constraint imposed on equation (1), there will be instability imposed upon the PM$_j$ and P$_j$ in equation (7'), and each one of the prices will interact with the other.

Imperfect Substitutes (Magee, 1975)

Depending on whether imports are substitutes or complements will determine whether imports will rise or fall. If there are uniform price changes, then only in the short term will changes take place; in the long term there will be no changes.

According to the evidence, there has been instability in the price elasticity of demand. Kemp found that Canadian imports exhibited a change in the price elasticity of demand from the period 1926–1939 to 1947–1955 (Kemp, 1962a). Even though some subgroups did not change, Rhomberg and Boisonneault indicated that U.S. imports changed between the periods 1948–1953 and 1954–1961. Finished manufactures undoubtedly changed their price elasticity of demand, and along with manufactures, semimanufactures also showed a shift in price elasticity (Rhomberg and Boisonneault, 1965).

Heien (1968) also indicated that the price elasticities of demand varied between the two periods 1950–1954 and 1955–1964.

Time Lag of Alterations of Competitiveness and Effect on the Current Account

It often takes time for the regressor to influence the regressand. In fact, former values of the regressor can influence the regressand, and the lag can be long.

Junz and Rhomberg reported that changes in prices may affect the exports of a nation for up to six years. They also derived short- and long-term elasticities of 3 and 5, respectively (Junz and Rhomberg, 1973).

Houthakker and Magee (1969) corroborated the findings of Junz and Rhomberg (1973). Specifically, they discovered that the long-term elasticities substantially exceeded short-term elasticities in the case of imports.

Grimm (1968) used a polynomial, distributed-lag approach and found different lags depending on the type of product being considered. However, he found lag lengths of up to seven quarters when he examined both exports and imports.

Artus did not support the findings of Grimm (1968) and reported lags of influence of up to eight months only (Artus, 1977).

Deppler gave evidence of lengthy lags of up to 4 years. Even though the lags of imports differed from those of exports, he basically supported the majority of the recent studies (Deppler, 1974). Finally, Dornbush and Krugman tested alterations of relative prices and export shares of manufactures. They found that the average mean lag was about 1½ years, although the adjustment could take as long as 43 quarters (Dornbush & Krugman, 1976).

INCOME EFFECTS

These are the three important aspects of the effects of the dependent variable, income, on trade: (1) size and sign of income elasticity of demand; (2) stability of income elasticity of demand; and (3) speed of adjustment of quantity responses to changes in income.

Size and Sign of Income Elasticity of Demand

We express the income elasticity of demand for imports as follows (Magee, 1975).

$$e_{my} = (D/M)e_{dy} - (S/M)e_{sy} \hspace{3cm} (4)$$

where:

e_{my} = income elasticity of demand for imports
e_{dy} = income elasticity of demand for importables
e_{sy} = income elasticity of supply for importables

Assuming that e_{dy} and e_{sy} have the same sign, in order to have a negative e_{my}, e_{sy} must be much greater than e_{dy}. Johnson (1967) described this type of occurrence and indicated that it was owed to ultra–trade-biased growth in supply, which more than offset ultra–protrade-biased growth in demand. The evidence on e_{my} showed it to be positive. Houthakker and Magee (1969) analyzed income elasticities of imports and exports for fifteen industrial countries and determined that all the income elasticities were positive and statistically significant. The values of the import elasticities varied from .90 to 2.25, and the values of the export elasticities, from .86 to 3.55. The researchers again found positive income elasticities when testing several underdeveloped and developing countries, which is very significant.

Houthakker and Magee (1969) found a positive sign for all coefficients with all the trading partners of the United States. Moreover, all the coefficients were significant. There is some evidence that the income elasticity was negative (Buckler and Almon, 1972). However, the negative sign applied to only 1 kind of commodity out of an aggregate of 50. The reason why it may be impossible to locate negative income elasticities the of demand are the following (Magee, 1975):

1. Omission of variables connected with the liberalization of trade.
2. Growth paths of demand and supply of import-competing products.
3. The mixing of cyclical and long-term elasticities.
4. Analysts' aversion to reporting negative income elasticities of demand.

The first reason indicates that effects are sometimes ascribed to income when in fact they should be ascribed to other factors. The second reason indicates that as long as demand overwhelms supply, the appropriate sign will be obtained. The third reason indicates that even though the long-term value of e_{my} is negative, it could be confused with the cyclical effect, which would make it positive. The true e_{my} is very difficult to calculate. In general, Khan found that the income elasticities of demand are lower than the price elasticities of demand and often are not statistically significant. Khan also found that import income elasticities were lower than export elasticities (Khan, 1974).

Stability of Income Elasticity of Demand

We can observe a few reasons why there can be instability in e_{my} by looking at equation (4). In total, there are four reasons for instability in e_{my}:

1. Instability in supply.
2. Instability in demand.
3. The fraction D/M in equation 4 changes in cases where the supply and demand elasticities are not equal, as we move through time. This can occur even if the demand and supply elasticities for importables (domestic goods) do not change over time.
4. Factor reversals (Johnson, 1967).

The reasons that make the exportable importable and vice versa (factor reversal) include: changes in factor taxes, either less or more unionization, changes in consumption taxes, changes in production taxes, and Vernon's product cycle (Vernon, 1966).

In most cases, the more trade is acted on by factor reversal, the more negativity e_{my} will achieve. Conversely, the less trade is affected by factor reversal, the more toward positivity e_{my} will go. Vernon's product cycle implies two tendencies. First, a change in the pattern of trade whereby industrial nations end up importing the technology-intensive good that they had initially been exporting, and second, movement of goods in some periods and movement of inputs in others.

Speed of Adjustment of Trade Account to Alterations in Incomes

The rapidity with which any changes in relative incomes between the focus nation and the rest of the world influence the trade flows between these nations is a critical piece of information. Using a Koyck distributed-lag approach, Houthakker and Magee (1969) calculated the long-run income elasticities of demand for imports. Their findings are very similar to other results that Magee (1970) calculated using nonlagged income variables. This result shows that income effects affect the trade balance faster than competitiveness, and that the effect ends in one year. Instead of income, Heien (1968) used consumption, which also corroborated the findings of Houthakker and Magee (1969).

QUALIFICATIONS TO THE BASIC MODEL

The construct we have used is true but incomplete. Specifically, we excluded certain issues, and consequently, our model suffers from these omissions. First, our model is a partial equilibrium one. In a general equilibrium model we would include many other factors, chief of which would be the capital account and the official reserves transactions balance. Consequently, our model is a depiction of only the current account, and not the full balance of payments. Additionally, we have not included the cause of the returns of the investment flows between nations. Thus, even the current account is not complete. Third, we have assumed a comparative static approach and not a dynamic one. Therefore, we have not examined the path of adjustment that an economy takes to adjust to international or national disturbances, a consideration that would be essential for policy makers.

However, given all these caveats, the model depicts the traditional view correctly and elaborately. The following chapters analyze the criticism of the Traditional approach and provide alternative views of adjustment of the international accounts.

REFERENCES

Adams, Gerard F., and Helen B. Junz. "The Effects of the Business Cycle on Trade Flows of Industrial Countries." *Journal of Finance*, 26 (May 1971): 251–268.

Armington, Paul. "A Theory of Demand for Products Distinguished by Place of Production." *International Monetary Fund Staff Papers*, 16 (March 1969): 159–179.

Artus, Jacques R. "The Behavior of Export Prices for Manufacturers." In *The Effects of Exchange Rate Adjustments*, ed. Peter B. Clark, Dennis E. Logue and Richard J. Sweeney. Proceedings of a conference sponsored by OASIA Research, Department of the Treasury, 1974, pp. 319–338. Washington, D.C.: U.S. Department of the Treasury, 1977.

Balassa, Bela. "Export Composition and Export Performance in the Industrial Countries, 1953–71." *Review of Economics and Statistics*, 61, no. 4 (November 1979): 604–607.

Ball, R. J., and K. Marwah. "The U.S. Demand for Imports, 1948–1952." *Review of Economics and Statistics*, 44 (November 1962): 395.

Branson, William H. "The Trade Effects of the 1971 Currency Realignments." *Brookings Papers on Economic Activity*, no. 1 (1972): 15–69.

Buckler, M., and C. Almon. "Imports and Exports in an Input-Output Model." Research Memorandum no. 38. Baltimore, Md.: Maryland Interindustry Forecasting Project, 1972.

Dornbusch, Rudiger, and Paul Krugman. "Flexible Exchange Rates in the Short-Run." *Brookings Papers on Economic Activity*, no. 3 (1976): 537–575.

Goldstein, Morris, and Mohsin Kahn, "The Supply and Demand for Exports—A Simultaneous Approach." *Review of Economics and Statistics*, 60 (May 1978): 275–286.

Goldstein, Morris, Mohsin Kahn and Lawrence H. Officer. "Prices of Tradable and Nontradable Goods in Demand for Total Imports." *Review of Economics and Statistics*, 62, no. 2 (1978): 190–199.

Grenfeld, Yehuda, and Zvi Griliches. "Is Aggregation Necessarily Bad?" *Review of Economics and Statistics*, 42 (February 1960): 1–13.

Heien, Dale M. "Structural Stability and the Estimation of International Import Elasticities." *Kyklos*, 21, Fasc. 4 (1968): 695–712.

Hooper, Peter. "The Construction of Trade Sector for the Michigan Quarterly Forecasting Model of the U.S. Economy, DHL-III." Unpublished paper, University of Michigan. Presented at the Winter Meetings of the Econometric Society, Toronto, December 28–30, 1972, p. 37.

Houthakker, Hendrik S., and Stephen P. Magee. "Income and Price Elasticities in World Trade." *Review of Economics and Statistics*, 51, no. 2 (May 1969): 111–125.

Houthakker, Hendrik S., and Lester D. Taylor. *Consumer Demand in the U.S.: Analysis and Projections*. Cambridge, Mass.: Harvard University Press, 1970.

Johnson, Harry G. *Money, Trade and Economic Growth*, Cambridge, Mass.: Harvard University Press, 1967.

Junz, Helen, and Rudolf R. Rhomberg. "Price Competitiveness in Export Trade among Industrial Countries." Discussion Paper no. 22, Board of Governors of the U.S. Federal Reserve, Division of International Finance, 1973.

Khan, Mohsin. "Imports and Export Demand in Developing Countries." *International Monetary Fund Staff Papers*, 21, no. 3 (November 1974): 678–694.

Kemp, Murray C. *The Demand for Canadian Imports: 1926–55*. Toronto: University of Toronto Press, 1962a.

Kemp, Murray C. "Errors of Measurement and Bias in Estimates of Import Demand Parameters." *Economic Record*, 38 (September 1962b): 369–372.

Laffer Arthur B. "Exchange Rates, the Terms of Trade and the Trade Balance." Mimeographed Manuscript, University of Chicago 1973.

Leamer, Edward, and Robert M. Stern. *Quantitative International Economics*. Chicago: Aldine Publishing Company, 1970.

MacDougall, G. B. A. "British and American Exports: A Study Suggested by the Theory of Comparative Costs, Part II." *Economic Journal*, 62 (September 1952): 493.

Magee, Stephen P. "A Traditional and Empirical Examination of Supply and Demand Relationships in the U.S. International Trade." Unpublished study for the Council of Economic Advisors, 1970.

Magee, Stephen P. "Prices, Incomes, and Foreign Trade." In *International Trade and Finance*, ed. Peter Kenen. Cambridge: Cambridge University Press, 1975, p. 178.

Murray, Tracy, and Peter J. Ginman. "An Empirical Examination of the Traditional Aggregate Import Demand Model." *Review of Economics and Statistics*, 58 (February 1976): 75–80.

Orcutt, Guy H. "Measurements of Price Elasticities in International Trade." *Review of Economics and Statistics*, 32 (May 1975): 117–132.

Rhomberg, Rudolf F., and Lorette Boisonneault. "The Foreign Sector." In *The Brookings Quarterly Economic Model of the United States*. Chicago: Rand McNally, 1965, pp. 375–406.

Vernon, Raymond. "International Investment and International Trade in the Product Cycle." *Quarterly Journal of Economics*, 80 (May 1966): 190–207.

White, William H. "Bias in Export Substitution Elasticities Derived through Use of Cross-Section (Sub-Market) Data." Mimeographed manuscript, International Monetary Fund, 1970.

Zellner, Arnold, and Claude Montmarquette. "A Study of Some Aspects of Temporal Aggregation Problems in Econometric Analyses." *Review of Economics and Statistics*, 53 (November 1971): 335–342.

Chapter 5

Empirical Evidence for the Monetary Approach to Balance of Payments Adjustments

Augustine C. Arize, Elias C. Grivoyannis,
Ioannis N. Kallianiotis and John Malindretos

The Monetary approach to the balance of payments can be judged by the accuracy of its predictions or the validity of its assumptions. The richness of testable hypotheses that underlie the Monetary approach to the balance of payments has led to a large body of empirical literature. The articles discussed here represent a sample of cases of empirical work that tested the predictions of the Monetary approach, and in the process attempted to refine variables in the monetary model and statistical tools.

The principal technique of testing the predictability of the monetary approach to the balance of payments is the formulation and estimation of a reserve-flow equation such as:

$$(R/B)\Delta\log R = a_1 \Delta\log P + b_1 \Delta\log y + c_1 \Delta\log i + d_1 \Delta\log m$$
$$+ e_1(D/B) \Delta\log D$$

where R is a country's international reserves, B is a country's monetary base, P is the price level, y is real income, i is the interest rate, m is the money multiplier, D is the domestic component of the monetary base, and $\Delta\log X$ is the rate of change in variable X.

This equation is then used to test the major premise of the Monetary approach, which claims that under a fixed exchange rate, changes in a country's reserves are a result of an excess demand for or supply of money. This implies that for a given amount of money demand and a given money multiplier, changes in the domestic component of the monetary base (D) will cause opposite and equal changes in international reserves (R). The coefficient of the domestic component of the monetary base (D) is known as the "offset coefficient." It shows the degree to which changes in the domestic component of the monetary base (ΔD)

are offset by changes in the international component (ΔR). The expected value of the offset coefficient is -1 because the Monetary approach postulates that under a fixed exchange rate, the change in international reserves induced by a change in the domestic component of the monetary base is equal in magnitude but opposite in sign. The monetarist prediction is validated as long as the estimated coefficient is statistically significant and not significantly different from the theoretically expected value of -1.

The coefficient d_1 on $\Delta \log m$ is an elasticity coefficient with an expected value of -1, because the money multiplier (m) is a multiplicative factor in the supply of money. The monetarist prediction is validated when the estimated coefficient is statistically significant and not significantly different from the expected value of -1.

Another technique of testing the predictability of the monetary approach to the balance of payments is the formulation and estimation of a capital-flow equation such as:

$$K = a_2\, \Delta Y + b_2\, \Delta i_w + c_2\, \Delta CA + d_2\, \Delta D + e_2\, DRR$$

where K is the net private capital inflow, ΔY is the change in nominal income, Δi_w is the change in the world interest rate, CA is the sum of the current account balance and the net flow of official capital (excluding international reserves), DRR is the change in the required reserves of commercial banks, and ΔD is the policy-induced change in the domestic component of the monetary base.

In all empirical studies, the predictive power of the Monetary approach is tested in terms of the predictability of the effects of the supply of money or determinants of this supply on the balance of payments and effects of the demand for money or its determinants. The effects of money supply are captured by the predictions of the values of the "offset" and "sterilization" coefficients and predictions of the effects of changes in the money multiplier or the money supply on the balance of payments. The effects of the demand for money are captured by the predictions of the changes in income, the price level, or the interest rate on the balance of payments.

In order to test the hypothesis that under fixed exchange rates, a country has no control over its money supply (the pursuit of any domestic objective, such as price stability, will, by altering the domestic component of monetary base, be frustrated by offsetting changes in the international component through reserve flows), a "sterilization equation" or "reaction function" of the monetary authorities is required. In such an equation, ΔD or its equivalent is the dependent variable, and ΔR or its equivalent is an explanatory variable. Where the model is based on a capital-flow equation, the single sterilization coefficient on ΔR may give way to two sterilization coefficients, on K and CA, because $\Delta R = K + CA$. The monetarist prediction is validated when the sterilization coefficient is not significantly different from its expected value of 0. If the sterilization coefficient is 0, the country will be unable to pursue sterilization policy. All the government will then be able to do is control the composition of the money supply (the division of the base into its domestic D and foreign R components), and not its level.

What follows is a sample of empirical studies, most of which were done in the decade of the 1970s when the Monetary approach to the balance of payments adjustment mechanism gained many converts and the validity of its predictions was widely debated with great concern.

ZECHER ON AUSTRALIA

Zecher (1976) estimated the reserve flow equation as follows:

$$(R/H)g_R = a_1g_y - a_2g_i + b_1g_P - b_2g_a - b_3(D/H)g_D + e'$$

and the demand for money equation as:

$$g_M = a_1'g_y - a_2'g_i + u$$

where g stands for growth rate; y is the permanent income (a sixteen-quarter weighted average of gross national product); R is the official international reserve holdings of the Australian Reserve Bank; i is the two-year Australian government bond rate; P is the consumer price index; $D = H - R$, where H is high-powered money; a is money multiplier; and M is currency plus all trading bank deposits owned by the public (roughly equivalent to U.S. M2).

Zecher assumes that (1) Australian reserve flows are dominantly influenced by the state of equilibrium in the market for Australian money, and (2) that the five other variables are dominantly influenced by factors outside the market for Australian money. Growth in real, permanent income is assumed to result primarily from growth in technology and factors of production. Both interest rates and prices are assumed to be dominantly influenced by world market conditions.

An estimation of money demand using quarterly data for the period 1950–1971 yields:

$$g_M = 0.74g_y - 0.075g_i,$$
$$\quad\;\; (6.19) \quad (-3.35)$$
$$R^2 = 0.30; D - W = 1.04,$$

where the numbers in parentheses are *t* statistics.

Estimation of the reserve flow equation with quarterly data for the same period yields:

$$(R/H)g_R = 1.11g_y - 0.035g_i + 0.65g_P - 0.89g_a - 1.06(D/H)g_D,$$
$$\quad\quad (6.54) \quad (-1.08) \quad (3.70) \quad (-12.77) \quad (-20.92)$$
$$R^2 = 0.89, D - W = 1.69$$

When annual data were used to estimate the two equations, the demand for money equation became:

$$g_M = 0.99g_y - 0.28g_i,$$
$$(7.05) \quad (-5.73)$$

$$R^2 = 0.77; D - W = 2.45$$

While the reserve flow equation became:

$$(R/H)g_R = 0.92g_y - 0.11g_i + 1.38g_P - 1.14g_a - 1.23(D/H)g_D,$$
$$(3.54) \quad (-0.75) \quad (2.56) \quad (-5.08) \quad (-7.97)$$

$$R^2 = 0.93, D - W = 2.13$$

The estimates of both the income and interest rate elasticities of demand for money have the expected sign and size, with a larger magnitude in the case of annual data. The estimation of the demand for money with annual data also provides a better R^2 value. In both estimations during the 1950–1971 period the demand for money in Australia has been a stable function yielding the expected results. All estimated coefficients of the reserve flow equations also conform to values implied by the Monetary approach to the balance of payments hypothesis.[1] The hypotheses that both economic growth and inflationary pressures lead to surpluses are supported by the evidence. The hypothesis that rising domestic interest rates lead to deficits is not inconsistent with the empirical results. Moreover, the domestic money stock variables g_a and (D/H) G_D have a dependable, negative effect on reserve flows, as expected.

Zecher's empirical results indicate that Australian international reserve flows over the 1950–1971 period support the hypotheses of the Monetary approach to the balance of payments. When the growth rate of the demand for money is greater than the growth rate of money supply due to domestic factors, international reserves tend to accumulate and to bring actual growth in the money stock closer to desired growth, and the converse. Growth in national output and the price level are associated with balance of payments surpluses, while growth in the domestic determined portion of the money stock tends to be associated with deficits and reserve outflows. The effect of the interest rate on reserve flows is weak but conforms to the negative relation implied by the Monetary approach to the balance of payments hypothesis.

GENBERG ON SWEDEN

Since the Monetary approach to the balance of payments stresses the importance of world rather than individual country equilibrium in the determination of prices and interest rates, Genberg (1976) used Sweden as a case study to empirically verify the most crucial hypotheses regarding the nature of a small economy and its relationship with the world.

By directly comparing price series in commodity and asset markets of several countries, Genberg determined how closely together they moved and compared them to Swedish data. Using a simple analysis of variance procedure, he examined the hypothesis that all countries have the same rate of inflation for the second quarter of 1959 through the second quarter of 1970. Quarterly OECD rates of change in the consumer price index were used for Austria, Belgium, Denmark, Finland, France, Germany, Ireland, Italy, Japan, the Netherlands, Norway, Portugal, Sweden, Switzerland, the United Kingdom, and the United States. His analysis of variance test rejected the hypothesis that inflation rates differ significantly between countries. His empirical evidence supported the view that Sweden was a small part of an integrated world commodities market.

Genberg also presented evidence consistent with the integrated asset markets hypothesis of the Monetary approach. By treating prices on the New York Stock Exchange as world market prices, he tested the single-market hypothesis as applied to Swedish stock prices. He ran the following regressions:

$$R_{i,t} = a_i + b_i R_{U.S.,t} + U_{i,t} \ (i = \text{Sweden, Germany}),$$

$$R_{Sweden,t} = a + b R_{U.S.,t} + c R_{Germany,t} + v_t$$

where R_t is the monthly rate of change in the relevant stock price index, namely, $R_t = \log(P_t/P_{t-1}; P_t) = $ index of stock prices at time t. The estimation gave the following results:

$$R_{Sweden} = 0.0031 + 0.37 R_{U.S.,t}; \quad R^2 = 0.12, \ D - W = 1.79$$
$$\qquad\quad (0.0028) \quad (0.09)$$

$$R_{Germany} = 0.0040 + 0.69 R_{U.S.,t}; \quad R^2 = 0.17, \ D - W = 1.65$$
$$\qquad\quad (0.0043) \quad (0.13)$$

$$R_{Sweden} = 0.0027 + 0.31 R_{U.S.} + 0.91 R_{Germany}; \quad R^2 = 0.14, \ D - W = 1.84$$
$$\qquad\quad (0.0028) \quad (0.09) \quad (0.057)$$

The coefficient estimates and their standard errors (given in parentheses) clearly support the unified equity market hypothesis. An analysis of the Swedish bond market also indicates that it is integrated with the Eurocurrency market despite the controls on capital movements.

Genberg also estimated long-run demand for money functions of the form:

$$\log(M/P)_t = k_0 + k_1 \log y_t + k_2 \log i_t$$

where i represents yields on other assets than money and y stands for permanent or current income, depending on which demand motive is considered. For his estimations Genberg used nominal and real M1 and M2 values along with permanent, transitory, or current income.

Using Sims's (1972) money-income causality test, Genberg concluded that income changes preceded changes in money in Sweden during the 1951–1970 period. He concluded that the demand for money has determined the stock of money in existence and monetary policy had no systematic effect on the flow of income. He also showed that neither commodity prices nor interest rates appear to be sensitive to domestic monetary forces unless these are in accord with world market conditions.

Following Johnson (1976), Genberg derived a reserve flow equation:

$$(R/H)g_R = g_M D - g_m - (D/H)g_D$$

where g stands for the relative growth rate of the variable appearing as a subscript, H is the monetary base, D is its domestic source component, R is its foreign source component, and m is a money multiplier. He computed a predicted time path for the balance of payments and compared that with the actual reserve flow during the period. The high correlation between the actual and predicted reserve flow series strongly support the monetary interpretation of balance of payments adjustments.

Finally Genberg simultaneously estimated the system:

$$[(R/H)g_R]_t = a_0 + a_1[(D/H)g_D]_t + a_2 g_{mt} + a_3(\log P_t - a \log P_{t-1})$$
$$+ a_4(\log y_t - a \log y_{t-1}) + a_7(\log i_t - a \log i_{t-1})$$
$$+ a_8 \log M_{t-1} + U_t$$

$$[(D/H)g_D]_t = b_0 + b_1[(R/H)g_R]_t + b_2 g_{\text{Govt. debt outstanding}} + V_t$$

where the first equation is the reserve flow equation and the second, a government policy reaction function. His estimates show that the sterilization hypothesis offers a very plausible alternative to his explanation of reserve flows. They also indicate that the Monetary approach passed his tests, both as far as its underlying view of the world is concerned and in its implications with respect to the balance of payments.

BEAN ON JAPAN

Some of the hypotheses of the Monetary approach to the balance of payments (like the price-taking assumption) pertain more to small country cases. Bean (1976) used post–World War II Japan to test the model's hypotheses.

She derived the following two equations from the money market equilibrium condition:

$$[R/(R + D)]d \log R = b_1 d \log P + b_2 d \log y + b_3 d \log i$$
$$+ b_4 d \log a + b_5 d \log[\{D/(R + D)\} d \log D] + e$$

$$d \log R = b_1 d \log P + b_2 d \log y + b_3 d \log i + b_4 d \log a$$
$$+ b_5[\{1 - r)/r\} d \log D] + e$$

where a is the money multiplier; H is high-powered money; R is the central authorities' international reserves; D is domestic credit issued to the government or commercial banks that is due to the central bank; i is interest rate; P is price level; y is real income; and $r = R/(R + D)$.

Bean estimated the equations using quarterly, seasonally adjusted data for the 1959–1970 period. During this period Japanese authorities were controlling reserve flows using their capacity as domestic credit creators. The monetary approach to the balance of payments provides a theoretical explanation for the effectiveness of this policy.

To test the price-taking assumption of the model, Bean used the U.S. consumer price index (CPI), the U.S. whole sale price index (WPI), the Japanese CPI, the Japanese WPI, and adjusted price indices for the Japanese CPI (ACPI) and WPI (AWPI). Those indices were constructed by multiplying the raw Japanese CPI and WPI data by a black market exchange rate factor. The colinearity between the U.S. WPI and Japanese WPI was higher when the Japanese prices were adjusted. These adjusted price series for Japan supported the price-taking hypothesis of the Monetary approach.

Bean reported results of eight different estimations for each one of her two specifications using combinations of the Japanese CPI, WPI, ACPI and AWPI with the U.S. treasury bill rate and the Japanese discount rate. The following specifications were, in general, statistically more significant, with higher R^2s, better Durbin-Watson statistics, and larger t statistics:

$$[R/(R + D)]d \log R = 1.31 \ d \log P + 0.56 \ d \log y - 0.05 \ d \log i$$
$$\qquad\qquad\qquad (6.34) \qquad\qquad (6.73) \qquad\qquad (-1.55)$$

$$-0.84 \ d \log a - 0.72 \ d \log[\{D/(R + D)\} \ d \log D],$$
$$(-5.42) \qquad\qquad (-9.20)$$

$$R^2 = 0.65, D - W = 2.3,$$

$$d \log R = 0.99 \ d \log P + 0.39 \ d \log y - 0.04 \ d \log i$$
$$\qquad\qquad (5.40) \qquad\qquad (4.84) \qquad\qquad (-1.42)$$

$$-0.80 \ d \log a - 0.55[\{(1 - r)/r\} \ d \log D],$$
$$(-4.71) \qquad\qquad (-6.54)$$

$$R^2 = 0.47, D - W = 1.84$$

In both cases the CPI is used as price index and the U.S. treasury bill rate as the interest rate. The t statistic is given in parentheses.

All the estimated coefficients have the expected sign. The income elasticity is consistently smaller than unity. The interest rate elasticity is larger when the

Japanese discount rate is used instead of the U.S. treasury bill rate, but the difference is not statistically significant. The money multiplier is not significantly different from its expected value of unity, while the estimates of the elasticity of the domestic component of the base are smaller than their expected magnitude. Bean's empirical analysis of Japan strongly supports the theses of the Monetary approach and suggests that it is a useful framework for analyzing these phenomena.

GUITIAN ON SPAIN

Guitian (1976) used data on the Spanish economy to test the theoretical proposition that the balance of payments is a monetary phenomenon. He investigated the relationship between the balance of payments in Spain and the rate of domestic credit expansion for the period 1955–1971. In his empirical investigation he tested: (a) the effect of domestic credit expansion on the balance on current account and on the overall balance of payments, (b) the connection between these two external accounts and the following variables: gross domestic product, domestic and foreign prices and the rate of domestic credit expansion. For his first test he estimated the following equations:

$$B_{CA} = F_{ij} [\Delta D_j]; j = 1, 2, \ldots, 10$$
$$\Delta B_{CA} = F_{2j} [\Delta^2 D_j]; j = 1, 2, \ldots, 10$$
$$B = F_{3j} [\Delta D_j]; j = 1, 2, \ldots, 10$$
$$\Delta B = F_{4j} [\Delta^2 D_j]; j = 1, 2, \ldots, 10$$

where B_{CA} and B stand for the balance on current account and the overall balance of payments, respectively, and the Δ_{js} are different concepts of domestic credit expansion. In his analysis Guitian considered ten such definitions focusing on both central bank and banking system credit variables. When the credit expansion variable was defined as $[\Delta D_1]$, representing the central bank net credit to the public sector, banking institutions and the private sector,[2] the estimation of the current account equation in levels gave:

$$B_{CA} = -0.6893 [\Delta D_1],$$
$$(10.03)$$
$$R^2 = 0.862, D - W = 2.05$$

The t value is given in parentheses.
Estimation of the same equation in differences gave:

$$\Delta B_{CA} = -0.622 [\Delta^2 D_1],$$
$$(5.173)$$
$$R^2 = 0.641, D - W = 2.61$$

Estimation in levels of the balance of payments equation with the same definition of domestic credit expansion gave:

$$B = -0.8356 \ [\Delta D_1],$$
$$(14.896)$$

$$R^2 = 0.932, \ D - W = 0.926$$

Its estimation in differences gave:

$$\Delta B = -0.8274 \ [\Delta^2 D_1],$$
$$(12.730)$$

$$R^2 = 0.915, \ D - W = 3.225$$

Guitian's results strongly reflect the monetary character of balance of payments disequilibria. They show a statistically significant relationship between the balance of payments (and the current account) and domestic credit for the economy of Spain during the 1955–1971 period.

In his empirical investigation Guitian also tested the connection between the current account (B_{CA}) along with the overall balance of payments (B) and the following variables: gross domestic product (Y), Spain's cost of living index (p), an index of foreign prices (ep_f) and the rate of domestic credit expansion (ΔD).[3] For this test he estimated the following equations both in levels and in differences:

$$B_{CA} = H_{1j} \ [Y, p, ep_f, \Delta D_j]; \ j = 1, 2, \ldots, 10$$
$$B = H_{2j} \ [Y, p, ep_f, \Delta D_j]; \ j = 1, 2, \ldots, 10$$

The estimation of the current account equation in levels gave (with t values in parentheses):

$$B_{CA} = 14.34 - 0.1709 \ Y - 0.4682 \ p + 0.1972 \ ep_f - 0.827 \ \Delta D_1,$$
$$(1.664) \qquad (0.943) \qquad (0.663) \qquad (7.228)$$

$$R^2 = 0.891, \ D - W = 3.07$$

The estimation of the current account equation in differences gave:

$$B_{CA} = 10.46 - 0.3148 \ Y - 0.2456 \ p + 0.5738 \ ep_f - 0.7428 \ \Delta D_1,$$
$$(2.508) \qquad (0.376) \qquad (0.911) \qquad (5.856)$$

$$R^2 = 0.711, \ D - W = 2.226$$

The estimation of the balance of payments equation in levels gave:

$$B = 5.493 - 0.08186 \ Y - 0.863 \ \Delta D_1,$$
$$(1.199) \qquad (11.351)$$

$$R^2 = 0.965, \ D - W = 2.525$$

When the estimated coefficient was not significantly different from zero, the corresponding variable was dropped.

The estimation of the balance of payments equation in differences gave:

$$B = 3.348 + 0.3286\ p - 0.2951\ ep_f - 0.8618\ \Delta D,$$
$$\quad\quad\quad (0.725)\quad\ (0.675)\quad\quad (9.750)$$

$$R^2 = 0.965, D - W = 2.53$$

Guitian's empirical results suggest that the safest way to cope with external imbalances in Spain is to control the rate of domestic credit expansion. Such control is consistent with the balance of payments constraint. If domestic credit expands in Spain at a larger rate than that at which the domestic economy wants to horde cash balances, an external deficit will tend to appear, and the reverse is also true.

The relationship between the exchange rate and the balance of payments was considered indirectly by incorporating it into an index of foreign prices. The empirical results indicate that exchange rate changes are effective only when they are accompanied by appropriate credit policies.

WILFORD AND ZECHER ON MEXICO

Wilford and Zecher (1979) examined the balance of payments and monetary policies in Mexico during the fixed exchange rate period of 1955–1975, using annual data. Their estimated equations are: (1) the real money demand equation, (2) the nominal money demand equation, and (3) the reserve flow equation.

$$g(M/P) = b_1 gy + b_2 gi + V \tag{1}$$

$$gM = b_1 gy + b_2 gi + b_3 gP + V \tag{2}$$

$$(R/H)gR = b_1 gy + b_2 gi + b_3 gp - b_4 ga - b_5 (D/H)D + u \tag{3}$$

where M represents the money stock in Mexico (M1 or M2), P is the price level, y is the real income, i is the interest rate, g is the growth rate of the variable that follows, R is the foreign reserves, a and D are domestic monetary variables, and V and u are stochastic disturbance terms.

The money demand equations were estimated for both M1 and M2, and all estimates had the expected sign. The estimated elasticities were significantly different from zero. The results are summarized in Tables 5.1, 5.2, and 5.3.

Equations (1) through (4) in Table 5.3 are nominal reserve flows, and equations (5) and (6) constrain the model to reflect the assumption of linear homogeneity in prices. The income elasticities are close to their expected value of +1 in all equations. The coefficients on the price indexes are close to 1 in both the cases where prices were proxied by the Mexican CPI and the U.S. CPI.

Table 5.1
Demand for Money in Mexico, 1955–1974 (Year over Year Percentage Change, M_1)

	Equation Number			
	1	**2**	**3**	**4**
Dependent variable	$g(M_1/P)$	$g(M_1/P)$	$g(M_1)$	$g(M_1)$
Income elasticity	0.985	1.040	1.121	1.176
	(0.124)	(0.171)	(0.161)	(0.175)
Mexican interest rate elasticity of money demand	-0.255 (0.168)		-0.141 (-0.810)	
U.S. interest rate elasticity of money demand		-0.064 (0.137)		-0.021 (0.125)
B_1 Mexican price elasticity of money demand			0.742 (0.168)	0.687 (0.157)
R^2	0.42	0.34	0.39	0.37
SE	0.038	0.040	0.035	0.036
D-W	1.69	1.91	1.86	1.86

Note: The standard error of the coefficient is reported in parentheses under the coefficient.

The Wilford-Zecher estimates indicate that the Mexican experience for the 1955–1974 period is consistent with the monetary model of the balance of payments. Both M1 and M2 demand specifications were stable over the estimation period, and the reserve flow equation was consistent with the predictions of the monetary model.

PUTNAM AND WILFORD ON EIGHT EUROPEAN COUNTRIES

Putman and Wilford (1978) estimated eight reserve flow equations for Austria, Belgium, Denmark, France, Germany, Italy, the Netherlands, and the United Kingdom for the period 1952–1971. Their article extended the empirical analysis of international reserve flows in two ways. First, they incorporated the interrelationship of the eight European countries' reserve-flow equations by applying the seemingly unrelated regressions technique.[4] Their intention was to empirically show that the international reserve flows of the eight countries under investigation were related through world goods, and capital markets, and that institutional arrangements (Bretton Woods) and economic shocks to the world system could impact that group of countries simultaneously. Second, Putnam

Table 5.2
Demand for Money in Mexico, 1955–1974 (Year over Year Percentage Change, M₂)

	Equation Number			
	1	**2**	**3**	**4**
Dependent variable	g(M₂/P)	g(M₂/P)	g(M₂)	g(M₂)
Income elasticity	1.015 (0.115)	1.057 (0.151)	1.210 (0.138)	1.205 (0.147)
Mexican interest rate elasticity of money demand	-0.116 (0.156)		0.029 (0.149)	
U.S. interest rate elasticity of money demand		-0.050 (0.122)		-0.006 (0.105)
B₁ Mexican price elasticity of money demand			0.655 (0.144)	0.668 (0.132)
R²	0.42	0.41	0.43	0.43
SE	0.035	0.036	0.030	0.030
D-W	1.65	1.77	2.02	1.99

Note: The standard error of the coefficient is reported in parentheses under the coefficient.

and Wilford integrated the purchasing power parity and interest rate parity assumptions directly into their reduced form tests. In addition to estimating equations specified solely with the domestic price level and interest rate as proxies for the world price level and interest rate, they substituted U.S. prices and interest rates for domestic variables to serve as alternative proxies for world variables. The first set of reserve-flow regression equation for the *j*th country was of the form:

$$(R_j/H_j)gR_j = b_1gY_j + b_2gi_j + b_3gP_j - b_4ga_j - b_5(D_j/H_j)gD_j + u_j$$

where R_j is the stock of international reserves held by authorities in country j; H_j is the stock of high-powered money in country j; Y is the level of output in country j; i_j is the interest rate in country j; P_j is the price level in country j; a_j the money multiplier in country j; D_j is domestic credit in country j; and gX_j = d ln X_j/dt = the rate of growth of the variable X in country j, where X = R, Y, P, i, a, and D. Putnam and Wilford point out that the reserve equation for the *i*th country may have an error that is related to the error of the *j*th country. As a result, if one is investigating the reserve-flow equation of n different countries and $Eu_j^t u_{j+1}^t$ is different than zero (t = time and u_j^t = the error in the

Table 5.3
Foreign Reserve Flow Equations for Mexico, 1955–1974 (Year over Year Percentage Change)

	Equation Number					
	1	2	3	4	5	6
Dependent variable	$(R/H)gR$	$(R/H)gR$	$(R/H)gR$	$(R/H)gR$	$(R/H)gR - gP$	$(R/H)gR - gP$
Income elasticity	1.090 (0.189)	1.097 (0.177)	1.260 (0.250)	1.212 (0.220)	0.888 (0.157)	0.851 (0.152)
Mexican interest rate elasticity	-0.038 (0.187)	0.046 (0.179)	0.199 (0.227)	0.270 (0.220)	-0.176 (0.179)	-0.125 (0.179)
B_1 price elasticity	0.711 (0.167)	0.657 (0.157)	1.187* (0.573)	1.265* (0.508)		
B_2 multiplier coefficient	-0.762 (0.117)	-0.661** (0.092)	-0.871 (0.155)	-0.774** (0.116)	-0.741 (0.123)	-0.0631** (0.102)
B_3 domestic credit coefficient	-1.023 (0.095)	0.964 (0.082)	-1.183 (0.139)	-1.134 (0.115)	-1.011 (0.101)	-0.946 (0.091)
R^2	0.91	0.92	0.85	0.88	0.89	0.89
SE	0.035	0.032	0.046	0.041	0.037	0.036
D-W	2.05	2.30	1.68	2.05	1.83	1.83

Notes: The standard error of the coefficient is reported in parentheses under the coefficient.
* The price variable is proxied by the U.S. consumer index.
** The money multiplier was determined from the broad definition of money, M2.

time t for the *j*th country), then a proper methodology for examining individual reserve-flow equations would involve estimating the equations jointly as one set. To increase efficiency, they estimated the coefficients of the reserve flow equations in a stocked format utilizing a generalized least squares (GLS) procedure.

The second set of estimating equations utilizes the same procedure of estimation except that the *j*th country's price variable is replaced by the U.S. CPI as a proxy of the movement in world price levels. The reserve flow regression equation for the *j*th country now becomes:

$$(R_j/H_j)gR_j = b_1 gY_j + b_2 gi_j + b_3 gP_{U.S.} + b_4 ga_j + b_5 (D_j/H_j)gD_j + u_j$$

The third set of estimating equations substitutes both the U.S. CPI and the U.S. interest rate for the domestic price level and interest rate variables for each country j as alternative proxies for the corresponding world variables.

Tables 5.4, 5.5, and 5.6 report the regression results for the eight countries, based on the three equation forms already described. Single equation estimation ordinary least squares (OLS) results as well as seemingly unrelated regression (GLS) results are reported for each country.

The income elasticity of money demand, b_1, is significantly different from zero and close to its hypothesized value of $+1$ in all cases except Denmark, and then only when the U.S. price level and interest rate are used as proxy for the world. The interest elasticity, b_2, is negative and relatively small in all cases except Denmark, conforming to a priori expectations of integrated world capital markets. The coefficient on prices, b_3, is close to $+1$ for all countries except France and England. The sign of the money multiplier variable coefficient, b_4, is negative in all cases and different from -1 with the exception of Denmark and Belgium, where they are very close to minus unity. The relative stability of this coefficient supports the hypothesis that a tightening of monetary policy in country j, ceteris paribus, will lead to reserve inflows. The coefficient on growth in domestic credit, b_5, is very close to its expected value of -1 and statistically significant in all cases. The stability of the money demand coefficients (b_1, b_2, and b_3) and the money supply coefficients (b_4, and b_5) over the three separate specifications, as well as the relative size and significance of these coefficients, strongly support the assumption of integrated world goods, services and capital markets, as espoused in the Monetary approach to the balance of payments.

AGHEVLI AND KHAN ON 39 LESS DEVELOPED COUNTRIES

Aghevli and Khan (1977) examine the balance of payments and monetary policies in 39 developing countries during the period 1955–1975, using cross-sectional data. Their first test was to estimate a demand for money function assuming homogeneity in prices. Their results were as follows:

Table 5.4
International Reserve Flows*, Domestic Prices and Interest Rates

COUNTRY J	Real Income	Interest Rate	Price Level	Money Multiplier**	Domestic Credit	Type	R^2
Austria	0.76 (5.66)	-0.24 (-4.19)	0.93 (4.53)	-0.50 (-2.95)	-1.21 (-8.12)	OLS	0.92
	0.69 (6.07)	-0.22 (-5.01)	1.05 (6.73)	-0.60 (-5.05)	-1.12 (-10.35)	GLS	
Belgium	0.69 (4.02)	-0.15 (-2.22)	0.85 (1.99)	-0.83 (-2.34)	-1.08 (-10.06)	OLS	0.88
	0.68 (4.22)	-0.01 (-1.76)	0.73 (1.80)	-0.75 (-2.33)	-1.11 (-11.19)	GLS	
Denmark	0.71 (3.58)	-0.27 (-1.33)	1.18 (4.98)	-0.99 (-4.20)	-0.98 (-8.93)	OLS	0.91
	0.69 (4.02)	-0.12 (-0.70)	1.10 (5.25)	-0.99 (-4.89)	-0.99 (-10.36)	GLS	
France	1.22 (5.91)	-0.37 (-3.98)	0.17 (1.10)	-0.43 (-1.34)	-0.95 (-9.29)	OLS	0.88
	1.32 (7.45)	-0.38 (-4.67)	0.15 (1.16)	-0.62 (-2.31)	-1.00 (-11.57)	GLS	
Germany	0.83 (8.34)	-0.04 (-3.09)	1.05 (3.43)	-0.54 (-3.62)	-1.08 (-18.07)	OLS	0.98
	0.84 (9.70)	-0.05 (-4.01)	1.12 (4.26)	-0.54 (-4.67)	-1.08 (-22.83)	GLS	
Italy	1.05 (5.18)	-0.09 (-1.06)	1.12 (2.53)	-0.49 (-6.22)	-0.82 (-6.98)	OLS	0.82
	1.02 (5.81)	-0.13 (-1.88)	1.21 (3.17)	-0.46 (-6.51)	-0.83 (-8.14)	GLS	
Netherlands	0.56 (3.69)	-0.13 (-1.91)	0.88 (3.03)	-0.52 (-3.45)	-1.13 (-24.51)	OLS	0.97
	0.61 (5.83)	-0.06 (-1.20)	0.70 (3.61)	-0.59 (-5.80)	-1.13 (-35.44)	GLS	
United Kingdom	0.91 (5.60)	-0.12 (-2.32)	0.30 (2.26)	-0.34 (-4.45)	-0.82 (-13.21)	OLS	0.94
	0.91 (6.20)	-0.10 (-2.20)	0.30 (2.48)	-0.32 (-5.24)	-0.84 (-16.90)	GLS	

Note: t statistics are in parentheses.
* Period: 1952–1971; reserves $(R_j/H_j)gR_j$.
** Calculated on basis of M1.
Source: International Financial Statistics, 1952–1971 (Washington, D.C.: International Monetary Fund).

Table 5.5
International Reserve Flows*, U.S. Prices and Domestic Interest Rates

COUNTRY J	Real Income	Interest Rate	Price Level	Money Multiplier**	Domestic Credit	Type	R^2
Austria	0.76 (3.53)	-0.21 (-2.64)	1.00 (1.98)	-0.71 (-2.99)	-1.19 (-5.70)	OLS	0.84
	0.69 (3.62)	-0.19 (-3.00)	1.09 (2.33)	-0.77 (-4.05)	-1.19 (-7.17)	GLS	
Belgium	0.81 (4.39)	-0.10 (-1.32)	0.22 (0.49)	-0.49 (-1.24)	-1.08 (-8.81)	OLS	0.84
	0.69 (4.41)	-0.05 (-0.94)	0.37 (1.00)	-0.54 (-1.87)	-1.04 (-11.47)	GLS	
Denmark	0.76 (2.36)	-0.03 (-0.09)	1.24 (1.91)	-1.01 (-2.92)	-0.96 (-5.94)	OLS	0.80
	0.61 (2.26)	-0.04 (-0.15)	1.18 (1.93)	-0.72 (-2.58)	-0.88 (-6.71)	GLS	
France	1.24 (5.48)	-0.42 (-3.97)	0.22 (0.49)	-0.43 (-1.28)	-0.94 (-8.93)	OLS	0.87
	1.22 (6.38)	-0.37 (-4.17)	1.13 (2.75)	-0.43 (-1.58)	-0.88 (-10.33)	GLS	
Germany	0.88 (8.33)	-0.05 (-3.44)	0.85 (2.86)	-0.59 (-3.72)	-1.05 (-16.69)	OLS	0.97
	0.84 (8.44)	-0.04 (-3.14)	0.89 (3.09)	-0.56 (-3.96)	-1.07 (-19.26)	GLS	
Italy	1.15 (5.95)	-0.03 (-0.34)	1.08 (2.12)	-0.52 (-6.13)	-0.79 (-6.56)	OLS	0.80
	1.03 (6.14)	-0.02 (-0.40)	1.38 (3.13)	-0.45 (-7.31)	-0.85 (-9.82)	GLS	
Netherlands	0.70 (4.74)	-0.13 (-1.54)	1.00 (2.12)	-0.57 (-3.02)	-1.07 (-20.39)	OLS	0.97
	0.54 (4.55)	-0.09 (-0.48)	1.29 (3.37)	-0.74 (-5.61)	-1.08 (-29.20)	GLS	
United Kingdom	0.83 (5.86)	-0.12 (-2.78)	0.59 (3.35)	-0.33 (-5.12)	-0.79 (-14.62)	OLS	0.96
	0.83 (5.98)	-0.01 (-2.61)	0.58 (3.33)	-0.33 (-5.38)	-0.80 (-15.43)	GLS	

Note: t statistics are in parentheses.
* Period: 1952–1971; reserves $(R_j/H_j)gR_j$.
** Calculated on basis of M1.
Source: International Financial Statistics, 1952–1971. (Washington, D.C.: International Monetary Fund).

Table 5.6
International Reserve Flows*, U.S. Prices and Interest Rates

COUNTRY J	Real Income	Interest Rate	Price Level	Money Multiplier**	Domestic Credit	Type	R^2
Austria	0.64 (2.71)	-1.21 (-1.46)	1.27 (2.11)	-0.81 (-2.93)	-1.36 (-6.27)	OLS	0.80
	0.60 (3.25)	-0.20 (-1.42)	1.30 (2.37)	-0.78 (-4.77)	-1.40 (-9.61)	GLS	
Belgium	0.78 (4.22)	-0.09 (-1.09)	0.12 (0.29)	-0.23 (-0.75)	-1.01 (-7.39)	OLS	0.84
	0.56 (4.54)	-0.10 (-1.35)	0.59 (1.88)	-0.41 (-2.49)	-0.93 (-12.96)	GLS	
Denmark	0.73 (2.37)	0.17 (1.15)	1.06 (1.78)	-1.10 (-4.03)	-0.99 (-8.04)	OLS	0.81
	0.40 (2.05)	0.17 (0.13)	1.33 (2.51)	-0.89 (-5.46)	-0.96 (-13.36)	GLS	
France	1.21 (4.95)	-0.34 (-3.34)	-0.37 (-0.89)	0.35 (1.07)	-0.78 (-7.06)	OLS	0.85
	1.21 (6.21)	-0.03 (-3.45)	-0.41 (-1.00)	0.36 (1.53)	-0.78 (-9.59)	GLS	
Germany	0.76 (5.78)	-0.07 (-0.71)	1.03 (2.57)	-0.23 (-1.49)	-1.10 (-13.60)	OLS	0.95
	0.72 (6.49)	-0.06 (-0.65)	1.09 (2.89)	-0.27 (-2.45)	-1.11 (-19.01)	GLS	
Italy	1.34 (7.54)	-0.24 (-2.53)	1.38 (3.12)	-0.52 (-7.39)	-0.91 (-8.83)	OLS	0.85
	1.13 (7.27)	-0.22 (-2.40)	1.67 (4.29)	-0.48 (-8.80)	-0.90 (-11.44)	GLS	
Netherlands	0.74 (5.18)	-0.15 (-1.78)	0.84 (2.07)	-0.50 (-2.96)	-1.08 (-22.16)	OLS	0.97
	0.58 (4.83)	-0.15 (-1.80)	1.22 (3.34)	-0.64 (-4.73)	-1.08 (-27.82)	GLS	
United Kingdom	0.89 (5.28)	-0.07 (-1.16)	0.47 (2.35)	-0.30 (-3.95)	-0.83 (-13.55)	OLS	0.93
	0.85 (5.27)	-0.05 (-0.89)	0.51 (2.56)	-0.31 (-4.42)	-0.87 (-15.30)	GLS	

Note: t statistics are in parentheses.
* Period: 1952–1971; reserves $(R_j/H_j)gR_j$.
** Calculated on basis of M1.
Source: International Financial Statistics, 1952–1971 (Washington, D.C.: International Monetary Fund).

$$[(dM/dt)/M - (dP/dt)/P] = -9.9207 + 2.8192(dY/dt)/Y \qquad (4)$$
$$(2.35)(3.55)$$

$$- 0.4566(dP/dt)\ P,$$
$$(3.31)$$

$$R^2 = 0.4751,\ SEE = 7.7753$$

where M is demand for nominal money balances; P is domestic price level; Y is level of domestic real income; P is rate of inflation, defined as $(dP/dt)(1/P)$; $(dX)/dt$ denotes a time derivative of the variable X; t values are in parentheses below the estimated coefficients; R^2 is the corrected coefficient of determination; and SEE is the estimated standard error of the regression.

Both, the income and the inflation elasticities have the correct signs and are significantly different from zero at the 1 percent level. The low R^2 value is not unusual for cross-sectional data.

The estimates of equation (4) could then be substituted into the following:

$$(DR/dt)/R = (H/R)\{[(dM/dt)/M - (dP/dt)/P] - (dm/dt)/m\} \qquad (5)$$
$$- [(D/H)(dD/dt)/D]$$

to yield the rate of growth in international reserves.

If it cannot be assumed that the demand for money function is homogeneous of degree one in prices, the function can be estimated in nominal terms. The estimation of such a function yields:

$$(dM/dt))/M = -3.810 + 0.2611(dP/dt)/P + 2.3575(dY/dt)/Y \qquad (6)$$
$$(1.22)(2.19)(4.20)$$

$$- 0.1142(dP/dt)P,$$
$$(1.03)$$

$$R^2 = 0.13374,\ SEE = 5.4479$$

The coefficient of the rate of growth in prices is significantly less than unity, so the assumption of homogeneity in prices is rejected.

The estimates of equation (6) could then be substituted into equation (7):

$$(DR/dt)/R = (H/R)\{[(dM/dt)/M] - (dm/dt)/m\} - [(D/H)(dD/dt)/D] \qquad (7)$$

to yield the rate of growth in international reserves.

Their second test was to estimate an unrestricted, reduced-form equation, which gave the following results:

$$(R/H)[(DR/dt)/R] = -4.2476 + 0.2569(dP/dt)/P + 1.0276(dY/dt)/Y \qquad (8)$$
$$(2.74)(3.39)(3.67)$$

$$- 0.1214(dP/dt)/P - 0.1452(dm/dt)/m$$
$$(2.00)(0.58)$$

$$- 0.4150[(D/H)(dD/dt)/D],$$
$$(6.62)$$

$$R^2 = 0.6244, \ SEE = 2.6921$$

All coefficients have the expected sign and all are significantly different from zero at the 5 percent level, except for the coefficient of the rate of growth in the money multiplier. The coefficient of the rate of inflation is substantially less than unity, suggesting a high degree of money illusion in the demand for money balances. The positive signs of the first two coefficients confirm two key monetary propositions, namely, that, ceteris paribus, an increase in inflation or in the rate of growth in income will lead to an improvement in the balance of payments. The estimated coefficient of the rate of growth in domestic assets is significantly different from unity, suggesting that some increases in this variable will fail to leak out in the balance of payments. This may be so because some of the assumptions behind the theory—for example, the exogenous nature of inflation—are not satisfied. To the extent that prices rise in response to an increase in net domestic assets, they will reduce the effect on the balance of payments.

Aghevli and Khan also estimated an equation in which the coefficients of the rates of growth in domestic assets and the money multiplier were constrained to be equal. Their results were as follows:

$$(R/H)[(DR/dt)/R] = -4.3246 + 0.2351(dP/dt)/P + 1.0437(dY/dt)/Y \qquad (9)$$
$$(2.78) \qquad (3.22) \qquad (3.73)$$

$$- 0.4045\{[(dm/dt)/m] + [(D/H)(dD/dt)/D]\},$$
$$(6.52)$$

$$R^2 = 0.6226, \ SEE = 2.6985$$

There is no major difference between the unconstrained and constrained equations. Aghevli and Khan argued that the results were biased because they included countries, such as Argentina, Brazil, Chile, Colombia, and Uruguay, with a very high rate of domestic inflation in comparison to the world rate.

The estimates obtained were used to simulate the rate of growth in international reserves, and the simulated values were compared with the actual values to test the model's tracking ability. The simple correlations between the actual and simulated values for the four cases were 0.7011; 0.7659; 0.8139, and 0.8069, respectively.

The results gave a strong indication of the usefulness of the monetary approach in explaining the rate of growth in the international reserves of developing countries.

KAHN ON PAKISTAN

To test the monetary approach, Kahn (1990) first estimated a very standard demand for money function for the period 1972–1973 through 1985–1986, which obtained the following results:

$$\log(M/P)_t = -6.971 + 1.207 \log y_t - 0.005 \, (d \, P_{t-1}/dt) \, P_{t-1},$$
$$(6.41) \qquad (12.39) \qquad (2.93)$$

$$R^2 = 0.961, \, D = W = 1.84, \, p = 0.509$$
$$(4.48)$$

where M is the stock of broad money balances (M2), y is real GNP, and P is the consumer price index. In his specification Kahn used the expected rate of inflation and approximated it by the previous period's percentage change in the consumer price index $(d \, P_{t-1} / dt)/P_{t-1}$. T values are reported in parentheses below the coefficients; and p is the estimated coefficient of first-order autocorrelation.

In the second stage, Kahn subtracted the fitted values of money balances ($\hat{M}$) from the stock of international reserves (in domestic currency terms) and ran it as a function of domestic credit. The results, in first-difference form (and correcting for first-order autocorrelation), were:

$$\Delta(R - \hat{M})_t = 1295.6 - 1.133\Delta D_t.$$
$$(0.67) \qquad (7.87)$$

$$R^2 = 0.872; \, DW = 2.10; \, p = -0.381$$
$$(1.31)$$

where R is the domestic-currency value of net foreign reserves, and D is domestic credit of the banking system. T values are presented in parentheses below the coefficients.

Kahn's results for the demand for money seem very reasonable. The coefficients have the right sign and are significant at the 1 percent level; the overall fit is good; and serial correlation in the errors was removed. The sizes of the estimated coefficients also seem plausible, with the long-run income elasticity above unity, as found in another study for Pakistan by Hasan, Kadir, and Mahmud (1988).

The coefficient for domestic credit is not significantly different from unity, thereby verifying the basic hypothesis of the Monetary approach to the balance of payments. The results here thus confirm that there is a close link between changes in domestic credit—the principal monetary policy instrument—and the balance of payments in Pakistan. One interesting implication of these results is that trade and exchange controls are far less effective than one might assume. If such controls had been binding, one would observe a much weaker relationship between the balance of payments and domestic credit expansion.

Kahn found that over the 1972–1973 through 1985–1986 estimation period there was a fairly close link between changes in domestic credit and the balance of payments—with an expansion in domestic credit being associated with international reserve losses. Consequently, Kahn observed that the government did tighten monetary policy when faced with an actual, or potential, reserve loss.

KAMAS ON MEXICO AND VENEZUELA

Kamas derives her monetarist specification of the balance of payments from a three-equation model: $M^d = 1(Y, P, i, W)$; $M^s = R + D$, and $M^d = M^s$, where M^d is money demand (nominal), Y is domestic income (real), P is the price level, i is domestic interest rate (nominal), W is wealth, M^s is money supply (nominal), R is foreign reserves, and D is net domestic credit. Solving these three equations for R, she obtained the monetarist balance of payments equation: $\Delta R = -\Delta D + 1'_y \Delta Y + 1'_p \Delta P + 1'_i \Delta i + 1'_w \Delta W$. This equation was estimated under the assumption of exogenous Y, P, and i, as justified by the assumptions of flexible wages, the law of one price, and perfect capital markets. The coefficient on ΔD is taken as an estimate of the offset coefficient. Using quarterly data from third-quarter 1971 to fourth-quarter 1981 for Mexico, and from fourth-quarter 1970 to fourth-quarter 1982 for Venezuela, Kamas estimated the following balance of payments equation:

$$\Delta R_t = a_0 + a_1 \Delta D_t + a_2 \Delta Y_t + a_3 \Delta P_t + a_4 \Delta i_t + u_{It}$$

This equation was estimated utilizing both ordinary least squares (OLS) and two-stage least squares (2SLS). Instruments were used for all the endogenous variables of the equation. The instruments utilized were the current and lagged values of the exogenous variables. Due to the lack of quarterly capital-account data for Venezuela, an estimate of total capital flows was obtained by subtracting the quarterly current account from the change in central bank reserves. Net domestic credit was adjusted to incorporate the impact of changes in reserve requirements on the money supply. Income was measured by the industrial production index for Mexico and by real commercial sales for Venezuela; prices were represented by the consumer price index for both countries. Bank time-deposit rates were used for the interest rate in Mexico, and short-term yields on government debt were used for Venezuela. The estimates are presented in Table 5.7.

The estimates for Venezuela provide some support for the monetarist prediction: the signs of all the coefficients are as predicted, and the R^2 in the OLS estimation is high. All the variables are significantly different from zero (at the 90 percent level or more) in the OLS estimation, but only ΔD and ΔY have significant coefficients in the 2SLS estimation. While the monetarist estimates of the offset are significantly different from minus one, they are large in absolute terms (-0.88 and -0.82).

Kamas's estimates for Mexico provide less support for the monetarist model: the R^2 is low, and ΔD and ΔY have the wrong signs. The price coefficient is positive and significant in both estimations, while the interest rate is significant at the 90 percent level in the 2SLS estimation. The estimated positive offset (0.046) is particularly troubling, as it indicates that monetary expansion results in higher foreign reserves. All the models predict a negative relationship; the

Table 5.7
The Monetarist Model for the Balance of Payments (ΔR_t)

	Constant	ΔD	ΔY	ΔP	Δi	SE	R^2	D-W
Venezuela								
OLS	279.0	-0.882	86.77	122.8	-4,924	1,098	0.898	2.339
	(239.8)	(0.046)	(15.27)	(61.8)	(2,413)			
2SLS	323.9	-0.823	95.15	88.5	-2,908	1,130		2.525
	(257.8)	(0.065)	(17.17)	(70.4)	(2,987)			
Mexico								
OLS	-554	0.046	-302.5	299.1	-981	4,585	0.301	1.484
	(1,144)	(0.019)	(222.4)	(137.1)	(2,669)			
2SLS	-1,445	0.041	-5.6	485.3	-7,079	5,010		1.838
	(1,324)	(0.025)	(304.5)	(184.4)	(4,003)			

Note: D, Y, P and i are treated as endogenous in the 2SLS estimation. The instruments used are current and lagged values of the government deficit, exchange rate, Eurodollar interest rate, U.S. income and prices, lagged inflation, trend income, time, seasonal dummies and a constant. For Mexico, the dummy representing the 1976 speculation is also used as an instrument. Numbers in parentheses are standard errors, SE is the standard error of the regression, and D-W is the Durbin-Watson statistic.

disagreement occurs over the size of the offset. The results are surprising in the light of other empirical studies for Mexico. Annual estimates for the offset are −0.46 in Blejer (1977) for 1950–1973; −0.61 in Gomez-Oliver (1976) for 1956–1973; and −1.02 in Wilford and Zecher (1979) for 1955–1974. Kamas concluded that structural change in the Mexican economy and policy in the 1970s was responsible for the difference in offsets.

The difference in the estimated offsets for Venezuela and Mexico is instructive. During the 1970s, the Mexican government played a large role in the economy, becoming involved in production, trade, and finance. Foreign borrowing was utilized extensively to finance current account and government deficits. This may explain the absence of a large offset to monetary policy, as government borrowing made up for reserve losses. The evidence then appears to support the existence of short- or medium-term autonomy for monetary policy in the presence of an active central government. On the other hand, in 1982 an economic crisis forced Mexico to devalue the peso and impose an austerity program. Thus, in the long run, the policies were unsustainable. Venezuela represents the case of a more open economy with a smaller role for the government, and the estimated offsets are in accordance with the predictions of theory.

GENERAL COMMENTS

This section summarized only a sample of empirical studies that attempted to test the monetary approach to the balance of payments adjustment process. No attempt was made here to compare the outcomes of these tests with those of other traditional approaches and reconcile their differences on empirical grounds.[5] As a result, no final conclusions can be drawn regarding the validity of the monetary approach predictions on the basis of empirical evidence. Nevertheless, a number of relevant comments could be made regarding the empirical evidence.

As Kreinin and Officer (1978) put it, a variety of statistical problems can adversely affect econometric testing of the monetary approach, just as they do the testing of any theory. Problems of simultaneity and omitted variables are conspicuous of the monetary theory. Johnson (1977, p. 13) is among the first to acknowledge the presence of a simultaneous-equation bias problem. He claimed that there is a dangerous temptation to test and confirm the monetary approach spuriously, by verifying statistically the tautology that an increase in domestic money must be provided either by domestic credit creation or by reserve acquisition. The use of ordinary least squares (OLS) to estimate either an offset or a sterilization coefficient results into a simultaneous-equation bias.[6] The existence of sterilization biases the OLS estimate of the offset coefficient, both in the capital-flow and the reserve-flow equations, in an upward direction in absolute value toward -1 rather than 0.[7] Moreover, the algebraic t value of the offset coefficient is biased in an upward direction, causing the statistical significance of the offset coefficient to be overstated.

The estimate of the offset coefficient is also biased because of a specification error of omitted variables.[8] The loss of reserves arising from a country's expansionary monetary policy must flow to other countries. Therefore, a country's change in reserves is influenced, not only by its own ΔD variable, which has a negative (and presumed unitary) coefficient, but also by the ΔD variables of each of its trade and payments partners, which have positive coefficients. Reserve-flow equations almost invariably omit foreign ΔD variables, perhaps in an effort to avoid multicollinearity or the loss of degrees of freedom. As a result, the omitted ΔD variables of other countries bias the offset coefficient toward 0 rather than -1.[9]

Another source of specification error of omitted variables is the fact that followers of the Monetarist approach emphasize monetary variables to the virtual exclusion of everything else in an effort to offer their approach as a complete substitute for the traditional approaches. For example, the speed of adjustment of the balance of payments to exchange rate changes is crucial, and devaluation can make a significant contribution. The speed of adjustment, though, depends to some degree on product-market elasticities, which are dismissed as irrelevant by the Monetary approach.[10]

The econometric problems associated with the specification and estimation of the monetary model indicate that the supportive empirical results were obtained, partly because of, rather than in spite of, the underlying assumptions of the Monetary approach.

The interpretation of the results of the empirical tests of the Monetary approach has been complicated by the controversy over the exogeneity assumptions underlying this approach that are implicit in those studies.[11] These include the exogeneity with respect to reserve flows of the determinants of the demand for nominal money balances as well as the domestic credit component of a country's money supply. If the monetary assumptions regarding exogeneity are not correct, then the otherwise identifying restrictions imposed on structural equations may not be sufficient to identify those equations, estimation procedures will be inconsistent, and the model cannot adequately portray the dynamics of the system it seeks to describe.

The empirical findings of the few studies reviewed here confirm the main propositions of the Monetary approach and support the view that the balance of payments deficits and surpluses in a given country cannot be understood without explicit reference to monetary policy and money market developments within the country and throughout the rest of the world.

NOTES

1. The estimated coefficients of g_P, g_a, and $(D/H)g_D$ are all within two standard errors of their expected values of $+1.0$ or -1.0.

2. This corresponds to the central bank's currency issue minus net foreign and other miscellaneous assets.

3. The foreign prices index was constructed by taking a weighed average (with import shares as weights) of the export prices of ten major European countries and of the United States which are the major trading partners of Spain. The index was converted to Spanish pesetas using the exchange rate.

4. For a good discussion of this approach, see Zellner (1962); Kakwani (1967); and Kementa and Gilbert (1968).

5. An interesting introduction to such a comparison can be found in Frenkel, Gylfason and Helliwell (1980), Kamas (1986), and Malindretos (1988).

6. See Johnson (1972), ch. 12. A detailed analysis of sources of least-squares bias can be found in Bronfenbrenner (1953).

7. See Kouri and Porter (1974), pp. 453–454; Magee (1976), p. 165; Kreinin and Officer (1978); and Frenkel, Gylfason and Helliwell (1980).

8. See De Grauwe (1975, 1976), and Rasulo and Wilford (1980).

9. The optimal solution to the problem of omitted variables is to estimate, simultaneously for n countries, the $n \times n$ matrix of offset coefficients (di_{ij} where i and j denote countries and d_{ij} is the effect on ΔD_j on ΔR_i. The monetary approach predicts $d_{ij} = -1$ for i = j and $d_{ij} \geq 0$ for i = j. See De Grauwe (1976).

10. For an attempt to reconcile the various approaches, see Kyle (1976).

11. See Johannes (1981).

REFERENCES

Aghevli, Bijan B., and Mohsin S. Khan. "The Monetary Approach to Balance of Payments Determination: An Empirical Test." In *The Monetary Approach to the Balance of Payments: A Collection of Research Papers by Members of the Staff of the International Monetary Fund.* Washington, D.C.: International Monetary Fund, 1977, pp. 275–290.

Bean, Donna L. "International Reserve Flows and Money Market Equilibrium." In *The Monetary Approach to the Balance of Payments*, ed. Jacob A. Frenkel and Harry G. Johnson. Toronto: University of Toronto Press, 1976, pp. 326–337.

Blejer, Mario. "The Short-Run Dynamics of Price and the Balance of Payments." *American Economic Review*, 67 (June 1977): 419–428.

Bronfenbrenner, J. "Sources and Size of Least-Squares Bias in a Two-Equation Model." In *Studies in Econometric Method*, ed. W. C. Hood and T. C. Koopmans. Cowles Foundation Monographs no. 14. New York: Wiley, 1953.

De Grauwe, Paul. "International Capital Flows and Portfolio Equilibrium: Comment." *Journal of Political Economy*, 83 (October 1975): 1077–1080.

De Grauwe, Paul. *Monetary Interdependence and International Monetary Reform.* Lexington, Mass.: Heath, 1976.

Frenkel, Jacob A., Thorvaldur Gylfason and John F. Helliwell. "A Synthesis of Monetary and Keynesian Approaches to Short-run Balance of Payments Theory." *Economic Journal*, 96 (September 1980): 582–592.

Genberg, Hans, A. "Aspects of the Monetary Approach to Balance of Payments Theory: An Empirical Study of Sweden." In *The Monetary Approach to the Balance of Payments*, ed. Jacob A. Frenkel and Harry G. Johnson. Toronto: University of Toronto Press, 1976, pp. 298–325.

Gomez-Oliver, Antonio. "La Demanda de Dinero en Mexico." In *Cincuenta Anos de Banca Central*, ed. E. Fernandez. Mexico: Fondo de Cultura Economica, 1976, pp. 275–327.

Guitian, Manuel. "The Balance of Payments as a Monetary Phenomenon: Empirical Evidence, Spain, 1955–71." In *The Monetary Approach to the Balance of Payments*, ed. Jacob A. Frenkel and Harry G. Johnson. Toronto: University of Toronto Press, 1976, pp. 338–356.

Hasan, Aynul S., Ghulam Kadir and S. Fakhre Mahmud. "Substitutability of Pakistan's Monetary Assets under Alternative Monetary Aggregates." *Pakistan Development Review*, 27, no. 3 (Autumn 1988): 317–326.

Johannes, James M. "Testing the Exogeneity Specification Underlying the Monetary Approach to the Balance of Payments." *Review of Economics and Statistics*, 62, no. 1 (February 1981): 29–34.

Johnson, Harry G. "The Monetary Approach to Balance-of-Payments Theory." In *The Monetary Approach to the Balance of Payments*, ed. Jacob A. Frenkel and Harry G. Johnson. Toronto: University of Toronto Press, 1976, pp. 147–167.

Johnson, Harry G. "Money, Balance of Payments Theory, and the International Monetary System." Essays in International Finance no. 124. Princeton University, Department of Economics, International Finance Section, 1977.

Johnson, J. *Econometric Methods.* New York: McGraw-Hill, 1972.

Kahn, Mohsin S. "Macroeconomic Policies and the Balance of Payments in Pakistan:

1972–1986." International Monetary Fund Working Paper 90/78. International Monetary Fund, Research Department, Washington, D.C., September 1990.

Kakwani, N. C. "The Unbiasedness of Zellner's Seeming Unrelated Equations Estimates." *Journal of the American Statistical Association*, 62 (1967): 141–412.

Kamas, Linda. "External Disturbances and the Independence of Monetary Policy under the Crawling Peg in Colombia." *Journal of International Economics*, 19 (November 1985): 313–327.

Kamas, Linda. "The Balance of Payments Offset to Monetary Policy: Monetarist, Portfolio Balance, and Keynesian Estimates for Mexico and Venezuela." *Journal of Money, Credit, and Banking*, 18, no. 4 (November 1986): 467–481.

Kementa, Jan, and R. F. Gilbert. "Small Sample Properties of Alternative Estimates of Seemingly Unrelated Regressions." *Journal of the American Statistical Association*, 63 (1968): 1180–1200.

Kouri, Pentti J. K., and Michael G. Porter. "International Capital Flows and Portfolio Equilibrium." *Journal of Political Economy*, 82 (May/June 1974): 46–89.

Kreinin, Mordechai E., and Lawrence H. Officer. "The Monetary Approach to the Balance of Payments: A Survey." Princeton Studies in International Finance no. 43. Princeton University, Department of Economics, International Finance Section, 1978.

Kyle, John F. *The Balance of Payments in a Monetary Economy*. Princeton, N.J.: Princeton University Press, 1976.

Magee, Stephen P. "The Empirical Evidence on the Monetary Approach to the Balance of Payments and Exchange Rates." *American Economic Review Papers and Proceedings*, 66 (May 1976): 163–170.

Malindretos, John. "The Keynesian and the Monetary Approaches to International Finance: A Reexamination." *International Journal of Finance*, 1, no. 1 (Autumn 1988): 46–89.

Putnam, Bluford H., and D. Sykes Wilford. "International Reserve Flows: Seemingly Unrelated Regressions." In *The Monetary Approach to International Adjustment*, ed. B. H. Putnam and D. S. Wilford. New York: Praeger Publishers, 1978, pp. 71–84.

Rasulo, James A., and D. Sykes Wilford. "Estimating Monetary Models of the Balance of Payments and Exchange Rates: A Bias." *Southern Economic Journal*, 47, no. 1 (July 1980): 136–146.

Sims, Christopher A. "Money, Income and Causality." *American Economic Review* (September 1972): 540–552.

Wilford, D. Sykes, and J. Richard Zecher. "Monetary Policy and the Balance of Payments in Mexico, 1955–75." *Journal of Money, Credit, and Banking*, 11, no. 3 (August 1979): 340–348.

Zecher, Richard. "Monetary Equilibrium and International Reserve Flows in Australia." In *The Monetary Approach to the Balance of Payments*, ed. Jacob A. Frenkel and Harry G. Johnson. Toronto: University of Toronto Press, 1976, pp. 287–297.

Zellner, Arnold. "An Efficient Method of Estimating Seemingly Unrelated Regressions and Tests for Aggregation Bias." *Journal of the American Statistical Association*, 57 (1962): 348–368.

Part III

Criticisms of the Keynesian and Monetary Views of Balance of Payments Determination

Chapter 6

A Critique of the Traditional Approach to International Finance

Theologos Homer Bonitsis and John Malindretos

INTRODUCTION

The Keynesian theory of external adjustment and payments has its roots in the second half of this century with the seminal contributions of Fritz Machlup (1943), Joan Robinson (1947), Sidney Alexander (1952) and James Edward Meade (1970). It is clear, therefore, that the Keynesian theory (also referred to as the Traditional approach in the literature) is essentially a *composite theory*, which includes the elasticities, relative price, absorption, and multiplier models of international adjustment and payments. Krueger (1969) pointed out that this theoretical school was well-established by the late 1950s as the dominant theory of international financial adjustment.

The objective of this research endeavor is to present a concise critical examination of the Keynesian theory of international financial adjustment and payments. In so doing, it takes the juxtaposition that the Keynesian approach, while insightful, ignores an array of significant contemporary and historical parameters that affect international trade and financial flows; this research, however, does not recommend discarding the Traditional approach, but suggests potential modifications and qualified extensions of the theory. Alternatively stated, this research finds that the Traditional approach is not extensive nor inclusive enough for use by policy makers and analysts of contemporary international payments and adjustment. This is shown by employing concise analyses-cum-conceptual extensions for ten broadly delineated inexactitudes of the Traditional approach to international finance. The brevity of the ten discourses are in the interest of breadth at the expense of depth; this chapter seeks to establish a general analytical framework so as to encourage ongoing rigorous research in this area. It follows that the general findings of this chapter achieve two timely goals: first, they enhance the realism, and by extension the policy potency, of the Traditional approach; and, second, the findings increase the theory's explanatory power of international financial accounts adjustment to external disturbances.

RELEVANCE OF MARKET IMPERFECTIONS

The existence of market imperfections in input and product markets is a noteworthy general criticism of the traditional approach. Gray (1976, ch. 3) noted that Keynesian international financial theory incorrectly presupposes that the input and product markets are perfectly competitive. The implication of employing this assumption is to imply perfect substitutability of inputs, whether employed or not, as well as perfectly homogenous products. Thus, this implies that the common practice of countries of adopting a macroeconomic expenditure-switching policy results in a country having no difficulty in shifting resources into expanding domestic industries. In the presence, however, of full employment of general resources or industry-specific resources, a greater supply of inputs will not be forthcoming; in short, an expenditure-switching policy will not achieve its intended policy goal.

Similarly, if goods are not perfectly interchangeable in consumption, an expenditure-switching measure will not be effective. Products may not be interchangeable in consumption for two reasons: they are differentiated or noncompetitive. In the case of differentiated goods, an expenditure-switching policy is effective only if it is severe enough to entice consumers to purchase domestic tradable goods in place of foreign ones, even if they are heterogeneous. Equally important, if the home country cannot produce some products that are imported, an expenditure-switching policy will not improve the international financial accounts. In fact, a country's external position will deteriorate if the product is of significant importance for domestic consumption and production.

In both these scenarios a general discretionary macroeconomic policy adopted to return a country to external balance has economy-wide deleterious effects. Clearly, the Traditional approach's structural assumption of perfectly competitive input and product markets is not realistic.

IMPOTENCY OF A FLEXIBLE EXCHANGE RATE REGIME TO RESTORE EXTERNAL BALANCE

The Traditional approach embodies the premise that a flexible exchange rate regime will restore a country to external equilibrium. However, for this to occur, several corollary factors must hold. The Marshall-Lerner condition, for example, must be satisfied; that is, the sum of the price elasticities of demand for imports and exports must be greater than unity; empirically, however, this is not always the case. Similarly, domestic prices are assumed to change by the equal percentage change in a country's currency, be it a depreciation or appreciation of the currency; in practice, firms may change their own-currency price so as to maintain a stable foreign-currency price. In the past, firms did this to maintain market share at the expense of profit margins. New technological innovations, however, now contribute to neutralizing exchange rate induced price changes while maintaining profit margins; two studies, by Bonitsis (1991) and Bonitsis and Tsanacas (1990), discussed this development.

Three other presuppositions are imbued in the efficacy of a flexible exchange rate system to achieve equilibrium of the international accounts: the domestic cost structure is not affected by a change in a currency's international value, the coefficients of the elasticities of supply for imports and exports are essentially infinite, and expectations of product quality, both by domestic and foreign residents, are stable. All these assumptions, like the two previous ones, are often empirically tenuous to defend.

It is clear, then, that the Traditional approach essentially ignores the domestic demand for foreign currency for purposes other than current account transactions. The Traditional approach essentially considers trade balance adjustments as the external equilibrating mechanism; all other accounts adjustments are "below-the-line" (i.e., the capital accounts), and are simply accommodating to the trade account. The contemporary world, however, is one in which autonomous capital flows, both short and long term, play an increasingly important roll; and there is no *a priori* reason for one exchange rate to be able to clear both current and capital accounts simultaneously, for the parameters that affect each account may differ. Indeed, the ongoing chronic surpluses and deficits of several large open economies under a flexible exchange rate regime may, concomitant with other developments, reflect this phenomenon.

RELEVANCE OF COUNTRY SIZE

Laffer (1972) pointed out that the Traditional approach assumes that in the pursuit of external adjustment, all countries are approximately equal in size. The Traditional approach, in short, states that there are no small price-taker countries or large price-setter countries. This view of the relative resource endowment and production capacity of countries of observably different economic magnitudes is unrealistic. Specifically, there are different implications for balance of payments adjustments from initiating monetary, fiscal, and exchange-rate policies depending on if a country is a small open economy or a large one. Miles (1978b), for example, has shown that a balance of payments deficit financed by a small country will not affect the external position of a large country. A large country's external deficit, in contrast, will significantly influence a small country's economy. In general, therefore, the outcomes of various policies to restore external balance depends on country size; this issue will be addressed with regard to monetary, fiscal, and exchange rate policies.

Monetary Policy

A small country pursuing an independent monetary policy will have a minor impact on a large country under fixed and flexible exchange rate regimes. Specifically, under fixed exchange rates the money supply of a large economy will rise slightly if a small economy follows an expansionary monetary policy and fall in response to a contractionary one. With a flexible exchange rate regime, the currency of a small country will depreciate with an expansionary monetary policy and appreciate with a contractionary one, with no significant effect on the large country.

Fiscal Policy

With fiscal policy, similarly, a small country will only insignificantly influence a large country, whereas a large country's fiscal actions will overwhelm a small country in terms of the international accounts and subsequent exchange-rate effects.

Exchange Rate Policy

If a small country alters its exchange rate to improve its balance of payments or its employment picture, this action will not significantly influence the balance of payments or employment in a large country. In contrast, a large country pursuing a devaluation of its currency to improve its balance of payments or domestic employment will drastically affect the balance of payments and employment in a small country.

RELEVANCE OF A COUNTRY'S INTERNATIONAL CURRENCY STATUS

Absence of a Reserve Country Status

The simple Traditional approach, as noted by Kemp (1975), does not embody into its theory the existence of a country that has special status in that its currency is used as international money. This is a major oversight within the Traditional model of international finance. It is well known that in the contemporary global economy, market forces have given several currencies international reserve status. In addition, political-economic institutions have transformed baskets of currencies into international reserve currencies. Two examples of this development are the special drawing rights (SDRs) created by the International Monetary Fund and the European currency unit (ECU) established by the European Union.

Reserve Currency Status, Exchange Rate Regimes and External Equilibrium

Swoboda (1978) pointed out that the traditional conclusions about the effects of exchange rates and international flows on a country change with the introduction of reserve currency status. In particular, a nonreserve country with a balance of payments deficit will lose money supply under a fixed exchange-rate regime; in contrast, under a flexible exchange-rate regime, a nonreserve country's currency will depreciate. These results differ for a reserve currency country: under a fixed exchange-rate regime, a reserve currency country will not lose money supply, whereas a flexible regime has no effect on the reserve country's currency as nonreserve countries will be willing to hold the reserve currency.

Reserve Currency Status and Monetary Policy Independence

Putnam and Wilford (1978) discussed at length the efficiency of monetary policy within the context of a country's reserve or nonreserve status.

Impotency of Nonreserve Country Monetary Policy

If a nonreserve country expands its money supply, most of it will be absorbed by the residents of the reserve country. The reserve country's residents will generally not be interested in holding this nonreserve currency and will exchange it for their own domestic reserve-status money. Further, if the citizens of the reserve-currency country exchange their own money for securities at the central bank, causing a return to some equilibrium of relative holdings of assets, the increase in the money supply will be eliminated via the international financial accounts. The implication of this scenario is that the nonreserve country does not increase its money supply since it loses it through its international financial accounts; its monetary policy is thus ineffectual. Moreover, the reserve country does not have its money supply increase as a result of an expansionary monetary policy of the nonreserve nation as the public will return to the central bank any money received through the international financial accounts. Thus, neither the nonreserve nor the reserve country has its money supply changed by an expansionary monetary policy enacted by the nonreserve country.

Potency of Reserve Country Monetary Policy

If the reserve country expands its money supply, the result will be diametrically different. This is because the nonreserve country will not necessarily return to the reserve country the reserve currency it acquires through its balance of payments, for its residents and central bank will hold some or all of it. This will result in an increase in the money supply of the nonreserve country, for the public will give some of the reserve currency to its central bank in exchange for domestic, nonreserve, currency. To receive a return on its holdings, the central bank of the nonreserve country will make a portfolio investment in securities of the reserve country; this action will increases the latter's money supply. In conclusion, an expansionary monetary policy enacted by the reserve country will increases its money supply and reserve country monetary policy is efficacious domestically and internationally.

Reserve Currency Status and Currency Substitution

Another important qualification to the basic theory of the Traditional approach is the issue of currency substitution. The Traditional approach assumes that all countries hold only their own currencies. The implication of this assumption according to Kindleberger (1970) is that under flexible exchange rates there is monetary *independence* across countries. In contrast, Miles (1978a) gave evidence of currency substitution between the United States and Canada and concluded that there is monetary *interdependence* among countries, even under a flexible exchange-rate regime. This is still a debatable issue, however, since Husted (1981) has questioned Miles's findings. However, if Miles's conclusions hold, however weakly, then the core Traditional theory needs to be modified to include currency substitution within its analytical framework. It is important to emphasize that currency substitution is not separate from the reserve-country status model, rather it is a unique outcome of the model.

EXCLUSION OF SOME OF THE INTERNATIONAL ACCOUNTS IN THE ANALYSIS OF EXTERNAL ADJUSTMENT

Kindleberger (1970) emphasized that the Traditional approach to international finance is exclusionary in its treatment of several accounts in the balance of payments. The Keynesian theory emphasizes the trade balance to the exclusion of other international financial accounts; these accounts, however, have significant historical and contemporary relevance.

The Transfer Account, and the Interest and Dividends Components of the Services Account

Machlup (1950) discussed the relevance of the transfer account and the interest and dividend components of the services account. The traditional approach, however, gives cursory attention to the unilateral transfers account, an account that Keynes (1929), interestingly, indicated may be of critical importance under certain conditions. Similarly, according to Cooper (1966), the Traditional approach fails to emphasize the interest and dividend financial components of the services account. Disregarding the importance of these two financial flows can be detrimental to a meaningful analysis of a country's external position.

The transfer account can enhance external equilibrium for countries receiving substantial amounts of development aid, war reparations and private remittances from its citizens abroad. Examples of these items, for the post–World War II era, would include aid received by less-developed countries, war damages received by Israel, and expatriate southern European workers' wage remittances; conversely, war reparations by Germany impacted negatively on the country's transfer account, and hence, external position. Similarly, dividend and interest inflows can be of significant positive importance for external equilibrium for countries with large present and past portfolio and direct foreign investments abroad. However, for a host country with an open-door policy toward foreign investment, large repatriations of dividend and interest payments will negatively affect the external position.

To summarize, a country may be facing a disequilibrium in the balance of payments that can be attributed to unilateral transfers as well as payments of dividends and interest to the rest of the world. The Traditional approach, with an emphasis on external adjustment through relative prices and incomes, fails to emphasize these types of external imbalances.

The Capital Account

Roosa (1970) noted that the Traditional approach to international finance does not integrate the capital account into its core theory, although for the contemporary integrated global economy the status of this account can be instrumental for a country to achieve external balance. The capital account consists of two parts: the short-term capital account and long-term capital account; referred to also as the liquid and illiquid capital accounts, respectively. The post–World War II period has seen the growth in the importance of the capital account, this is a reflection of the internationalization of the money and capital markets. Recently, for example, the net flow on the capital account for the United States roughly equaled the U.S. trade balance deficit. Similarly, the experience of Mexico in 1995 indicates how international portfolio adjustments by private investors can quickly affect a country's external position. Financial flows of these magnitudes makes the exclusion of the capital account from discussions of international adjustment an egregious oversight.

The Long-Term Capital Account

The long-term or illiquid capital account has two principal components, both of which constitute investment flows with a maturity duration in excess of one year. These components are the portfolio and direct foreign investment components of the capital account.

Foreign Portfolio Investment. Foreign portfolio investment is investment in financial instruments with a maturity of more than one year, inclusive of equity investments of less than 10 percent ownership. Foreign portfolio investment is mainly investment in long-term securities such as bonds and equities. This type of investment is passive (i.e., with no active role by the investor).

Branson (1968) argued that relative incomes and prices do not influence the flows of portfolio investment globally as they do for the flow of goods and services. Other variables influence portfolio investment, such as relative interest rates, wealth, and the marginal propensity of the home country's acquisition of securities to those of the rest of the world. Hence, for the Keynesian theory to become a comprehensive international financial theory of external equilibrium adjustment, it must explicitly introduce foreign portfolio investment into its theoretical framework.

Foreign Direct Investment. Foreign direct investment is an external flow of funds to purchase common stock of 10 percent or more of the voting stock of the company. The acquisition of common stock could be in the form of a new firm, an ongoing concern, or an extension of an operational firm. It is instructive to mention that any acquisition by individuals of land or real estate is considered foreign direct investment. In practice, the percentage devoted to the business side of direct foreign investment is much greater than that devoted to the individual side. Therefore, this discussion concentrates on business foreign direct investment.

Researchers have proposed diverse motives for foreign direct investment. Nehrt and Hogue (1968) emphasized strategic factors, such as seeking markets, materials, knowledge, production efficiency and political certainty. Simon (1947) and Aharoni (1966) emphasized behavioral motives. Other motives for direct foreign investment are clearly dynamic economic ones: Hymer (1976) discussed product and input market imperfections; Horst (1972), economies of scale; Servan-Schreiber (1968), managerial and marketing expertise; Gruber, Mehta, and Vernon (1967), technology; Grubel (1968), financial diversification and strength; Caves (1971), differentiation of goods; and Vernon (1966), product cycles. However, there are also defensive economic reasons for firms to pursue such international investment activity: following the leader, as in Knickerbocker (1973); and growth to survive, as in Eiteman and Stonehill (1986) and Rugman (1980). Given this body of research, it is appropriate to conclude that relative prices and incomes are not the prime motivating factors behind foreign direct investment. Thus, the traditional theory of international payments and adjustment must be modified to include the factors for pursuing foreign direct investment. Indeed, if a country experiences a balance of payments deficit because of foreign direct investment outflows (e.g., the United States during the 1960s), an appropriate policy framework needs to be employed to remedy the external deficit without adverse effects on the host country. For empirical research, see, for example, Bonitsis and Aggarwal (1990), who showed the importance of direct foreign investment on an emerging economy.

The Short-Term Capital Account

The short-term, liquid part of the capital account consist of inflows and outflows of financial capital with a maturity of less than one year. These financial flows are determined by relative country interest rates, wealth and tastes of domestic and foreign residents. As a result of their short-term incentive nature and high mobility, these financial flows are very liquid. It is argued that these international financial flows, in toto, can be a destabilizing factor for a host economy; hence, they are now referred to in the popular press as "hot money." Indeed, recent events indicate that abrupt, private, short-term portfolio adjustments have the potential to wreak havoc on a country's balance of payments and exchange rate. (The 1995 experience of Mexico is a prime example.) Hence, it is necessary to recognize that corrective policies for the short-term capital account will, *prima facie*, differ from those used to remedy a trade balance disequilibrium.

The Official Reserves Transactions Balance

The Keynesian theory does not include the official reserves transactions balance (i.e., the money account), as an integral part of the international financial accounts. The Traditional approach has always considered the official reserves transactions balance as a residual balance resulting from ''above-the-line,'' autonomous, market-motivated, balance-of-trade transactions, and occasionally from capital account transactions. This perspective is, *prima facie*, not appropriate in the contemporary, open-economy world, for the official reserves transactions account balance is not necessarily a result of accommodating transactions; in fact, the account's balance may be a reflection of explicit policy actions and consequently must be treated as an autonomous account.

In contrast to the Traditional approach, a theory has emerged that emphasizes the importance of the official reserves account. It is known as the Monetary approach to the balance of payments; Frenkel and Johnson (1976) are its seminal contributors. This theory addresses many of the deficiencies of the Traditional approach in the area of the money account. Indeed, the Monetary approach attempts to rigorously analyze international financial flows and their causes by giving preeminence to the money account, whether a country is trading under a fixed, flexible, or mixed exchange-rate regime. Even though the Monetary approach is extreme in many of its theoretical and policy implications, it is a timely development toward a comprehensive theory of international financial flows and adjustment.

The Traditional approach appropriately discusses trade flows in goods and services, but it lacks theoretical insight into trade in money and securities. Indeed, monetary factors can, and often are, the source of an external disturbance to an economy. In such a case the traditional approach's cache of analytical tools is insufficient to effectively resolve the external disequilibrium. The traditional approach—which is essentially a theory of trade balance adjustments—needs to be complemented by the monetary approach via a theory of official reserves transactions balance determination. If this is done successfully, a complete theory of international finance will emerge—items both above and below the line will thus be fully integrated into a theory of international financial payments and adjustment.

Succinctly stated, following Johnson (1977), the Monetary approach to the balance of payments states that it is excessive money supply or insufficient money demand that causes a deterioration in a country's balance of payments under a fixed exchange-rate regime and in the value of the currency under a flexible exchange-rate regime. In principle, any disturbance to the international accounts is resolved through the money market; money demand and money supply determine the balance of payments and, as such, are key to ameliorating external disequilibria.

RELEVANCE OF MONETARY VARIABLES

The Traditional approach does not place theoretical weight to an economy's monetary parameters; this nonrelevance of monetary factors is a significant shortcoming. That is, the Keynesian approach discards the notion that the balance of payments can be a monetary phenomenon even though the trade balance reflects the net exchange of goods for money, while the capital account is an exchange of securities for money. Intuitively, the money account can be seen as the net reflection of the trade balance and the capital accounts; money is intricately involved in every one of the accounts.

RELEVANCE OF THE DISPOSITION OF REVENUES AND FINANCING OF DISCRETIONARY INTERNATIONAL POLICIES

Disposition of Tariff Revenue

If a country has a trade deficit, it may impose a tariff, *ceteris paribus*, on imported goods and services. This will result in tariff revenues as well as an improvement in the country's balance of payments. How will the government use the tariff revenue? It may distribute it to the general population by reducing income taxes. However, if residents spend some or all of this incremental income on foreign tradable goods, the trade balance will again deteriorate. Thus, depending on the disposition of funds generated from a trade policy, the Traditional approach may not unequivocally achieve its anticipated policy goals.

Disposition of an Export Tax

An export tax placed on products whose price elasticity of demand is less than unity will result, *pari passu*, in a trade balance improvement. However, the disposition of the export tax needs to be considered. If a country decreases its income tax, its residents will be wealthier after taxes. Given a positive marginal propensity to import, the home country residents will return to foreigners some or all of the revenues generated by the export tax. In principle, both actions can be offsetting, resulting in a status quo trade balance. Hence, the appropriate theoretical condition for a trade balance improvement, given the export tax income redistribution, is that the price elasticity of demand for exports must be less than one minus a country's marginal propensity to absorb.

Financing an Export Subsidy

A government may pay an ad valorem subsidy to producers to encourage them to reduce their price in order to enhance export sales. If the price elasticity of demand of the products is greater than unity, the export subsidy will induce an improvement in the trade balance. This is not an unequivocal outcome, however. If one considers the mechanism by which a government finances an ad valorem export subsidy. This may occur by a general increase in income taxes on the nonexporting sector. The population will become less wealthy after taxes and will consume less goods, including foreign goods; the trade balance will thus receive an additional boost. Consequently, the trade balance will improve as a result of an export subsidy if the price elasticity of demand for exports exceeds one minus the home country's marginal propensity to import. This is a less stringent condition than the Traditional one, which precludes the financing aspect.

MULTIPLE CAUSES OF EXTERNAL DISEQUILIBRIA

An important major shortcoming of the Traditional approach is that it only discusses, in its attempt to explain external disequilibria, intermediate parameters such as relative incomes, prices and interest rates, and not the *causal-root* parameters. This oversight was discussed by Malindretos (1991). Optimal policy formulation, however, requires that the root cause of the disturbance be determined, for otherwise international trade and financial flow disequilibria will not be optimally remedied by policy actions. Alternatively stated, the traditional approach looks at the vehicles of transmission of disturbances, not their causal parameters. James E. Meade (1970), for example, elaborately delineated alternative adjustment mechanisms by dividing them up into two groups—those of price and income adjustments. However, he gave cursory treatment to the nature of the root causes of a disturbance that induces an external account adjustment.

Some theorists have made attempts to include into the Traditional approach the nature of the causes of the various disturbances; this has been reflected in the research of Machlup (1964), Roosa (1970), and Gray (1974). Unfortunately, they do not delve deeply enough into the nature of the root causes of the disturbances to a country's external position. Given numerous root disturbances, their categorization is perhaps optimally based on three criteria: the accounts they affect, their duration, and repetitiveness. Malindretos (1988) presented the following seven types of disturbances: random and seasonal, structural, cyclical, overabsorption, noncompetitiveness, capital account, and the official reserves transactions balance. Malindretos and Tsanacas (1997) gave an analysis and policy recommendations to respond to these types of disturbances.

RELEVANCE OF THE SUPPLY SIDE

The adjustment mechanism under the Traditional approach does not introduce a discussion of supply-side economics, for the theory implicitly assumes that income expansions are demand-side induced. This implies that income expansions, which increase the demand for foreign, tradable goods via the marginal propensity to import, cause a deterioration in the trade account. A decline in national income, in contrast, will result in an improvement in the trade balance. This conceptual framework excludes the possibility of export-led growth, which is a supply-side phenomenon. It is empirically observable that export-led growth policies have resulted in income expansions concomitant with an improved international accounts position. This is the recent experience for the newly industrialized countries of Asia.

NONRELEVANCE OF A GENERAL EQUILIBRIUM FRAMEWORK

The Keynesian theory of international finance was developed within the framework of the neoclassical world of general equilibrium. However, this is a static equilibrium model, whereas the international financial system operates within a state of continuous disequilibrium, as noted by Davidson (1978). He argued that several factors cause this, namely, uncertainty, time irreversibility, money and exogenous factors (e.g., natural and political events).

CONCLUSIONS

This chapter is a commentary on the Traditional approach to international finance. The criticisms of the theory are put into ten broad categories. First, it contains unrealistic assumptions concerning perfect input and product markets. Second is the inability of a flexible exchange rate regime to achieve external balance. Third is the theory's erroneous treatment of countries as being of equal economic size. Fourth is the absence of a reserve-currency country. Fifth is the lack of integration of components of the current, capital, and official reserves accounts into the general theory. Sixth is the absence of the importance of monetary variables in external adjustment. Seventh is the lack of consideration of the disposition of revenues and sources of financing of discretionary international policies. Eighth is the problem that the Traditional approach does not distinguish between the various root causes of external disturbances, nor does it satisfactorily separate between monetary and real causal parameters. Ninth, the theory fails to consider the importance of the supply side to achieve external balance. Finally, the Traditional approach inaptly assumes that external accounts' adjustments occur within a general equilibrium framework. It is important to emphasize that even though these items are discussed within *ceteris paribus* contexts, all items are intricately connected within the general framework of the Traditional theory of external adjustment.

The ten inexactitudes in the Keynesian approach to international finance are, for the most part, a reflection of an analytic-historic emphasis on adjustments to the trade balance as the modus operandi to achieve overall external balance.

In light of these imperfections, this chapter shows that the Traditional approach to international finance can provide a useful theoretical and policy framework to resolve issues of external disequilibria; however, the theory needs to be modified with new insights and extensions to adjust for shortcomings. Specifically, this research indicates that the theory can be expanded with complementary theoretical constructions to become a comprehensive model, the details of which need to be theoretically conceptualized and integrated into the general framework of the Keynesian approach to international finance.

REFERENCES

Aharoni, Yair. *The Foreign Investment Decision Process*. Cambridge, Mass.: Harvard Graduate School of Business Administration, Division of Research, 1966.

Alexander, Sidney. "Effects of a Devaluation on a Trade Balance." *International Monetary Fund Staff Papers*, 2 (April 1952): 263–278.

Bonitsis, Theologos Homer. "Dollar Exchange Rate Indices and U.S. Exports: Is There an Intertemporal Linkage?" *Journal of Business and Economic Studies*, 1, no. 2 (Fall/Winter 1991): 1–10.

Bonitsis, Theologos Homer, and Raj Aggarwal. "U.S. Direct Foreign Investment and Economic Growth in Brazil: An Econometric Causal Analysis." *International Journal of Finance*, 2, no. 2 (Spring 1990): 12–19.

Bonitsis, Theologos Homer, and Demetri Tsanacas. "Yen Appreciation, Hysteretic Effects, and Japanese Micro-Adjustments." *Detroit Business Journal*, 3, no. 1 (Spring 1990): 1–10.

Branson, William H. *Financial Capital Flows in the U.S. Balance of Payments*. Amsterdam: North Holland Publishing Company, 1968.

Caves, Richard. "International Corporations: The Industrial Economics of Foreign Investment." *Economica*, 38, no. 149 (February 1971): 1–27.

Cooper, Richard N. "The Balance of Payments in Review." *Journal of Political Economy*, 74, no. 4 (August 1966): 379–395.

Davidson, Paul. *Money and the Real World*. 2nd ed. London: Macmillan, 1978.

Eiteman, David, and Arthur Stonehill. *Multinational Business Finance*. 4th ed. New York: Addison-Wesley, 1986.

Frenkel, Jacob A., and Harry G. Johnson, eds. *The Monetary Approach to the Balance of Payments*. Toronto: University of Toronto Press, 1976.

Gray, H. Peter. *An Aggregate Theory of International Payments Adjustment*. London: Macmillan, 1974.

Gray, H. Peter. *A Generalized Theory of International Trade*. London: Macmillan, 1976.

Grubel, Herbert G. "Internationally Diversified Portfolios: Welfare Gains and Capital Flows." *American Economic Review*, 58, part 1 (December 1968): 1299–1314.

Gruber, W., D. Mehta and R. Vernon. "The R&D Factor in International Trade and Investment of U.S. Industries." *Journal of Political Economy*, 75, no. 1 (February 1967): 20–37.

Horst, Thomas. "Firm and Industry Determinants of the Decision to Invest Abroad: An Empirical Study." *Review of Economics and Statistics*, 54, no. 3 (August 1972): 258–266.

Husted, Stephen. "A Transactions Model of Currency Substitution." Mimeo, University of Pittsburgh, Department of Economics, October 1981.

Hymer, Stephen. *The International Operations of National Firms: A Study of Direct Foreign Investment*. Cambridge, Mass.: MIT Press, 1976.

Johnson, Harry G. "The Monetary Approach to the Balance of Payments: A Nontechnical Guide." *Journal of International Economics*, no. 7 (August 1977): 251–268.

Kemp, Donald S. "A Monetary View of the Balance of Payments." *Federal Reserve Bank of St. Louis Review* (April 1975): 14–22.

Keynes, John M. "The German Transfer Problem." *Economic Journal*, 39 (March 1929): 1–7.

Kindleberger, Charles P. "The Case for Fixed Exchange Rates." In *International Adjustment Mechanism*. Conference Series No. 2. Boston: Federal Reserve Bank of Boston, March 1970, pp. 93–108.

Knickerbocker, Fred T. *Oligopolistic Reaction and the Multinational Enterprise*. Cambridge, Mass.: Harvard Graduate School of Business, 1973.

Krueger, Anne O. "The Balance of Payments Theory." *Journal of Economic Literature*, 7, no. 1 (March 1969): 1–26.

Laffer, Arthur B. "Monetary Policy and the Balance of Payments." *Journal of Money, Credit and Banking*, 4, no. 1 (February 1972): 13–22.

Machlup, Fritz. *International Trade and the National Income Multiplier*. Philadelphia: Blakiston, 1943.

Machlup, Fritz. "Three Concepts of the Balance of Payments and the So-called Dollar Shortage." *Economic Journal*, 60, no. 1 (March 1950): 46–68.

Machlup, Fritz. "The Terms of Trade Effects of Devaluation upon Real Income and the Balance of Trade." *Kyklos*, 9 (1956): 417–452.

Machlup, Fritz, "Adjustment, Compensatory Correction, and Financing of Imbalances in International Payments." In *Trade, Growth and the Balance of Payments: Essays in Honor of Gotfried Haberler*, ed. Richard E. Caves, Harry G. Johnson and Peter B. Kenen. Chicago: Rand McNally, 1964.

Malindretos, John. "A Critique of the Keynesian International Financial Theory of Disequilibrium and Adjustment: Under the Regime of Fixed Flexible Exchange Rates." *Journal of Business and Society*, 1, no. 1 (1988): 4–38.

Malindretos, John. "An Examination of the Two Views of International Finance for an Advanced, Medium-Sized, Reserve Currency Country." In *Advances in Quantitative Analysis of Finance and Accounting*, ed. Chen-Few Lee. Greenwich, Conn.: JAI Press, 1991, pp. 183–214.

Malindretos, John, and Demetri Tsanacas. "A Policy Orientation of the Criticism of the Traditional Theory of International Finance in the Context of Fixed Exchange Rates." In *Quantity and Quality in Economic Research: Studies in Applied Business Research*, vol. 4, ed. Theologos Homer Bonitsis and Roy C. Brown. Hampshire, U.K.: Ashgate Publishing, 1997.

Meade, James Edward. *The Theory of International Economic Policy*, Volume 1: *The Balance of Payments*. London: Oxford University Press, 1970.

Miles, Marc A. "Currency Substitution, Flexible Exchange Rates, and Monetary Independence." *American Economic Review*, 68, no. 3 (June 1978a): 428–436.

Miles, Marc A. *Devaluation, the Trade Balance and the Balance of Payments*. New York: Marcel Dekker, 1978b.

Nehrt, Lee, and W. Dickerson Hogue. "The Foreign Investment Decision Process." *Quarterly Journal of AISEC International* (February–April 1968): 43–48.

Putnam, Bluford H., and D. Sykes Wilford. "Money, Income, and Causality in the United States and the United Kingdom." *American Economic Review*, 68, no. 3 (June 1978): 423–427.

Robinson, Joan. "The Foreign Exchanges." In *Essays in the Theory of Employment*. 2nd ed. Oxford, U.K.: Blackwell, 1947.

Roosa, Robert V. "Capital Movements and Balance-of-Payments Adjustment." In *Money, and Policy Essays in Honor of Karl R. Bopp*, ed. David P. Eastburn. Philadelphia: Federal Reserve Bank of Philadelphia, 1970, pp. 171–194.

Rugman, Alan. "Internationalization as a General Theory of FDI: A Re-Appraisal of the Literature." *Weltwirtschftliches Archiv*, 110, no. 2 (1980): 365–379.

Servan-Schreiber, J. J. *The American Challenge*. London: Hamish Hamilton, 1968.

Simon, Herbert. *Administrative Behavior*. New York: Macmillan, 1947.

Swoboda, Alexander K. "Gold, Dollars, Euro-Dollars, and the World Money Stock under Fixed Exchange Rates." *American Economic Review*, 68, no. 4 (September 1978): 625–642.

Vernon, Raymond. "International Investment and International Trade in the Product Cycle." *Quarterly Journal of Economics*, 80 (May 1966): 190–207.

Chapter 7

The Monetary Theory of the Balance of Payments: A Retrospective Analysis

H. Peter Gray

In 1976, I wrote a taxonomic paper on the Monetary theory of the balance of payments, necessarily drawing a comparison between it and the Absorption theory. The paper was never submitted to a journal, but it served the very useful purpose of making me think through the implications of the Monetary theory. On rereading it for possible inclusion in this volume, I was reminded of critiques of taxonomic theory (Johnson, 1951; Day, 1955) and the dangers of excessive verbiage.

The Monetary theory does contain some elements of truth which the Absorption theory bypasses (and vice versa). This chapter seeks to address the current relevance of the Monetary theory of the balance of payments in the modern institutional context and will again use the Absorption approach as a basis for comparison.[1] Of course, the institutional context can vary significantly among countries so that the contents of this chapter must be seen from the perspective of a modern state with a national currency that financial and nonfinancial firms use in globalized financial and goods markets. The relevance of the Monetary theory as described here would be sharply different for France, Germany (which acts as central banker to the European system of fixed exchange rates), Brazil, India, Korea or Poland. Still further, as will be shown, the value of the Monetary theory as a basis for policy in the nation whose national currency is the main transaction vehicle for global trade must be minimal because the role of hegemon demands that the national interest be subjugated to the role of supplier of international public goods. It is equally clear that the Absorption approach cannot be applied directly to the United States since capital flows dominate current transactions of the monetary hegemon.[2]

The basic question concerns the value of the two theories in explaining the elimination of a deficit (see next section): this serves to highlight the methodological differences between the two approaches. The following section examines an empirical test of the Monetary theory emanating from the University of Chicago, which is of interest because of the combination of its provenance and its slipshod empirical model. The final section considers the implications of the two theories for central banking in the modern institutional setting.

ELIMINATING AND DEFINING A DEFICIT UNDER THE TWO THEORIES

The orthodox or Absorption approach uses proactive policies to attack an imbalance on current account and illiquid capital transactions.[3] It does so by bringing the current account into balance with the so-called autonomous balance on illiquid capital transactions. This approach has a Keynesian flavor, and the policy makers are required to recognize the interaction between domestic aggregate demand and the rate of exchange (the terms of trade of current transactions) by imposing, at the same time (possibly with an allowance for lags), expenditure reduction and expenditure-switching policies.[4] The expenditure-switching policies include depreciation of the currency,[5] and expenditure reduction is intended to hold the level of economic activity constant—presumably in the realm of a satisfactorily high level of activity—by curtailing domestic aggregate demand to allow for an expansion of net foreign demand. In practice, the Absorption approach puts greater stress on expenditure reduction policies (monetary and fiscal policies) than on devaluation/depreciation of the currency, which is designed to generate aggregate demand from abroad when an under-utilization of domestic resources has been achieved. Under the Bretton Woods system, expenditure-switching policies were scarce because rates of exchange were fixed and price levels moved more or less independently of rates of exchange.

Adherents of the Monetary approach suggested that the Absorption approach was compatible with very long periods of uninterrupted surplus or deficit. Here, the monetarists misinterpreted the approach. The Absorption approach could countenance a change in policy (i.e., policy was not immutable through time), but it could also countenance the building up of assets abroad by running current account surpluses as a target.[6] Logically, the benefit of additional holdings of foreign assets would diminish as international net worth grew, and a surplus country would be induced, albeit probably too slowly, to take steps to reduce its surplus. On the other hand, a deficit nation would be forced to eliminate its deficit quite quickly, and the disappearance of a deficit would also require the disappearance of the surplus. The Absorption approach did not confront the means by which surplus-seeking countries would be forced to reduce their surpluses, and indeed, this problem has not been solved by any system. In the fourteen years ending in 1995, Japan ran a cumulative current surplus of over a trillion U.S. dollars and had fourteen consecutive years of surplus—financed largely by an even larger cumulative deficit on the part of the United States (see

Table 7.1). While such protracted imbalances represent questionable policies, they do exist, and the Absorption approach can hardly be cited as unrealistic on this count.[7]

The Monetary approach is very reminiscent of David Hume's price specie flow mechanism, but its direct antecedent was Milton Friedman's domestic analysis, with its preference for the elimination of the discretion of the Federal Reserve System in the formulation of monetary policy. The approach measures an imbalance (below-the-line transactions) by the sum of all transactions that have a direct effect on the money supply, including short-term capital movements which, in a simple exposition, may be seen as the balancing item in a world of fixed exchange rates. The Monetary approach also has a very distinctive assumption about the sensitivity of the current account to a change in relative prices of home and foreign goods: the elasticity of substitution is deemed to be infinite, and the approach is then able to assume that long-run equilibrium price relationships can be taken as constant (Johnson, 1972, pp. 26–27). Effectively, then, the Monetary approach eliminates from its domain the existence of real shocks or disturbances in the market for goods (such as the harnessing of North Sea energy by the British and the Dutch, changes in the prices of primary products and/or wars), and the terms of trade among nations are effectively fixed. Imbalances derive exclusively from events that take place in the monetary sector. Since any payments deficit or surplus affects the monetary base of the economy, the equality between the demand for real balances and the supply of money must be consonant with balanced payments. An excess of money deriving from a payments surplus will lead to an unloading of money balances and stimulate the demand for both goods and assets. That portion of the surplus demand devoted to foreign goods and assets will allow the excess money balances to disappear into trading partner nations.[8] A second problem of the Monetary theory is immediately apparent: the theory is unaffected by changes in the international net worth of one nation vis-à-vis others, and therefore assumes away any changes in international payments of dividends and interest. The Monetary approach is set in a stationary state world and allows for complete passivity on the part of policy makers.

In contrast, the Monetary approach does have value in determining a global rate of inflation, as became apparent when the United States ran large deficits during the period of the Vietnam War and, because other nations were unwilling voluntarily to contract their own money supplies (to provide the necessary international saving), a global demand-pull inflation resulted.

In the Absorption approach, proactive measures are required if a deficit is to be eliminated, and in the Monetary approach, the rate of absorption changes as required by events (but is assumed to be constant), and the change is enforced through the interplay of the demand for real balances and the national money supply, i.e. by market forces. This is, of course, consonant with Milton Friedman's well-known libertarian bent.[9]

The great contribution of the Monetary approach is to emphasize the cash-flow aspects of an international deficit by emphasizing the role of monetary variables and to illustrate that devaluations of a currency can easily be eradicated by lax monetary policy so that relative prices in a single numeraire (the real rate of exchange) revert back to the predevaluation level. Policies, be they passive or proactive, Monetarist or Keynesian, will not be effective unless they are allowed to take hold and force the economy to conform to the prevailing conditions.

A DEFICIENT TEST OF THE EFFECTIVENESS OF DEVALUATIONS

Miles (1979) tested the effectiveness of devaluation in reducing a trade deficit by using pooled cross-section results for a number of countries whose currencies were devalued within the period from 1956 through 1972.[10] The regression equation used was:

$$\Delta(TB/Y)_i = a_0 + a_1\Delta(g_i - g_r) + a_2\Delta(M_i - M_r) + a_3\Delta(G_i - G_R) + a_4\Delta ER_i$$

where $(TB/Y)_i$ is the trade balance as a percentage of the level of output in country i; g is the rate of economic growth; M is the ratio of high-powered money to output; G is the ratio of government consumption to output; and ER is the exchange rate defined in terms of a specified group of other countries defined as the rest of the world and represented by the subscript R.

The major weakness of the empiricism was, by itself, sufficient to render the empirical work valueless. Because it used aggregate annual data for the dependent variable, the rate of exchange variable was measured by year-end data. If rates of exchange as of the end of December are to be used to explain annual trade data, then the devaluation should take place early in the year so that in a model with no built-in lags, an instantaneously acting devaluation could register its effect on the dependent variable over the whole year.[11] Nine devaluations in 1967 (sterling, the Irish pound, the Danish krone, the Icelandic krona, the Spanish peseta, the New Zealand dollar, the Guyana dollar, the Israeli pound and the Ceylon rupee) took place between November 18 and 22—allowing approximately six weeks of the new exchange rate to affect a year's trade balance *and to overwhelm the effects of the first 10½ months.* Out of sixteen devaluations included in the pooled data set, two others took place in August and September.[12]

A second major weakness was the failure of the analysis to be able to allow for the implementation of other policy measures simultaneously with the devaluation. Commercial or macroeconomic policies measures can affect the success of a devaluation, just as the elimination of previously imposed deficit-suppressing measures can weaken its effects. This omission was particularly troublesome in the analysis of British devaluation since large-scale tariff surcharges had been imposed to defend sterling in October 1964 (all manufactures were subjected to a 15 percent surcharge on cost-insurance-freight (c.i.f.)

cost over and above existing tariffs rates). Severe deflation was imposed in Britain in mid-1966, but the surcharge was eliminated in December 1966 as a result of political pressure from trading partners. A flood of imports in early 1967 caused the devaluation of sterling by 12½ percent in November. The equation simply cannot catch this multivariability of economic policy.

This piece of empirical work illustrates the difficulty of identifying the effectiveness of a combination of instruments on policy targets. Individual countries faced different individual reasons for the need for devaluation. The fact that some countries faced real shocks (which are not allowed for in the Monetarist model) and others faced excessive rates of inflation shows the impossibility of comparing two theories based on different sets of assumptions. It is probably fair to say that the relative strength of the Monetary or the Absorption theory in any single country study depends on the degree to which the country's experience fits the assumptions of one of the two models.

This article is a blatant example of the difficulties in social science of separating the reviewing process from established belief. It was published in a University of Chicago journal, and it is difficult to avoid the conclusion that the refereeing process is less searching when the empirical work produces results consonant with the views of the referees—in this case, by people predisposed to accept the Monetary theory. The article was cited by McKinnon (1981) as evidence of the unreliability of the effectiveness of devaluation. McKinnon had the right to expect that a piece of empirical work published in a front-line economics journal was methodologically reliable.[13]

THE PROBLEMS FACING CENTRAL BANKERS

The deregulation and globalization of financial markets that has occurred recently has clearly put stress on both theories designed to explain the international flows of funds and the problem of bringing them into balance (however defined). The institutional setting has changed drastically since the time when the two theories were promulgated. In part this is due to the elimination in many nations of controls over currency transactions and of reduced regulation of financial intermediaries and, in part, to the liberalization of the global economic régime through the reduction of impediments to international trade and the the liberalization of both financial and direct international investments. These events have facilitated variability in the income velocity of money in individual nations through the adaptation of institutions to the new conditions and the new technologies in communications and information. It is also necessary to recognize the de facto integration of erstwhile national capital markets in OECD countries. In this, multinational firms and multinational banks (Gray and Gray, 1981) are able, possibly after taking covered positions in derivatives, to hold their real balances in a variety of currencies. Multinational corporations seek to achieve economies of common governance by so doing (Eiteman, Stonehill, and Moffett, 1992). The total real balances of a nation are not now defined in a single currency because many important economic entities diversify their liquid assets across currencies;[14] even individuals are able to diversify their portfolios across national boundaries by relying on the expertise of mutual funds.[15] The consequence of this internationalization or globalization of money is pervasive, and the global integration of money markets may well be shown to be a major cause of the breakdown in the historically tight relationship between the money supply and economic activity.

There are now two basic problems: (1) the problem of ensuring balance in the international payments of a single nation without creating drastic instability in the exchange rate of its currency and, consequently, large real costs of adjustment; and (2) the problem of maintaining the stability of the international financial system (i.e. of maintaining reasonable stability in domestic and international asset values). The latter problem applies most directly to the United States and the Group of Seven (G-7), and the former to individual countries (though, clearly, the reserve currency must also retain its value if it is to preserve its status and the viability of the existing international financial system).

The essential national problem that precludes constructive international financial policy is the apparent desire of politicians and the business community to have fixed rates of exchange in a world in which real shocks are common and, on occasion, mutually reinforcing and in which it is possible to finance current deficits by short-term borrowing for a surprisingly long time (see Table 7.1). [16] The Monetary theory assumes that monetary variables are allowed to do their work and are not suppressed: this is simply not a valid assumption about the modern world any more than is the idea that the Absorption approach will be effective if policy makers refuse to inflict postponable pain on their own electorates.

The development of private financial markets has made any distinction between illiquid and liquid financial assets and liabilities meaningless: both long-term and short-term maturities are easily cashable, and the threat of massive currency movements is huge. This situation has led some to urge for the institution of sand in the international monetary mechanism (Eichengreen, Tobin, and Wyplosz, 1995).

Both problems revolve around the possibility that monetary flows will, either through market forces or as a result of central bank laxity, finance deficits that are not subject to some automatic reversal (i.e., are likely to continue for a period exceeding that for which the confidence of foreign investors in the country's assets can be sustained). Inevitably, on occasions such as this when the currency is maintained at an overvalued rate, current account deficits mean a substantial reduction in the international net worth of the country and support of the currency means a reduction of the net worth of the central bank. Foreign investors will ultimately lose confidence, and a crisis can occur in foreign exchange markets in the country's currency. Large, real adjustment costs are inflicted on the home economy, usually involving severe expenditure reductions following the forced expenditure switch. If the causal disturbance is real (an adverse shift in the terms of trade compatible with balanced payments), the

Table 7.1
Cumulative Current Balances, 1982–1995[a] (Billions of U.S. Dollars)

Country	Cumulative Surplus (deficit = -)	Longest Number of Consecutive Years with Same Sign[b]	Cumulative Balance as Percent of 1995 Exports of Goods and Services
Australia	-160.2	14*	233
Belgium	+66.9	11*	40
Canada	-164.8	11*	57
France	-14.1	6[c]	4
Germany	+171.0	9[c]	28
Italy	-36.8	6[c]	12
Japan	+1,021.0	14*	308
Netherlands	+109.2	14*	49
Taiwan	+141.2	14*	112
United Kingdom	-138.0	10*	44
United States	-1,443.0	14*	179

[a] These data must be viewed as orders of magnitude because statistical discrepancies (errors and omissions) can be substantial.
[b] An asterisk denotes that the longest consecutive sequence is unended in the last year for which data are available.
[c] France had a string of six deficits prior to four surpluses beginning in 1992; Germany had nine consecutive surpluses prior to four deficits beginning in 1992; Italy had six consecutive deficits prior to three years of surplus beginning in 1993. These intra-EU phenomena are undoubtedly related to the realignment of exchange rates in 1992 and to the reunification of Germany.
Sources: International Monetary Fund, International Financial Statistics (various issues). For Taiwan: The Statistical Yearbook of the Republic of China, 1995, and International Commerce Bank of China Economic Review, Taipei, September/October 1992.

Monetary theory has little to offer: if the causal disturbance is one of domestic inflation, then the Monetary theory fails because it cannot countenance the possibility that capital movements can be destabilizing over a period of time. The experiences of the United Kingdom and Italy in 1992 are classic examples of this problem, which was aggravated by the ability of speculators to precipitate the crisis (Salvatore, 1995).

While the experience of powerful countries, such as France, Great Britain and Italy, can send tremors through their own financial markets, they are unlikely, except in a very fragile setting (Gray, 1992), to bring about a global collapse of the magnitude experienced between 1929 and 1933. Such a situation, deriving from the inability of the hegemon and other nations to sustain viability of the extant international financial system, is not impossible at the present time because the ostensible hegemon of the world's financial system (the United States) has allowed its cumulative international dissaving to be financed largely by easily cashable liabilities of private financial institutions (see Tables 7.2 and

7.3). A run from the U.S. dollar by foreign creditors and American residents is not an impossibility: such a run would have to have the ability to overcome efforts to sustain the dollar's value by central banks, but cohesion among central banks (an effective "committee hegemon") is not always assured. It is very difficult to identify the circumstances that would trigger such a flight, but the conditions are likely to be mutually reinforcing. A large overhang of private dollar-denominated liabilities held by foreigners whose functional currency is not the dollar impairs the resilience of foreign exchange markets: the possibility of a speculative flight by national residents thus becomes greater. Once a flight is set in motion, it becomes cumulative (Gray, 1992) and brings down, along with the value of the currency, the value of dollar-denominated assets of equities and of corporate and even government bonds, as assets are liquidated to be transferred into other currencies.

This is merely a larger-scale version of the problem outlined in the previous paragraph. In both sets of circumstances, the Monetary assumption of a stable demand for real balances in an individual currency is rendered invalid.

CONCLUSION

At a national level, the Monetary approach has lost such validity as it may once have enjoyed. However, this does not mean that control over the money supply of an individual nation is not important—merely that a passive stance can no longer suffice. It is necessary that policy makers (central banks) identify the strength or lack of strength of the currency and adjust monetary conditions accordingly. As is explicit in the Absorption approach, this requires that fiscal policy and monetary policy be integrated.

There remains a problem, identified by McKinnon (1990), that in a world of free financial flows and floating exchange rates, a depreciation of a currency can only occur in response to actual (or the expectation of future) monetary ease. Monetary ease is expansionary and will aggravate the current deficit. McKinnon identifies the need for tightening fiscal policy as a means of reducing any current account deficit. Such a policy on the part of a major nation requires the assumption that other (surplus or creditor) nations will expand aggregate demand in order to avoid a global recession. Such an arrangement would need to be worked out before the deficit nation can introduce fiscal discipline (even if its politicians have the stomach for the task).

It is necessary to add to McKinnon's concerns about the problems facing a single nation and to consider the implications of his analysis for global financial fragility. Given that the main hegemon of the global financial system is steadily engaged in reducing its international net worth and increasing its easily-encashable liabilities to firms and individuals who use a foreign currency as their functional currency, it is vital that the United States reduce the current deficit and, if possible, even increase its current account to surplus. This has two major implications: there is a lower limit to the degree which the United

Table 7.2
U.S. International Net Worth (INW) (with Direct Investments at Current Cost, Billions of Dollars at Year-End)[a]

	1983	1984	1985	1986	1987	1988	1989	1990	1991	1992	1993	1994	1995	1996
INW at End of Prior Year	+324.7	+303.4	+167.7	+60.1	-13.4	-54.8	-161.8	-243.8	-246.4	-326.0	-473.0	-370.1	-411.7	-687.7
Current Account Balance	-40.1	-99.0	-122.3	-152.1	-167.4	-128.4	-106.7	-94.7	-9.5	-62.6	-90.8	-133.5	-129.1	-148.2
Total Adjustments[b]	-2.0	-53.9	-2.8	+48.9	+133.7	+39.0	-23.9	+67.2	-24.0	-40.8	+188.1	+95.2	-132.0	+11.4
Statistical Discrepancy[c]	+16.8	+17.2	+17.5	+29.7	-7.7	-17.6	+48.6	+24.9	-46.1	-43.6	+5.6	-3.3	-14.9	-46.0
INW at End of Year	+303.4	+167.7	+60.1	-13.4	-54.8	-161.8	-243.8	-246.4	-326.0	-473.0	-370.1	-411.7	-687.7	-870.5
Memorandum With Direct Investments at Market Value	+232.5	+109.2	+72.0	+78.1	+27.6	-12.5	-70.5	-207.0	-319.9	-529.5	-274.9	-321.5	-637.5	-831.3

[a] Gold is valued at year-end market price (see n. 7 above). INW at market valuations is given in the memorandum. For detail, see sources.
[b] This number includes value changes of both real and financial assets as well as net capital flows. This number is clearly sensitive to changes in exchange rates.
[c] When positive, the "statistical discrepancy" shows "unexplained credits." Clearly, incomplete data tend to reduce the reduction in INW.
Sources: Survey of Current Business, July 1997, p. 33, 64–65; Landefeld and Lawson (1991); Scholl (1991, 1997).

Table 7.3

Outstanding Financial Assets of Non-Americans in U.S. Financial Markets (End of Year Data in Billions of U.S. Dollars)

	1982	1985	1989	1992	1995
Official Assets	189.1	202.5	341.9	442.8	678.5
Private Financial Assets	428.5	806.2	1,542.0	1,854.9	2,627.5
U.S. Treasury Securities	25.8	88.0	166.5	225.1	389.4
Other Bonds	16.7	82.3	231.7	319.8	465.4
U.S. Currency	54.2	68.9	90.1	137.7	192.3
Stocks	76.3	125.6	251.2	300.4	338.9
Liabilities of Non-bank Concerns	27.5	87.0	167.1	220.7	232.9
Liabilities of Banks	228.0	354.5	635.5	651.0	813.4

Source: Survey of Current Business, July 1997, p. 33.

States can reduce its interest rate in order to depreciate its dollar for fear of inducing a flight from the dollar; and the United States is currently playing the role of the nth country in terms of global aggregate demand. A sudden switch in that pattern (reducing global aggregate demand by about $100 billion per annum) would bring about a dislocative recession unless surplus/creditor nations are capable of expanding their aggregate demand. This inflicts major difficulties on governments of surplus/creditor nations if the ability of multinationals corporations to maintain their market share will be reduced by a substantial strengthening of the national currency (Milberg and Gray, 1992).

NOTES

1. Interestingly, the two approaches were both outlined in Johnson (1957): in my opinion this is the single most insightful article ever written on balance of payments adjustment with the exception of Kindleberger (1969), which stresses the international net worth aspects.

2. This fact allows the key-currency nation to accumulate huge indebtedness to foreigners without encountering a balance of payments constraint—see Table 7.1. For an analysis of the problem of the indebtedness of the key-currency nation, see Gray (1996b).

3. The original article identified the basic balance (current account plus direct investment plus long-term capital flows) as the focus of the Absorption approach. Since then, evolution in the financial markets has made long-term bonds virtually as easily encashable as treasury bills, so "illiquid capital movements" is a better, though still imperfect, definition. This distinction would be important in any analysis of the stability implications of the balance of payments of the hegemon (Gray, 1996a).

4. Keynes does not seem to have countenanced a situation in which the hegemon (the United States) was unable to fulfill its appointed task. Gray (1996a) uses the Absorption approach to uncover the burdens imposed on the hegemon and to speculate about the possibility of the role of hegemon being adequately performed in a country with universal suffrage and a high rate of social discount.

5. The implicit assumption is that the "sum of the elasticities" exceeds unity by a substantial margin so that currency depreciation will lead to a significant switch in expenditure patterns.

6. For an analysis showing the interrelationship between current account balances and international net worth, see Gray and Gray (1988–1989). That the acquisition of foreign assets could be a legitimate national strategy to prevent the strengthening of the currency is conceived in Milberg and Gray (1992).

7. It seems improbable that deficits of the magnitude recorded in Table 7.1 could exist except as a result of the utter neglect by policy makers in the country willing *and able* to allow its international net worth to sink into a seemingly bottomless pit. On the costs of servicing the debt, see Godley and Milberg (1994).

8. This mechanism correctly identified the ability of the United States to implement inflationary pressures throughout the world during the Vietnam War because the United States increased the global money supply by running international current and/or basic deficits and also because the other nations in the world were unable or unwilling to reduce their money supplies by the amount needed to keep world prices stable.

9. In practice, the observed consistency of the monetarist relationships has collapsed in the United States. Benjamin Friedman (1988, pp. 51–52) reports, "Relationships connecting income and prices to the monetary base, or to measures of credit, fell apart just as visibly as did those centered on M1" between mid-1982 and 1987. This was also the period of President Ronald Reagan's tax cuts and of large increases in the deficit and the current account deficits.

10. In my criticism of this article, I hold the members of the author's dissertation committee and the Department of Economics at the University of Chicago primarily responsible for the unsatisfactory specification of the model.

11. In fact, Dornbusch and Krugman (1976) reported adjustment lags after devaluations running to years rather than quarters.

12. The devaluation of the French franc in August 1969 was most effective, but that may be because the devaluation merely brought the official exchange rate into line with the forward rate, which had been at a discount for most of the year ("M. Pompidou's First Strike," *The Economist*, August 16, 1969, p. 49).

13. A similar problem exists in the work of Evans (1985), which tested the hypothesis that large government deficits do not contribute to higher interest rates. He did not include inflows of foreign funds in the equation, and in this way he ignored a substantial source of financing of the federal deficit. Neither editor was prepared to publish a note pointing out the fallibility of the modeling, suggesting that editors are prone to resist acknowledging their own errors and putting the reliability of economic scholarship under suspicion.

14. Behrman (1993) showed that multinational corporations now command a major part of global trade and investment. Consequently, it is impossible to analyze global phenomena without taking their influence into account.

15. These exist in terms of money market instruments, bonds and equities.

16. Apart from the inability of economists and central bankers to reliably foresee future events.

REFERENCES

Behrman, Jack N. "World Investment Report, 1993: Transnational Corporations and Integrated International Production." *Transnational Corporations*, 2 (December 1993): 149–162.

Day, A. C. L. "The Taxonomic Approach to the Study of Economic Policies." *American Economic Review*, 45 (March 1955): 64–78.

Dornbusch, Rudiger, and Paul Krugman. "Flexible Exchange Rates in the Short Run." *Brookings Papers on Economic Activity*, no. 3 (1976): 537–575.

Eichengreen, Barry, James Tobin and Charles Wyplosz. "Two Cases for Sand in the Wheels of International Finance." *The Economic Journal*, 105 (January 1995): 162–172.

Eiteman, David K., Arthur I. Stonehill and Michael H. Moffett. *Multinational Business Finance*. 6th ed. Reading, Mass.: Addison-Wesley, 1992.

Evans, Paul. "Do Large Deficits Produce High Interest Rates?" *The American Economic Review*, 75 (March 1985): 68–87.

Friedman, Benjamin. "Lessons of Monetary Policy from the 1980s." *Journal of Economic Perspectives*, 2 (Summer 1988): 51–72.

Godley, Wynne, and William S. Milberg. "U.S. Trade Deficits: The Recovery's Dark Side?" *Challenge* (November/December 1994): 40–47.

Gray, H. Peter. "Hicksian Instability in Asset Markets and Financial Fragility." *Eastern Economic Journal*, 18 (Summer 1992): 249–258.

Gray, H. Peter. "The Burdens of Global Leadership." In *International Trade in the 21st Century*, ed. Khosrow Fatemi. London: Pergamon, 1996a.

Gray, H. Peter. "The Ongoing Weakening of the International Financial System." *Banca Nazionale del Lavoro Quarterly Review*, 49, no. 197 (June 1996b): 165–186.

Gray, Jean M., and H. Peter Gray. "The Multinational Bank: A Financial MNC?" *Journal of Banking and Finance*, 5 (March 1981): 33–63.

Gray, H. Peter, and Jean M. Gray. "International Payments in a Flow-of-Funds Format." *Journal of Post Keynesian Economics*, 7 (Winter 1988–1989): 241–260.

Johnson, Harry G. "Towards a General Theory of the Balance of Payments." In *International Trade and Economic Growth*. London: George Allen and Unwin, 1958, pp. 153–168.

Johnson, Harry G. "The Monetary Approach to Balance-of-Payments Theory." *Economic Notes*, 1 (Spring 1972): 20–39.

Johnson, Harry G. "Why Devaluations Often Appear to Fail." *Eastern Economic Journal*, 1 (October 1974): 231–238.

Kindleberger, Charles P. "Measuring Equilibrium in the Balance of Payments." *Journal of Political Economy*, 77 (November–December 1969): 873–891.

Landefeld, J. Steven, and Ann M. Lawson. "Valuation of the U.S. Net International Investment Position." *Survey of Current Business* (May 1991): 40–49.

McKinnon, Ronald I. "The Exchange Rate and Macroeconomic Policy: Changing Postwar Perceptions." *Journal of Economic Literature*, 19 (June 1981): 531–557.

McKinnon, Ronald I. "The Exchange Rate and the Trade Balance: Insular Versus Open Economies." *Open Economies Review*, 1, no. 1 (1990): 17–37.

Milberg, William S., and H. Peter Gray. "International Competitiveness and Policy in

Dynamic Industries." *Banca Nazionale del Lavoro Quarterly Review* (March 1992): 59–80.

Miles, Marc A. "The Effects of Devaluation on the Trade Balance and the Balance of Payments: Some New Results." *Journal of Political Economy*, 87 (June 1979): 600–620.

Salvatore, Dominick. "European and International Monetary Systems: Problems and Prospects." *The International Trade Journal*, 9 (Winter 1995): 453–474.

Scholl, Russel B. "The International Investment Position of the United States in 1990." *Survey of Current Business* (June 1991): 23–35.

Scholl, Russel B. "The International Investment Position of the United States in 1996." *Survey of Current Business* (July 1997): 24–36.

Part IV

A Theoretical Comparison of the Keynesian and Monetary Theories to the Balance of Payments

Chapter 8

Keynesian and Monetary Approaches to the Balance of Payments

*Melvin Johnson, Krishna M. Kasibhatla
and John Malindretos*

INTRODUCTION

The purpose of this chapter is to review the Keynesian and Monetary approaches to the balance of payments, with specific emphasis on the assumptions and conclusions of each. The main proponents of the Keynesian approach are Keynes, C. F. Bickerdike, J. Robinson, F. Machlup, S. S. Alexander, A. P. Lerner, G. Haberler, S. Lauren, and L. A. Metzler. The Keynesian approach to the balance of payments, which to a large extent is an extension of the income expenditure model, consists of three subtheories: (1) the elasticities view, which is a short-run examination and explanation of the balance of payments; (2) the multiplier approach, which is a medium-term view of the balance of payments; and (3) the absorption model, which is a general analysis of the balance of payments. The multiplier model incorporates both the elasticities and the absorption views. The focus of the Keynesian approach is the trade balance, or the current account, and how it is determined (Krueger, 1969). In the early 1960s, the capital account—the inflows or outflows of capital—was integrated into the mainstream Keynesian approach. In this chapter a distinction is made between Keynes and the Keynesians.

The main proponents of the Monetary approach to the balance of payments are R. A. Mundell, H. Johnson, J. A. Frenkel, D. F. Meiselman, M. Mussa, M. Miles, and A. B. Laffer. The Monetary approach to the balance of payments is a long-run theory and originated much earlier than the Keynesian approach. The main components of the balance of payments are the current account, the capital account, and the official reserve transactions balance, which is an equilibrating account between the current account and the capital account.

KEYNESIAN AND MONETARY APPROACHES TO THE BALANCE OF PAYMENTS

The Keynesian and Monetary approaches view the balance of payments differently. The Keynesians, for example, focus on goods and services in their analysis of the balance of payments. The Monetarists, on the other hand, look upon the current account, the capital account, and the official reserves transactions balance as the main components of the balance of payments. The main difference between the two approaches revolves around the assumptions regarding the existence of general equilibrium and the role of money.

General Equilibrium

General equilibrium, in the Walrasian sense, is defined as an economic world characterized by the simultaneous clearing of all markets (termed Walras's Law). Keynes and some of his followers did not subscribe to the existence of general equilibrium, whereas Keynesians do believe in its existence (Leijonhufvud, 1973). On the other hand, the Monetary approach is completely posited within the general equilibrium framework (Frenkel, 1976).

Keynes's approach rejects the general equilibrium framework. In its place, Keynes used a short-run model incorporating the uncertainties that can affect the balance of payments. Keynes argued that for a general equilibrium framework to be appropriate in an economy set on high employment, the following conditions must hold: (1) a high employment equilibrium must currently exist or be quickly restored following a disturbance; (2) the social cost of restoring high employment equilibrium should be very small or negligible; (3) the policies designed to restore high employment equilibrium should not create further unemployment (Gray, 1974).

Keynes strongly believed that it was quite unlikely for these conditions to hold in face of uncertainties and other disturbances (Whitman, 1975). The factors creating disturbances in the economy that prevent the restoration of equilibrium include time, central bank interference, instability of capital flows, exogenous factors, full employment, and purchasing power parity.

Time

The time frame on which a problem is recognized and policy is designed and implemented may not coincide with the emergence of an economic problem. The time lag in recognizing a problem may delay or prevent the economy from adjusting toward an equilibrium. In addition, institutional rigidities may not allow the quick design and implementation of appropriate policy responses. Furthermore, the adjustments needed in input and output prices may not be sufficiently instantaneous to move the economy back to equilibrium. Finally, in an environment of business cycles, an identified exchange rate path consistent with a specific growth rate may cause policy makers to miss the target by over- or undershooting.

Central Bank Interference

The price specie flow mechanism assumes an automatic adjustment in exchange rates in response to price-level changes among nations. However, central monetary authorities can, intentionally or unintentionally, thwart the automatic adjustment process (Barro, 1993).

Instability of Capital Flows

The economy can be prevented or delayed from reverting to equilibrium as a result of inordinate delays in the stock adjustment process and uncertainties associated with the political climate.

Exogenous Factors

General equilibrium implicitly assumes that there are no changes in the exogenous variables relating to economic, social, and political factors. Included among those variables are technology, government expenditures and regulation. Since this is a very restrictive assumption, the existence of general equilibrium is questionable. In addition to general equilibrium, the other key assumptions of the Monetary approach include full employment, the law of one price, and the importance of the money market to the balance of payments.

One of the basic assumptions of the Monetary approach is that in the long run, economies tend toward full employment. This assumption is based on Walras's Law, which states that in the long run, there are no excesses of supply or demand for goods and services; hence, full employment is the inevitable outcome. In Keynes's world, however, Walras's Law does not hold because an excess supply of labor (unemployment) can exist, primarily due to the unique characteristics of money (i.e., its zero substitutability and productivity) (Davidson, 1974). An excess demand for money will not be eliminated by an excess supply of goods and services as, according to Keynes, money and goods are not substitutable. Furthermore, the downward inflexibility of prices and wages will allow an excess supply of labor to exist. This unique characteristic of money and the downward rigidity of prices and wages will prevent general equilibrium from occurring. Keynesians who believe in general equilibrium hold that unemployment is basically due to the downward rigidity of prices and wages.

The monetary approach assumes that the purchasing power parity (PPP) condition holds. According to PPP, price differences of goods and services between countries are eliminated, and in the long run, uniform prices will prevail. The PPP condition is known as the law of one price (Cassel, 1928). In contrast to the Monetary approach, Keynes's approach does not accept the PPP condition; this is due to the belief that perfect competition does not exist in the world markets and because of the limited elasticity of substitution in production (Whitman, 1975). From the Keynesian perspective, differences in the prices of goods and services between countries are most likely to exist. Keynes concluded that there would be no rationale for the existence of international trade if the law of one price held (Ohlin, 1933).

Keynes totally rejected the assumption of PPP, which is the bedrock of the Monetary approach. For Keynes, changes in inflation rates and exchange rates between countries are very important factors, which influence the balance of payments. Inflation is important since if domestic prices in a country increase faster than foreign prices, the exchange rate must increase (the domestic currency will be devalued). In a similar situation, the Monetary approach assumes that inflation rate differentials will bring about arbitrage actions until prices are equalized (Mundell, 1975). Exchange rates are important to Keynes since a deficit in the balance of payments would require a devaluation of the domestic currency vis-à-vis the foreign currency to eliminate the deficit. The Monetary approach, on the other hand, assumes that a devaluation will not accomplish the objective of closing the balance of payments deficit. As a result, the adjustment to an imbalance in the balance of payments must occur through the money markets (Laffer, 1974).

Money and capital accounts are the centerpiece of the Monetary approach to the balance of payments. In Keynes's world, money and capital accounts are not part of balance of payments analysis. The Keynesian approach does incorporate the capital account as part of its balance of payments theory. According to the Monetary approach, however, the domestic money market determines the balance of payments in a country. An assumption with which both Keynes and the Keynesians disagree. In this approach, any disequilibrium in the money market is attributed to a disequilibrium in another market. Appropriate price and output movements in the goods and services market would eventually restore equilibrium following a disturbance in the money market (Kemp, 1975).

In the case of flexible exchange rates, changes in the exchange rate resulting from a money market disequilibrium will be instrumental in restoring balance of payments equilibrium. If a monetary authority expands the money supply (assuming that money demand is constant), the domestic currency will depreciate vis-à-vis foreign currencies. Consumer goods will become more expensive relative to foreign goods. In the long run, however, this depreciation will finally make domestic goods as expensive as foreign goods, even though they were cheaper initially.

In an environment of fixed exchange rates, an excess supply of money will flow abroad and spill over in the demand for foreign goods, services, and financial assets. When excess supply and demand are eliminated, equilibrium is restored. In this case, it is quantity rather than price changes that are responsible for restoring equilibrium. In the case of a dirty float (floating exchange rates with government intervention), the restoration of equilibrium occurs through price and quantity changes rather than through price and quantity movements alone.

Keynes's Critique of General Equilibrium

Keynes did not believe that money and general equilibrium were compatible, especially in a world of uncertainty. However, Keynesians do not harbor the same reservations concerning money and general equilibrium. For Keynes, there is no gross substitutability between goods and money. In the case of an expansionary monetary policy, Keynes would argue that there would be no greater desire for the public to change its money balances once it is acquired. Under this policy, the public prefers to hold on to cash when interest rates are low, which is a "liquidity trap."

Keynes believed money to be substitutable with financial assets such as equity or debt, but not with real assets. For Keynes, because general equilibrium does not exist in a Walrasian sense, an excess supply of money cannot be eliminated (Davidson, 1974). It follows that if general equilibrium does not exist in a closed economy, it will exist in an open economy. Thus, the money account will not materially affect the balance of payments. According to Keynes, any adjustment in the balance of payments must occur through the interest rate. An excess money supply will lead to a decrease in the interest rate and the flow of domestic capital abroad in search of higher returns from foreign securities. However, the balance of payments will worsen because the capital account is not affected; this is because money is not exchanged for goods and services. Excess money supply will flow abroad in exchange for foreign securities through the capital account.

Keynesians do not agree altogether with Keynes. The specific disagreement between Keynes and the Keynesians concerns the relationship between money market disturbances and the capital account. Keynesians do not believe that money market disturbances influence the capital account. An excess supply of money will lead to a decrease in the domestic interest rate and an increase in investment, employment, income and output. Since production takes time, increases in output may lag behind increases in income and in the demand for goods and services. In other words, in the short run, domestic absorption may rise faster than output. This excess demand for goods and services in the domestic market can only be met by increases in the import of goods and services in the interim. In this case, provided all the changes occur above the "liquidity trap," a disturbance in the money market can influence the current account balance.

The Money Supply and the Balance of Payments

The question that is often raised is "why the expansion in the money supply does not first encourage an expansion in economic activity before it seeks foreign lands and foreign goods" (Malindretos, 1984, p. 37). This is due primarily to the assumption of full employment and gross substitutability in the Monetary approach. In contrast, this need not be the case for Keynes or the Keynesians since they do not assume full employment. From the perspective of Keynes and the Keynesians, the most likely outcome of an expansion of the money supply is to move the economy a step closer to full employment. The excess supply of money need not be exported. With an initial expansion of the money supply, the residents of a country will import money from abroad in order to meet the increase in money demand. This will result in an increase in the capital account surplus, which may more than offset the deficit in the trade account. The Keynesian prediction would result in a better outcome for the balance of payments. Clearly, this approach predicts a different outcome resulting from a disturbance in the money market. These differences in predicted outcomes lead to different policy recommendations.

The Balance of Payments: A Monetary or Real Phenomenon?

The main point of contention for the various approaches is whether the balance of payments in general is a monetary or real phenomenon. The Monetary approach stresses that the balance of payments is essentially a monetary phenomenon. To be specific, it claims that money plays a vital role in determining the balance of payments. This approach does not deny the importance of nonmonetary factors such as productivity changes, tariffs, government spending and taxation on the balance of payments. Indeed, it stresses the links between these factors and the money market (Rivera-Batiz and Rivera-Batiz, 1994) The Monetary approach does not assert that balance of payments problems are caused solely by monetary mismanagement or that monetary policy is the only possible cure. Rather, it emphasizes that ''the monetary process will bring about a cure of some kind (not necessarily very attractive) unless frustrated by deliberate monetary policy action. Policies that neglect or aggravate the monetary implications of deficits or surpluses will not be successful in their declared objectives'' (Rivera-Batiz and Rivera-Batiz, 1994, p. 430).

The Monetary approach to the balance of payments applies specifically to a fixed exchange-rate regime. In this environment, it is the money supply that adjusts to money demand through international flows of money, which brings about equilibrium in the balance of payments. In this case, the money market determines the balance of payments. In a regime of flexible exchange rates, it is the money demand that adjusts to the money supply, which in turn is determined by the central bank. In a ''managed float'' scenario, both international money flows and exchange rate changes are anticipated, given the nature of the central bank intervention (Rivera-Batiz, and Rivera-Batiz, 1994).

The Keynesian approach focuses mainly on the merchandise trade account, with the capital account incorporated in the analysis at a later date. Disequilibrium in the balance of payments is caused by both the current account and the capital account. The current account, however, is considered to be more important than the capital account for the balance of payments disequilibrium. The relative prices and relative income levels of domestic and foreign countries are responsible for the balance of payments disequilibrium condition (Malindretos, 1984).

The relative prices and exchange rate of a country, vis-à-vis its trading partners, will determine the competitiveness of that country's goods and services. An adverse movement in the relative price structure of a country, ceteris paribus, would decrease its competitiveness relative to its trading partners. Keynesians argue that a devaluation of a country's currency will improve the trade account and enhance competitiveness. In time, equilibrium will be restored in the trade account. From the Monetary approach's point of view, the money market is the principal vehicle, if not the only one, that is responsible for a balance of payments disequilibrium. For the Keynesians, it is differences in relative prices and domestic absorption rates that determine the balance of payments outcome. In short, real factors are more important than monetary factors in determining the balance of payments outcome.

Short Run versus Long Run

The Monetary approach states that in the long run, monetary variables cannot affect real variables such as output, employment and, in the case of the balance of payments, the trade account. In the short run, monetary variables will affect real variables (Friedman, 1965). This is true in the case of the money supply, money demand, exchange rates, and interest rates. The influence of interest rates on direct foreign investment is not made clear in the Monetary approach. This is because the approach does not distinguish between different types and durations of capital flows and the money account.

The Keynesian approach considers the balance of payments as a real phenomenon. Factors such as relative prices, devaluations, and aggregate demand affect the real variables in the short as well as the long run. In addition, capital flows are divided into short and long term. Protagonists of this approach argue that it is the short-term capital flows and long-term portfolio investments that respond to monetary factors (Gray, 1976).

Stability of Money Demand

For the Monetary approach, the demand for money is a stable function of a few variables (Davidson, 1982). In a world of stable money demand functions, the assumptions of this approach are all valid. However, the Keynesian approach is not anchored on the premise of a stable demand function. In fact, for Keynesians, money demand functions are not considered stable since velocity is not stable. Hence, the Monetary approach's conclusions are not valid for the Keynesians. The Monetary approach does not specifically identify whether it is the current account or the capital account that is responsible for a balance of payments deficit or surplus. However, it may be important to be able to clearly attribute the deficit or surplus to either the current account or the capital account. This would have an implication on the determination of the net worth of a country. For example, a change in the net worth of country will occur if the capital account is in deficit, ceteris paribus. However, net worth declines if the deficit is in the current account. The Keynesian approach specifically identifies which account is responsible for balance of payments deficits or surpluses. The reason for this identification is due to the importance of a country's net worth over time.

Asymmetry in Money Supply Changes

The Monetary approach argues that the response of wages to a change in the money supply is not symmetric (Gray, 1976). This is due to resistance from workers and unions to wage reductions following a decrease in the money supply. Conversely, with an increase in the money supply, wages rise following an increase in prices caused by the money supply expansion. Strong resistance to a drop in wages may be due to contractual agreements and institutional rigidities. According to the Monetary approach, a given change in the money supply is similar to a change in exchange rates in terms percentage changes. For the Keynesians, however, this is not the case. It is their belief that in the real world, exchange rates are motivated in part by political reasons as well as economic and monetary factors. Keynesians argue that the reaction of wage earners and unions to a decrease in the money supply compared to their reaction to a devaluation is different. A decrease in the money supply will reduce nominal wages, and such a reduction is unacceptable to labor and labor unions. On the other hand, all other things remaining equal, a devaluation lowers the real wage rate by increasing domestic prices. However, a devaluation normally does not bring forth resistance from labor unions, despite the fact that an outcome similar to a decrease in the money supply is produced. It is possible that labor unions tend to focus on the immediate, direct effects on wages rather than on the delayed, indirect effects produced by a devaluation. In essence, the results of a decrease in the money supply or a devaluation are the same in the Keynesian view.

Exchange Rate as a Relative Price

The Keynesian approach regards the exchange rate as a relative price of domestic and foreign goods (Humphrey and Lawler, 1978). A change in relative prices will lead to a decrease in exchange rates. In the case of a devaluation, domestic prices of the devaluating country will decline in terms of foreign (goods) prices by the amount of the devaluation in percentage terms. In a regime of flexible exchange rates, the outcome of the current and capital accounts determines the exchange rate. According to the Keynesians, it is the capital account that exerts a more significant influence on exchange rates. This view is different from the Monetary approach, which argues that it is the money market outcome—money supply and money demand—that determines the exchange rate. The factors that influence the money supply and money demand will indirectly influence the exchange rate.

Currency Substitution

The two approaches hold different views on currency substitution (Miles, 1978). The Monetary approach assumes the substitution of currencies and believes that in practice, this occurs to a high degree. This implies that monetary policy is independent. In the Keynesian approach, currencies of different countries are not really substitutable, and hence, monetary policies are not independent. In a managed-float regime, changes in exchange rates as well as monetary flows will occur to restore equilibrium in the monetary market and in the balance of payments. In this case, because of the money flows generated by "intervention," central banks cannot truly be independent in conducting their monetary policies.

SUMMARY AND CONCLUSION

In summary, this analysis discussed the differences between the Monetary and the Keynesian approaches to the balance of payments. As can be seen, there are fundamental and striking differences between the two approaches, and past efforts to reconcile or synthesize the differences between them have not been very successful.

REFERENCES

Barro, R. *Macroeconomics*. New York: John Wiley and Sons, 1993.

Cassel, G. *Postwar Monetary Stabilization*. New York: Columbia University Press, 1928.

Davidson, P. "A Keynesian View of Friedman's Theoretical Framework for Monetary Analysis." In *Milton Friedman's Monetary Framework: A Debate with His Critics*, ed. R. J. Gordon. Chicago: University of Chicago Press, 1974, pp. 100–101.

Davidson, P. "Money and General Equilibrium." *Economie Appliqué*, 30, no. 4 (1977): 541–563.

Davidson, P. *International Money and the Real World*. London: Macmillan, 1982.

Frenkel, Jacob A. "A Monetary Approach to the Exchange Rate: Doctrinal Aspects and Empirical Evidence." *Scandinavian Journal of Economics* (May 1976): 200–224.

Frenkel, J. A., and H. G. Johnson, eds. *The Monetary Approach to the Balance of Payments*. Toronto: University of Toronto Press, 1976.

Friedman, M. "The Role of Monetary Policy." *American Economic Review*, 58, no. 1 (March 1958): 1–17.

Gray, H. P. *An Aggregate Theory of International Payments Adjustment*. London: Macmillan, 1974.

Gray, H. P. "The Monetary Approach to International Payments Theory: A Critique." Mimeo, Rutgers University, March 1976.

Humphrey, T. M., and T. A. Lawler. "Factors Determining Exchange Rates: A Simple Model and Empirical Tests." In *The Monetary Approach to International Adjustment*, ed. B. H. Putnam and D. S. Wilford (rev. ed.). New York: Praeger Publishers, 1978, pp. 134–146.

Kemp, Donald S. "A Monetary View of the Balance of Payments." *Federal Reserve Bank of St. Louis Review*, 57, no. 4 (April 1975), pp. 14–22.

Krueger, Anne O. "The Balance-of-Payments Theory." *Journal of Economic Literature*, 7, no. 1 (March 1969): 1–26.

Laffer, A. B. "Exchange Rates, the Terms of Trade, and the Trade Balance." In *The Effects of Exchange Rate Adjustments*, ed. Peter B. Clark, Dennis E. Logue and Richard J. Sweeney. Proceedings of a conference sponsored by OASIA Research, Department of the Treasury, 1974. Washington, D.C.: Department of the Treasury, 1977, pp. 32–44.

Leijonhufvud, Axel. *On Keynesian Economics and the Economics of Keynes: A Study in Monetary Theory*. New York: Oxford University Press, 1973.

Malindretos, J. "The Traditional and Monetary Approaches to the Balance of Payments: A Theoretical Comparison." *American Business Review*, 2 (June 1984): 31–42.

Meiselman, D. I. "Worldwide Inflation: A Monetarist View." In *The Phenomenon of Worldwide Inflation*, ed. D. I. Meiselman and A. B. Laffer. Washington, D.C.: American Enterprise Institute for Public Policy Research, 1975, pp. 69–112.

Miles, M. A. "Currency Substitution: Perspective, Implications, and Empirical Evidence." In *The Monetary Approach to International Adjustment*, ed. B. H. Putnam and D. S. Wilford. New York: Praeger Publishers, 1978, pp. 171–183.

Mundell, R. "Inflation from an International Viewpoint." In *The Phenomenon of Worldwide Inflation*, ed. D. I. Meiselman and A. B. Laffer. Washington, D.C.: American Enterprise Institute for Public Policy Research, 1975, pp. 141–152.

Ohlin, B. *Interregional and International Trade*. Cambridge, Mass.: Harvard University Press, 1933.

Rivera-Batiz, F., and L. Rivera-Batiz. *International Finance and Open Economy Macroeconomics*. 2nd ed. New York: Macmillan, 1994.

Whitman, M. V. N. "Global Monetarism, and the Monetary Approach to the Balance of Payments." *Brookings Papers on Economic Activity*, no. 3 (1975): 491–555.

Part V

Empirical Comparisons of the Keynesian and Monetary Theories of Balance of Payments Determination

Chapter 9

International Adjustment for Kenya: The Relevance of the Traditional and Monetary Approaches

Luis Eduardo Rivera-Solis, Krishna M. Kasibhatla and John Malindretos

INTRODUCTION

The purpose of this chapter is to empirically compare the Traditional and Monetary approaches of international adjustment during a period of quasi-flexible exchange rates in the small, agricultural, advancing country of Kenya. With so many such countries competing in the global economy, it is important to determine the applicability of these two theories in these cases.

This issue was studied on an empirical basis by Malindretos (1984) and Bonitsis, Kasibhatla, and Malindretos (1995). Malindretos's (1984) study focused on the Federal Republic of Germany, a large, developed country, and derived ambiguous results. In about half the instances, the Traditional approach is supported, and in the other half, the Monetary approach is supported. In examining the small, open economy of South Korea, the econometric results of Bonitsis et al. (1995) supported the Monetary approach.

THEORETICAL PERSPECTIVE

The Monetary Approach

The Trade Balance Model

Magee (1976) provides the theoretical framework for the balance of trade model, which is given by the multivariate equation (1):

$$(EXP - IMP) = F[(Y_d - Y_f), (P_d - P_f), (M_d - M_f)] \tag{1}$$

EXP and IMP represent the money value of exports and imports; Y_d is domestic income and Y_f, foreign income; P_a represents the domestic price level and P_f, the foreign price levels; M_d is the domestic money supply and M_f, the foreign money supply.

According to the Monetary approach, the trade account balance is influenced by the money supply. It stipulates that if a country has an excess supply of money, this excess will flow abroad in exchange for goods and/or securities. This will lead to a worsening of the balance of payments since the trade balance will worsen. Alternatively, if there is an excess demand for money, foreign reserves will be exchanged for goods and securities. This will, in essence, lead to an improvement in the trade, capital account, and, above all, the balance of payments.

Given this framework, we can analyze the effect of the independent variables M, Y_d, and P on the trade balance. An increase in domestic real income creates greater demand for money. Goods and securities are sent abroad in exchange for foreign reserves, which affects trade positively. An increase in foreign income has the opposite effect on a country's trade balance from that of income expansion in the country itself. Thus, growth will worsen a country's trade balance (Mundell, 1968).

The domestic price level affects the trade balance in the same way as the growth of domestic income. A rise in the domestic price level relative to the foreign price level increases the demand for money, which effectively improves the balance of payments. This also results in an improvement in the trade balance. On the other hand, the price increase results in an excess demand for money, which is satisfied by importing reserves. In essence, the foreigner's price has an inverse relationship with the trade balance (Laffer, 1974).

The variable that affects both the trade balance and the balance of payments, according to the Monetary approach, is the money market. A decrease in the domestic money supply improves the trade balance, but an increase in domestic money supply impacts the trade balance negatively. An increase in foreign money supply improves the trade balance because foreigners will send more money abroad in exchange for goods and services. However, as the foreign money supply declines, foreigners will import money from abroad and export goods and services to pay for it. This improves their own trade balance but worsens that of the focus country.

The Balance of Payments Model

Johnson (1976) provided the theoretical framework utilized to examine the balance of payments according to the Monetary approach, as specified in equation (2):

$$IR = G[(Y_d - Y_t), (P_d - P_t), (M_d - M_t)], (i_d - i_t), ER] \tag{2}$$

where IR is the level of international reserves and ER is the nominal exchange rate (the other variables were already defined).

The Monetary approach is really a theory of the balance of payments rather than a trade balance theory. The trade balance is affected only in that it is part of the international financial accounts. The key variable in the balance of payments equation, just as in the trade balance equation, is the money market. Thus, the balance of payments must be considered as a "monetary phenomenon," that is, an interaction of supply of, and demand for, money. The money supply, income, and price regressors influence the official reserves transactions account in the same fashion as they influence the trade balance, and for the same reasons.

The demand for international reserves is considered similar to the demand for domestic reserves. This is depicted in the way interest rates relate to foreign currency: there is a negative relationship. An increase in the interest rate causes the foreign exchange to fall in demand, and a decrease in the interest rate makes the foreign exchange holdings rise. This view of the interest rate is not traditional, since it treats international reserves as domestic money in terms of their relationship with the interest rate (Zecher, 1976).

The exchange rate influences the balance of payments. If a country devalues, it makes its money holdings fall in real terms. To return to equilibrium, the country then must import money from other nations and pay with goods and/or securities (Miles, 1978).

Traditional Approach

Trade Balance Model

Houthakker and Magee (1969) provided the theoretical framework for the balance of trade model according to the Traditional approach, which is expressed by equation (3):

$$(EXP - IMP) = F^*[(Y_d - Y_t), (P_d - P_t), ER] \tag{3}$$

The variables specified have already been defined. However, the signs of the Traditional approach parameters are different from what the Monetary approach generally contends. This is due to the underlying assumptions stipulated by each approach. Domestic income has an inverse relationship with the trade balance. A rise in domestic income increases absorption and, therefore, increases imports. The effect of income is inherent in the absorption side of the Traditional approach. Competitiveness is also an aspect of this approach. This applies to the price level and exchange rate of the focus country's currency in relation to those of the rest of the world. (MacDougall, 1951) The lower the price level in the focus country in terms of world price levels, the more its exports will be demanded, while there will be less of a demand for imports. Therefore, when prices rise, the focus country's trade balance worsens, but when the price of its imports rises, its trade balance improves. Another variable that determines the price of goods in relation to imports is the exchange rate. The Traditional approach assumes that the trade balance will improve after a devaluation as long as the right elasticities exist. Conversely, a revaluation will lead to an unfavorable trade balance. The exchange rate and the trade balance have an inverse relationship. When a nation's exchange rate is low (i.e., the country's currency is strong), its trade balance will worsen. Conversely, the trade balance will improve when the exchange rate is high (i.e., the focus country's currency is weak) (Robinson, 1947).

The Balance of Payments Model

The Traditional approach for the balance of payments model is expressed by equation (4):

$$IR = G^*[(Y_d - Y_t), (P_d - P_t), (i_d - i_t), ER] \qquad (4)$$

The variables have already been defined. The domestic and foreign incomes will have the same signs as those obtained in the balance of payments for the Traditional approach. Similarly, the signs of the coefficients of the domestic and foreign price will be the same in the balance of payments model as in the trade model under the Traditional approach. Domestic interest rates relate positively to the available reserves. As domestic rates rise, the country attracts foreign capital and at the same time retains domestic capital (Branson, 1968). An increase in foreign interest rates will have a negative influence on the focus country's balance of payments.

Both the exchange rate and the price level determine the competitiveness of a country's goods and services. The exchange rate relates negatively to the reserve flow. If a country depreciates its currency, its exports will rise while its imports will fall, which will improve its balance of payments. The balance of payments may initially worsen because it takes time to adjust to the change in the exchange rate. Thus, a J effect will result. After the adjustment, the balance of payments should improve, given the right elasticities. If, on the other hand, a country's currency appreciates, its balance of payments will improve and an inverted J-curve effect may result, again depending on whether the right elasticities are in effect (Dornbusch and Krugman, 1976).

EMPIRICAL RESULTS

The empirical analysis of this study uses the Time Series Processor (TSP) software, and the statistical tool is ordinary least squares (OLS), adjusted for auto-correlation by the Cochrane-Orcutt technique. The model is structured in a polynomial distributed-lag method, which is lagged in an Almon fashion (Almon, 1965). This model was chosen for the following reasons: first, if the Almon technique has few lags, it will provide more than one coefficient sign and, for that matter, the true statement concerning the signs of the regression coefficients. Second, it takes time for adjustments in the international accounts to take effect.

The Almon procedure allows for this. As a result, the use of lagged determining variables is both appropriate and meaningful.

The data for this study was obtained from various issues of the International Monetary Fund's *International Financial Statistics*. Quarterly data for Kenya for the period 1972–1982 were compiled. The reason for conducting this study was purely to test and determine the appropriate approach for a small country like Kenya to employ to cause an adjustment in its international accounts. The statistics indicate a perennially unfavorable balance of payments for Kenya, which is quite characteristic of developing countries.

The theoretical relationships (presented in the previous section) to be investigated are expressed by equations (5) and (6):

$$(EXP_t - IMP_t) = \alpha + \beta(Y_d - Y_f) + \tau(P_d - P_f) + \delta(M_d - M_f) \qquad (5)$$
$$+ \phi(i_d - i_f) + \Phi ER_t + u_1$$

$$IR = \alpha + \beta(Y_d - Y_f) + \tau(P_d - P_f) + \delta(M_d - M_f) \qquad (6)$$
$$+ \phi(i_d - i_f) + \Phi ER_t + u_2$$

All of the variables were defined in the previous section. Domestic and foreign income are measured by industrial production. All foreign parameters are aggregate OECD measures. Both domestic and foreign price levels are represented by the consumer price index. To maintain similarity and consistency, the two equations are identical for both international financial theories.

In view of the small size of the sample, only four independent variables were used. As a result, equations (5) and (6) were tested by constructing a composite parameter for the price level and exchange rate parameters. This parameter is called the competitiveness ratio (CR); it is the product of Kenya shilling and the ratio of foreign to domestic price levels.

The models examined in this study estimate the Almon polynomial distributed-lag structure. The Traditional and Monetary approaches are deemed valid only if the variables are statistically significant and have the expected theoretical signs. The models in this study are estimated using the Almon polynomial structure of degree two with a lag of six quarters. In addition, one model structure has zero restrictions on both head and tail lag values, whereas the other model structure has zero restriction on the head lag values only. There are four models, two for the trade balance account and two for the balance of payments account. Each empirical equation is corrected for autocorrelation in the residuals with the Cochrane-Orcutt technique.

The regression coefficients are tested for statistical significance using either a one- or two-tailed t test to validate the applicability of each approach to international competitive adjustment. The signs are also tested to verify whether they have the signs expected by theory.

The money stock is expected to be significant and negative under the Monetary approach to the trade balance. This may be verified with a one-tailed t test

Table 9.1

Almon Polynomial Distributed Lag Model (Zero Restrictions on Head and Tail Values): Degree Two and Six Quarterly Lags

A. Balance of Trade Model

Parameter	$M_d - M_f$	$Y_d - Y_f$	$i_d - i_f$	CR
Sum of Coefficients	-1.22	0.69	133.16[a]	-85.7
	(9.01)	(4.35)	(49.22)	(85.3)
Mean Lag	19.99	-35.94	1.64	-0.8
	(27.76)	(21.88)	(1.21)	(3.4)

$R^2 = .803$, DW = 1.988, SSR = 0.35E+7, SE = 383.93
N = 37, d.f. = 32

B. Balance of Payments Model

Parameter	$M_d - M_f$	$Y_d - Y_f$	$i_d - i_f$	CR
Sum of Coefficients	5.13[b]	-0.67	23.55	-10.55
	(2.73)	(1.53)	(15.20)	(26.38)
Mean Lag	2.17	4.87	4.73	-3.57
	(1.62)	(9.25)	(1.91)	(7.95)

$R^2 = .893$, DW = 1.88, SSR = 88007.8, SE = 60.555
N = 37, d.f. = 32

Note: Both models have zero restrictions on the head and tail values of the Almon polynomial lag.
[a] Significant at the 1% level.
[b] Significant at the 10% level.

of the regression parameter. On the other hand, the Monetary approach and the Traditional approach predict different signs for the income coefficient in the trade balance equation. Using a two-tailed *t* test of significance, we may confirm with which theory the regression outcome is consistent. Furthermore, the mean lag of the significant coefficients can be analyzed to determine the speed of adjustment of a specific independent variable: variables having larger and shorter mean lags under one approach will indicate a dominance in the international accounts by that approach.

Table 9.1 reports the econometric findings for the Almon polynomial distributed-lag model for six quarters and four explanatory variables for both the balance of trade and the balance of payments (i.e., international reserves equations).

Section A of Table 9.1 for the trade balance model indicates the following: a one-tailed *t* test for the monetary parameter is statistically insignificant, having a negative sign and a mean lag adjustment of 19.99 quarters. Although it is statistically insignificant, the findings are consistent with the Monetary approach. The income coefficient is also statistically significant, even though its positive sign is consistent with the Monetary approach. The interest rate parameter is statistically significant, but its sign is not consistent with the Monetary approach. The exchange rate parameter is also statistically insignificant, and the parameter's direction is inconsistent with both theories of international adjustment. The independent variables in the model explain roughly 83 percent of the variation in the balance of trade.

Part B of Table 9.1 provides the results for the international reserves model. The monetary parameter is statistically significant and positive, with a mean lag adjustment of 2.17 quarters. The income parameter is negative and insignificant, with a mean lag of 4.87 quarters. These findings are not in agreement with the Monetary approach to the balance of payments. The interest rate and exchange rate parameters are not statistically significant; they have positive and negative signs, respectively. The direction of these signs was not under the Monetary approach. Thus, the empirical evidence is not supportive of the Monetary approach.

The results for the trade balance equation in Table 9.2 indicate that the monetary parameter is negative and insignificant, with a mean lag of 2.50 quarters. The sign of monetary parameter is consistent with the Monetary approach. The income parameter is also a negative and insignificant, with a mean lag of 2.50 quarters. This sign is not consistent with Monetary approach. The interest rate parameter is significant and has a positive sign (which is not consistent with the Monetary approach to the balance of trade), with a mean lag of 2.5 quarters. The competitiveness ratio is also insignificant and has a negative sign; this is not consistent with either approach. Sixty-nine percent of the variation in the trade balance can be explained by the four independent variables.

Part B of Table 9.2 displays very disappointing results. All the variables were statistically insignificant and the Durbin-Watson statistic was 1.43. As far as the speed of adjustment is concerned, the Monetary approach expects adjustments to the trade balance and the balance of payments to occur within the time horizon of two years. The findings in this study are consistent with that approach.

The disappointing results are probably due to the fact that Kenya is a small country and its effects on the rest of the world are minor.

SUMMARY AND CONCLUSION

The results do not support one theory or the other. Each theory has only partial support. Frenkel and Razin (1987) are correct in arguing that the original policy is the determining factor for the signs of the coefficients. Depending on the original policy, the sign may be negative or positive for the same independ-

Table 9.2
Almon Polynomial Distributed Lag Model (Zero Restrictions on Head Values):
Degree Two and Six Quarterly Lags

A. Balance of Trade Model

Parameter	$M_d - M_f$	$Y_d - Yf$	$i_d - i_f$	CR
Sum of coef.	-6.69	-3.17	120.55[a]	-16.12
	(9.05)	(5.98)	(42.93)	(97.18)
Mean Lag	2.50	2.50	2.50	2.50
	(3.58)	(5.31)	0.88	15.44

$R^2 = .69$, DW = 1.99, SSR = 0.559, SE = 418.05
N = 37, d. f. = 32

B. Balance of Payments Model

Parameter	$M_d - M_f$	$Y_d - Y_f$	$i_d - i_f$	CR
Sum of coef.	6.08[a]	-0.85	17.32	-40.78
	(3.14)	(2.12)	(16.11)	(29.97)
Mean Lag	2.50	2.50	2.50	2.50
	(1.20)	(9.12)	(2.27)	(1.85)

$R^2 = .84$, DW = 1.43, SSR = 128390, SE = 63.34
N = 37, d.f. = 32

Notes: Both models have zero restrictions at the head of the Almon Polynomial lag.
[a] Significant at the 1% level.

ent variable. This indicates that different policies are affecting it on different occasions with dissimilar impacts.

We are thus unable to provide support for either of the two theories. Therefore, our policy recommendation is to include both theories in a comprehensive theory of adjustment to disequilibrium in either the real or the financial international accounts.

REFERENCES

Almon, Shirley. "The Distributed Lag between Capital Appropriations and Expenditures." *Econometrica*, 33, no. 1 (January 1965): 178–196.
Bonitsis, Theologos Homer, Krishna M. Kasibhatla and John Malindretos. "A Comparison of the Monetary and Traditional Approaches to International Competitive

Adjustment: The Case of South Korea." *Journal of International Economic Studies*, no. 9 (1995): 123–138.

Branson, William H. *Financial Capital Flows in the U.S. Balance of Payments*. Amsterdam: North Holland Publishing Company, 1968.

Dornbush, Rudiger, and Paul Krugman. "Flexible Exchange Rates in the Short Run." *Brookings Papers on Economic Activity*, no. 3 (1976): 537–575.

Frenkel, Jacob A., Thorvaldur Gylfason and John F. Helliwell. "A Synthesis of Monetary and Keynesian Approaches to Short-Run Balance of Payments Theory." *Economic Journal*, 96 (September 1980): 582–592.

Frenkel, Jacob A., and Assaf Razin. "The Mundell-Fleming Model, a Quarter Century Later." *International Monetary Fund Staff Papers*, 34 (December 1987: 567–620.

Gujarati, Damodor. *Basic Econometrics*. New York: McGraw-Hill, 1978.

Houthakker, Hendrik S., and Stephen P. Magee. "Income and Price Elasticities in World Trade." *Review of Economics and Statistics*, 51 (May 1969): 111–125.

International Monetary Fund. *International Financial Statistics*, various issues.

International Monetary Fund. *The Monetary Approaches to the Balance of Payments*. Washington, D.C.: International Monetary Fund, 1977.

Johnson, Harry G. "The Monetary Theory of Balance of Payments Politics." In *The Monetary Approach to the Balance of Payments*, ed. Jacob A. Frenkel and Harry G. Johnson. Toronto: University of Toronto Press, 1976, pp. 262–284.

Laffer, Arthur B. "Exchange Rates, the Terms of Trade, and the Trade Balance." In *The Effects of Exchange Rate Adjustment*, ed. Peter B. Clark, Dennis E. Logue and Richard J. Sweeney. Proceedings of a conference sponsored by OASIA Research, Department of the Treasury, 1974. Washington, D.C.: Department of the Treasury, 1977.

MacDougall, G. B. A. "British and American Exports: A Study Suggested by the Theory of Comparative Costs." *Economic Journal*, 61 (December 1951); 697–724.

Magee, Stephen. "The Empirical Evidence on the Monetary Approach to the Balance of Payments and Exchange Rates." *American Economic Review Papers and Proceedings*, 66 (May 1976): 163–170.

Malindretos, John. "The Traditional and Monetary Approaches to the Balance of Payments: A Theoretical Comparison." *American Business Review*, 2 (June 1984): 31–42.

Malindretos, John. "An Examination of the Two Views of International Finance for an Advanced, Medium Sized, Reserve Currency Country." In *Advances in Quantitative Analysis of Finance and Accounting*, vol. 1, part B, ed. Chen-Few Lee. Greenwich, Conn.: JAI Press, 1991, pp. 183–214.

Meese, Richard. "Currency Fluctuations in the Post–Bretton Woods Era." *Journal of Economic Perspectives*, 4 (Winter 1990): 117–134.

Miles, Marc A. *Devaluation, the Trade Balance and the Balance of Payments*. New York: Marcel Dekker, 1978.

Mundell, Robert A. *International Economics*. New York: Macmillan, 1968, pp. 111–133.

Mundell, Robert A. "Barter Theory and the Monetary Mechanism of Adjustment." In *Monetary Theory, Inflation, Interest Rates and Growth in the World Economy*. Pacific Palisades, Calif.: Goodyear Publishing, 1971, pp. 147–169.

Robinson, Joan. "The Foreign Exchanges." In *Essays in the Theory of Employment*. 2nd ed. Oxford, U.K.: Blackwell Publishing Company, 1947, pp. 221–228.

Whitman, Marina V. N. "Global Monetarism and the Monetary Approach to the Balance of Payments." *Brooking Papers on Economic Activity*, no. 3 (1975): 491–555.

Wilson, William. "J-Curve Effect and Exchange Rate Pass-Through: An Empirical Investigation of the United States." *International Trade Journal*, 7, no. 4 (Summer 1993): 463–483.

Zecher, Richard. "Monetary Equilibrium and International Reserve Flows in Australia." In *The Monetary Approach to the Balance of Payments*, ed. Jacob A. Frenkel and H. G. Johnson. Toronto: University of Toronto Press, 1976, pp. 287–297.

Chapter 10

A Comparison of the Monetary and Traditional Approaches to International Competitiveness

*Krishna M. Kasibhatla, John Malindretos
and Paul R. Kutasovic*

INTRODUCTION

Although there is very little theoretical literature on the comparison of the Traditional Approach (TA) and the Monetary Approach (MA), Marina V. Whitman investigated the two views hypothetically and presented many of the theories (Whitman 1975). Malindretos interpreted the assumptions underlying the two theories and showed the conditions under which the two theories would be similar. Malindretos also compared the two views empirically and found that in half the instances the TA is supported; in the other half, the MA is supported (Malindretos, 1991).

In the work, "A Synthesis of Monetary and Keynesian Approaches to Short-Run Balance of Payment Theory" (1980), Frenkel, Gylfason and Helliwell strove to unite the two theories. They argued that the impact of the independent variables on the official reserves transactions balance (ORTB) or the trade balance (TB) can be either positive or negative. The outcome depends on whether a monetary or fiscal policy action triggered the change (Frenkel, Glyfason and Helliwell, 1980).

The intention of this chapter is to empirically compare the Traditional and Monetary approaches of international adjustments for an advancing country such as Taiwan. The empirical test will concentrate on the trade balance (TB) and the balance of payments (BOP).

MONETARY APPROACH

The Monetary approach postulates that the cause of an imbalance in the TB is a monetary phenomenon determined by the supply of, and demand for, money. An excess demand for money results in an improvement in the TB, capital account and BOP. This is because the shortage of money causes an inflow of foreign reserves, which are used to purchase goods and services as exports. Conversely, with an excess supply of money, individuals and firms act to reduce their money stocks by increasing their purchases of foreign goods, thereby causing a deterioration, first in the TB and then in the BOP.

The TB equation for the MA is:

$$(X - M)_t = b_0 + b_1(Yd - Yf)_t + b_2(Pd - Pf)_t + b_3(Md - Mf)_t \tag{1}$$

where:

X = the monetary value of exported goods or services
M = the monetary value of imported goods or services
D = change in a certain variable
b_0 = the constant of the regression equation
b_1 = coefficient of income regressor
b_2 = coefficient of price regressor
b_3 = coefficient of money regressor
Yd = domestic income (i.e., industrial production)
Yf = foreign income (i.e., foreign industrial production)
Pd = domestic price, namely, domestic (OECD) CPI
Pf = foreign price, namely, foreign (OECD) CPI
Md = domestic money supply
Mf = foreign (OECD) money supply
t = certain time period

This equation shows the basic relationship of the MA to the TB. Exogenous shifts in the domestic money supply or in domestic income relative to the foreign money supply or real income will cause the TB to improve. Similarly, higher domestic inflation relative to foreign inflation raises the demand for money and then improves the TB. Thus, increases in domestic income, money supply and the price level are positively related to the trade balance.

The second equation to be estimated is an examination of the BOP. For the MA we shall test the following equation:

$$DR = b_0 + b_1(Yd - Yf)_t + b_2(Pd - Pf)_t + b_3(Md - Mf)_t$$
$$+ b_4(id - if)_t + b_5(ER_t) \tag{2}$$

where ER is the exchange rate, which is the amount of foreign currency attainable for the unit of home currency.

Like the TB, the BOP should be looked at as a "monetary phenomenon," namely, an interaction of the supply of, and the demand for, money. The money supply, income and price regressors influence the ORTB in the same way as they affect the TB, and for the same reasons. In addition, there is a direct relationship between interest rates and the BOP. The idea is that higher interest rates cause a decrease in the demand for money and a fall in international reserves.

Finally, the ER influences the BOP in that if the country devalues, it makes its money holdings fall in real terms. In order to return to equilibrium, the country will import money from foreign countries and pay with goods and/or securities. This improves the BOP and either the TB or the KA.

TRADITIONAL APPROACH

The TB regression equation for TA is given as:

$$(X - M)_t = b_0 + b_1(Yd - Yf)_t + b_2(Pd - Pf)_t + b_3(ER)_t \tag{3}$$

The Traditional Approach explains international payment adjustments in terms of changes in real expenditures rather than in terms of money demand and supply. As a result, the signs of the TA and MA parameters are different. Relative faster growth in domestic income compared to foreign income now has an inverse relation to the TB as a rise in domestic income increases the absorption of imports.

Competitiveness, as measured by the price level and exchange rate, is a key focus of the TA. Lower domestic price compared to foreign price will prompt the demand for exports to rise and the demand for imports to fall. Thus, when domestic prices fall relative to foreign prices, the TB improves.

Exchange rates also determine the relative price of domestic versus foreign goods. The TA presumes that the TB will improve after a devaluation as long as we have the correct elasticities. A revaluation, in contrast, will lead to an unfavorable TB. Thus, the ER and TB have an inverse relationship (Goldstein and Khan 1978).

The BOP equation for the Traditional Approach is given by the following:

$$DR = b_0 + b_1(Yd - Yf)_t + b_2(Pd - Pf)_t + b_3(ER)_t + b_4(id - if)_t \tag{4}$$

In this equation, the coefficients for domestic and foreign incomes and prices will have the same signs as those obtained in the TB for the TA. Domestic interest rates are positively related to the reserves available. This follows since when domestic interest rates rise, the nation attracts foreign capital and at the same time retains domestic capital. Foreign interest rates, however, are negatively related to the reserves available. In this instance, when interest rates rise, domestic residents will be eager to send their capital abroad and foreigners will be less willing to let go of their capital and will invest domestically.

Together the exchange rate and the price determine the competitiveness of the country's goods and services. If a country depreciates its currency, its exports will rise while its imports will fall, which will certainly improve its BOP. It is important to note that the BOP may initially worsen because it takes time to adjust to the change in ER. As an end result, a J-curve effect will result. After the adjustment, the BOP should rise given the proper elasticities. Thus, the country's BOP and the exchange rate are inversely related.

EMPIRICAL TEST

The TA and BOP equations specified in the previous sections were estimated using ordinary least squares (OLS) corrected for autocorrelation by the Cochrane-Orcutt method. A dynamic structure was incorporated into the equation using the Almon distributed-lag method. This specification was preferred for two reasons. First, the Almon lag has few terms and will give us more than one coefficient sign, and second, adjustments in international accounts take time to become effective, and thus, using lagging determining variables is both meaningful and appropriate (Almon, 1965).

The country under investigation is Taiwan from 1972 to 1982. This study was set out to test and discover the appropriate approach that a small country like Taiwan can employ to bring about an alteration in its international accounts.

The equation to estimate the trade balance is:

$$
\begin{aligned}
(X - M)_t = {} & b_0 + b_1(Yd - Yf)_t + b_2(Pd - Pf)_t + b_3(Md - Mf)_t \\
& + b_4(id - if)_t + b_5(ER_t)
\end{aligned} \tag{5}
$$

The equation to estimate the balance of payments is:

$$
\begin{aligned}
DR = {} & b_0 + b_1(Yd - Yf)_t + b_2(Pd - Pf)_t + b_3(Md - Mf)_t \\
& + b_4(id - if)_t + b_5(ER_t)
\end{aligned} \tag{6}
$$

To maintain similarity and consistency, the two equations were specified identically for both international financial theories. The study compared the two theories using two tests. First, the signs of the coefficients of the regressors were compared to determine which theory was supported. The second test examined the speed of the adjustment of the regressands to the real and monetary regressors. In addition, it examined the speed of adjustment of the TB versus the ORTB.

The results of our study do not give definitive support to either one of the theories. In the majority of cases, the evidence supported both theories approximately equally. This is so for the correctness of signs, the swiftness of the real versus the monetary regressors, and finally, the swiftness of the adjustment of the TB in contrast to the ORTB. Thus, we derived no definitive results.

CONCLUSION

It can be seen through this study that both the theories have explanatory power for the international accounts, and thus both theories are useful. The MA is incorrect in saying that the IR is the autonomous account and the TA is incorrect in saying that the TB is the autonomous account. We give specific evidence that in some instances, either the IR or the TB may have the slower speed of adjustment.

Most important, real variables do not overwhelm the real account and nominal variables do not, by themselves, determine the money account. The conclusion formed is that both real and monetary variables determine each of the two accounts. Therefore, both theories are promoted.

We recognize that both theories are verified only under certain instances; thus, there is no support for either of the two theories. After careful study, we conclude that both theories are correct. Our policy recommendation is to include both views in a systematic theory of adjustment to disequilibria in the international accounts.

REFERENCES

Almon, S. "The Distributed Lag between Capital Appropriations and Expenditures." *Econometrica*, 33 (1965): 178–196.

Frenkel, J. A. T. Gylfason, and J. F. Helliwell. "A Synthesis of Monetary and Keynesian Approaches to Short-Run Balance of Payments Theory." *Economic Journal*, 96 (September 1980): 582–592.

Frenkel, J. A., and H. G. Johnson, eds. *The Monetary Approach to the Balance of Payments.* Toronto: University of Toronto Press, 1976.

Goldstein, M., and M. S. Kahn. "The Supply and Demand for Exports: A Simultaneous Approach." *Review of Economics and Statistics*, 60 (May 1978): 275–286.

Malindretos, J. "An Examination of the Two Views of International Finance for an Advanced, Medium-Sized Reserve Currency Country." In *Advances in Quantitative Analysis of Finance and Accounting*, vol. 1, part B, ed. Chen-Few Lee. Greenwich, Conn.: JAI Press, 1991, pp. 183–214.

Whitman, M. V. N. "Global Monetarism and the Monetary Approach to the Balance of Payments." *Brookings Papers on Economic Activity*, no. 3 (1975): 491–555.

Chapter 11

The Keynesian and Monetary Approaches to International Accounts Adjustment: Some Heuristics for Germany

Theologos Homer Bonitsis and John Malindretos

INTRODUCTION

The goal of this chapter is twofold: on the one hand, to discuss and formally present the theoretical relationships for the Keynesian and Monetary paradigms of international payments and adjustment, and on the other hand, to report the results of a heuristic model that allows for intertemporal relationships among the theoretical parameters of the two approaches. It is important to note that for the theoretical and empirical presentation, this research draws extensively from Bonitsis, Kasibhatla and Malindretos (1995).

There have been some studies that compared the Keynesian and Monetary paradigms of external accounts equilibrium determination. Whitman (1975) and Malindretos (1984) are two noteworthy endeavors; their studies examined the Monetary approach within the context of the Keynesian approach and provided a useful framework for the comparative analysis of the two theories. Frenkel, Gylfason and Helliwell (1980) theoretically integrated the two theories. Their research indicated the need to identify the original jolt or policy action on the balance of trade account and/or official reserves account as the only means of determining the impact of the initial change. This implies that if the original policy action is fiscal or monetary, a parameter may have either a positive or a negative intertemporal effect on the various international accounts. Two important policy questions arise from this line of inquiry and are addressed by this research. First, what is the disturbance's character? Second, how does this affect the international accounts and, by extension, the external competitive position of a country?

This research presents comparative intertemporal heuristic findings covering the period from the first quarter of 1972 through the fourth quarter of 1983 that cast light on the Keynesian and Monetary approaches to international accounts equilibrium for the large open economy of Germany. Traditionally, the existence of a large open economy implies a country that is a price-setter for its exports and imports. With the planned integration of national economies, as in the European Union (EU), it follows that the policy pertinence of this research concerns the applicability of the two theories of international accounts determination for large open economies.

This chapter is organized as follows: the theoretical frameworks for the Keynesian and Monetary approaches are presented in the second and third sections, respectively; the fourth section discusses how the size and pace of adjustment of the parameters for each approach are determined as well as the policy significance of these findings; the actual empirical findings are presented in the fifth section; and the final section summarizes and discusses policy implications and suggests future extensions of this research.

A THEORETICAL FRAMEWORK FOR THE KEYNESIAN APPROACH

The Balance of Trade Relationship

Houthakker and Magee (1969) suggested the following theoretical structure for the Keynesian trade model relationship:

$$TB_t = F[(Y_t - Y_t^*), (P_t - P_t^*), ER_t], \tag{1}$$

where domestic parameters are denoted without an asterisk and foreign, rest of the world, parameters have an asterisk. Hence, TB_t is the trade balance, the difference between nominal exports and imports; Y_t and Y_t^* are domestic and foreign incomes, respectively; P_t and P_t^* are the domestic and aggregate foreign price levels, respectively; and ER_t is the nominal exchange rate.

The total differential of the trade balance model indicates the expected effects of changes in individual parameters, as well as simultaneous changes in several parameters, on a country's balance of trade. This is given by equation (2):

$$dTB_t = \frac{\partial TB_t}{\partial (Y_t - Y_t^*)} d(Y_t - Y_t^*) + \frac{\partial TB_t}{\partial (P_t - P_t^*)} d(P_t - P_t^*) + \frac{\partial TB_t}{\partial ER_t} dER_t. \tag{2}$$

The *ex ante* signs of the partial derivatives—which give the effect on the trade balance from *ceteris paribus* changes in a particular parameter—are negative, negative, and positive, respectively. For example, a positive change in the domestic-foreign income difference has a negative effect on the trade balance because residents of the domestic country will import more as their incomes grow at a faster rate than foreign incomes. Similarly, an increase in the domestic-foreign price level difference increases the absorption of foreign tradable goods and services, since their relative price is lower. The higher domestic price level, in essence, encourages imports and discourages exports; hence the negative effect. Finally, both Robinson (1947) and Meese (1990) emphasized the positive nominal exchange-rate effect on the trade balance. When the exchange rate is increasing (i.e., the domestic currency is weakening internationally), a country's tradable goods and services become more attractive to foreigners: exports increase and imports decline, improving the balance of trade. Needless to say, a country's domestic price level and exchange rate are key determinants of its international competitive position because the foreign price of domestic tradable goods and services is the product of the domestic price and the exchange rate.

The Balance of Payments Relationship

The Keynesian theoretical specification of the balance of payments relationship is given by equation (3):

$$IR_t = G[(Y_t - Y_t^*), (P_t - P_t^*), (i_t - i_t^*), ER_t]. \tag{3}$$

The signs of the partial derivatives of this equation's total differential capture the expected effect on international reserves $(IR)_t$—namely, the balance of payments—from a *ceteris paribus* change in a specific independent variable. The total differential of equation (3) is given by equation (4):

$$dIR_t = \frac{\partial IR_t}{\partial (Y_t - Y_t^*)} d(Y_t - Y_t^*) + \frac{\partial IR_t}{\partial (P_t - P_t^*)} d(P_t - P_t^*)$$
$$+ \frac{\partial IR_t}{\partial (i_t - i_t^*)} d(i_t - i_t^*) + \frac{\partial IR_t}{\partial ER_t} dER_t, \tag{4}$$

where all parameters are as defined earlier and i_t and i_t^* are the domestic and foreign interest rates, respectively. The *ex ante* signs of the partial derivatives are negative for the income and price-level parameters and positive for the interest rate and exchange rate parameters.

It follows from the previous subsection that increases in the domestic-foreign income and price level differences will impact adversely on international reserves because they both cause an outflow of foreign currencies as individuals purchase foreign tradable goods and services. In contrast, following Branson (1968), international reserves are favorably affected by an increase in the domestic-foreign interest rate difference because residents desire to hold more of their own capital domestically and foreign capital, seeking a higher return, flows in. Finally, an increase in the exchange rate (i.e., a depreciation in the currency) will enhance exports and depress imports resulting in an inflow of foreign exchange; albeit, in the presence of a J-curve effect, as shown by Wilson (1993), the improvement may occur with a significant time lag. Interestingly, Dornbusch and Krugman (1976) note that an inverted J-curve effect can exist for a decrease in the exchange rate (i.e., a strengthening of the currency internationally).

In closing this section, it is important to note the historical emphasis that the Keynesian approach places on exchange rate adjustments to secure trade and overall balance of payments equilibrium. However, empirical studies, such as Bonitsis (1991) and Bonitsis and Tsanacas (1990), have indicated that such exchange rate effects may have lost their potency to secure external equilibrium. This development is a reflection of innovative entrepreneurial responses, made possible by continuing technological advances, that offset the price effects of exchange-rate fluctuations.

A THEORETICAL FRAMEWORK FOR THE MONETARY APPROACH

The Balance of Trade Relationship

The essence of the Monetary approach is that the balance of trade is exclusively a monetary phenomenon. It is the result of the interaction of the supply and demand for money. In the presence of an excess supply of money, residents will exchange this excess cash for foreign products, services, and financial assets, causing the balance of trade and the overall balance of payments to deteriorate. In contrast, if there is an excess demand for money relative to supply, a country's residents will obtain the additional cash by exporting more goods, services, and financial assets. This results in an increase in the level of foreign reserves, and hence leads to an improvement in the balance of payments. Two volumes of collected articles, by the International Monetary Fund (1977) and Frenkel and Johnson (1976), contain the seminal research done in the Monetary approach to external adjustment.

Magee (1976) discussed the theoretical specification for the trade balance model consistent with the Monetary approach. It is summarized by equation (5):

$$TB_t = H[(Y_t - Y_t^*), (P_t - P_t^*), (M_t - M_t^*), (i_t - i_t^*)] \tag{5}$$

M_t is the domestic stock of money and M_t^* is the foreign aggregate money stock; all other relevant parameters are defined as in the second section. However, the theoretical signs of the parameters for the Monetary approach differ from those for the Keynesian approach, for the postulated theoretical adjustment mechanisms of the two approaches differ in their philosophical underpinnings. Taking the total differential of the trade balance relationship gives equation (6):

$$dTB_t = \frac{\partial TB_t}{\partial(Y_t - Y_t^*)}d(Y_t - Y_t^*) + \frac{\partial TB_t}{\partial(P_t - P_t^*)}d(P_t - P_t^*) \tag{6}$$
$$+ \frac{\partial TB_t}{\partial(M_t - M_t^*)}d(M_t - M_t^*) + \frac{\partial TB_t}{\partial(i_t - i_t^*)}d(i_t - i_t^*),$$

where the expected sequential signs of the partial derivatives are positive for the first two derivatives and negative for the last two.

The adjustment mechanism for the balance of trade under the Monetary approach can be described as follows. First, growth in the domestic-foreign income difference increases the demand for money, resulting in an increase in goods, services and securities available to be sold to foreigners. As Mundell (1968) stated, this augments a country's foreign reserves position, positively impacting the trade balance. Second, an unanticipated increase in the domestic-foreign price level difference increases the demand for money, which encourages exports so as to obtain cash balances. This ameliorates the balance of payments via a trade balance improvement. Conversely, as Laffer (1974) emphasized, a decrease in the domestic-foreign price level difference has an adverse effect on the domestic country's balance of trade by reducing the demand for money as domestic residents rid themselves of excess cash balances by exchanging them for foreign tradable items.

The third and *dominant* variable that affects both the trade balance and the balance of payments in the Monetary approach is the domestic-foreign money supply difference. On the one hand, a decrease in the domestic money supply relative to demand will improve the trade balance. On the other hand, an increase in the domestic money supply relative to demand adversely affects the trade balance. An increase in the foreign money stock, in contrast, improves the balance of trade as foreigners reduce their excess holdings of money by importing the domestic country's products, services, and financial assets. It is clear, as noted by Mundell (1971), that an organic automatic adjustment process exists under the Monetary approach to the balance of payments; its roots can be found in David Hume's price specie flow mechanism of classical economics.

Finally, an increase in the domestic-foreign interest rate difference decreases the demand for money as residents exchange excess cash balances for foreign goods, services and securities. As a result, there will be an unequivocal deterioration in the balance of trade and payments. However, a decrease in the domestic-foreign nominal interest-rate difference increases the domestic demand for money. In order to obtain the increase in optimal cash balances, there is an increase in exports and a decrease in imports; the balance of trade will be positively affected.

The Balance of Payments Relationship

The Monetary approach is *intrinsically* a theory of balance of payments adjustment. The trade balance is affected only as part of the international accounts. It follows that the *ex ante* signs of the partial derivatives in equation (8) are similar to those in equation (6), meaning that unanticipated changes in the money supply, income-level and price-level parameters affect the official reserves transactions balance by the same mechanisms detailed in the previous subsection and indicated mathematically in the following discussion. Further, the dominant independent variable is clearly the monetary stock parameter, reflecting the concept that the balance of payments is considered solely a "monetary phenomenon."

Following Johnson (1976), a theoretical specification for the balance of payments consistent with the Monetary approach is represented by equation (7):

$$IR_t = J[(Y_t - Y_t^*), (P_t - P_t^*), (M_t - M_t^*), (i_t - i_t^*), ER].$$ (7)

All parameters were defined previously. Taking the total differential of international reserves gives equation (8):

$$dIR_t = \frac{\partial IR_t}{\partial(Y_t - Y_t^*)} d(Y_t - Y_t^*) + \frac{\partial IR_t}{\partial(P_t - P_t^*)} d(P_t - P_t^*)$$ (8)

$$+ \frac{\partial IR_t}{\partial(M_t - M_t^*)} d(M_t - M_t^*) + \frac{\partial(IR_t)}{\partial(i_t - i_t^*)} d(i_t - i_t^*)$$

$$+ \frac{\partial(IR_t)}{\partial(ER_t)} dER_t.$$

The *ceteris paribus* expected effects of the independent variables on international reserves are favorable for the income and price-level parameters, adverse for the money supply and interest-rate parameters, and favorable for the exchange-rate parameter. Mathematically stated, the expected signs of the partial derivatives in equation (8) are positive, positive, negative, negative, and positive, respectively.

It is important to emphasize that a unique assumption of the Monetary approach is that the demand for domestic and international money is interchangeable. Hence, the domestic-foreign interest rate difference is inversely related to the demand for foreign currency. Specifically, an increase in this parameter will cause the demand for domestic and foreign money to decline; a decrease in this parameter, in contrast, will result in increased holdings of domestic and foreign money. Thus, international reserves are treated as domestic money in terms of their respective relationship to the interest rate. It is clear that this interest rate effect is very different from that of the Keynesian approach to external adjustment. Zecher (1976) discussed this unique aspect of the Monetary approach in detail. Therefore, the official reserves account and the domestic-foreign interest rate difference are inversely related.

Turning to the exchange-rate parameter, Miles (1978) pointed out that the real stock of domestic money will decline if the domestic currency depreciates (i.e., the country's exchange rate increases). Hence, residents will restore their optimal money stock by increasing the level of exports in the form of tradable goods and services as well as financial assets. This results in an inflow of foreign reserves via the trade and capital accounts with the commensurate improvement in the overall balance of payments.

SIZE AND PACE OF ADJUSTMENT OF THE TWO
APPROACHES' PARAMETERS

As stated in the first section, this research endeavored to determine whether the Keynesian or Monetary approach characterizes external adjustment for the large open economy of Germany. However, a corollary investigation, which is of significant relevance to policy makers, is the determination of the size and pace of adjustment of each approach's parameters with regard to the trade account and the official reserves transactions account. In principle, the approach to international accounts adjustment, whose statistically significant parameters have a greater size and faster pace of adjustment, would have larger empirical regression coefficients and smaller time-mean lags of adjustment.

With respect to the Monetary approach, a balance of payments disequilibrium is the exclusive result of disequilibrium is the money market. Hence, monetary parameters such as the stock of money and interest rates, independent of the particular international account, are instrumental for the speed and pace of adjustment relative to real parameters (e.g., real income and relative prices). Alternatively stated, optimally managed monetary variables, which can be targeted by policy makers, lead to stability and equilibrium in a country's international accounts. Real variables, in contrast, are not considered as possible root causes of significant external disequilibrium. Hence, the heuristic results would indicate that monetary variables, relative to real variables, have empirical coefficients of greater magnitudes and smaller time-mean lags of adjustment for the international accounts.

In contrast, as Malindretos (1991) pointed out, the Keynesian approach would predict that real parameters have larger empirical coefficients as well as shorter time-mean lag adjustment values relative to the Monetary approach's coefficients. Monetary variables, in essence, would not dominate international accounts adjustment because their effect on the accounts are channeled only through real variables.

Policy makers and international financial analysts seek to predict the effect (i.e., both the magnitude and adjustment period) that changes in choice and/or nonchoice parameters will have on a country's international accounts. Equations (2), (4), (6) and (8), which provide the total differentials of the trade and balance of payments models under both theories, indicate the practical difficulty of such a task. While the *ex ante* partial effect of each independent variable is known, a simultaneous change in several parameters—which is reflective of real-world occurrences—may yield an indeterminate effect on the international accounts. It may, in practice, be impossible to ascertain if positive or negative effects dominate; nonetheless, it may be possible to ascertain the effect of a sizable, obviously dominant disturbance on the external position of a country. Equally important is the ability of a country to borrow internationally for a prolonged period, for such a capacity will delay the required adjustments. It is clear, therefore, that predicting the path of the balance of trade or payments for a country may be a somewhat precarious endeavor.

HEURISTIC MODELS AND FINDINGS

Empirical Techniques and Data

The heuristic equations employed to test the theoretical relationships for Germany are given in concise form by equations (9) and (10):

$$TB_t = \alpha_1 + \beta_1 \Delta Y_t + \gamma_1 \Delta P_t + \delta_1 \Delta M_t + \phi_1 \Delta i_t + \psi_1 ER_t + \varepsilon_{1t}. \tag{9}$$

$$IR_t = \alpha_2 + \beta_2 \Delta Y_t + \gamma_2 \Delta P_t + \delta_2 \Delta M_t + \phi_2 \Delta i_t + \psi_2 ER_t + \varepsilon_{2t}. \tag{10}$$

The variables are defined in the second and third sections; parameters with the difference operator, Δ, represent the difference between domestic and foreign magnitudes. Industrial production and the consumer price index are used as proxy variables for both domestic and foreign incomes and price levels, respectively; while M1 is the monetary aggregate used for domestic and foreign money stocks. It is important to note that aggregate OECD magnitudes are the measure for all foreign parameters.

Equations (9) and (10) have similar independent variables to allow for a general testing of the applicability of the Keynesian and Monetary approaches to external adjustment for Germany for the historical period under study. If the regression coefficients are statistically significant and have the *ex ante* signs of a particular theory, then the results are consistent with that theory. The two equations' innovations are assumed to be white noise: $\varepsilon_{1t} \sim N(0, \sigma_1^2)$ and $\varepsilon_{2t} \sim N(0, \sigma_2^2)$; $E[\varepsilon_{1s}, \varepsilon_{1t}] = 0 = E[\varepsilon_{2s}, \varepsilon_{2t}]$ for $s \neq t$, and $E[\varepsilon_{1s}, \varepsilon_{2t}] = 0$ for all s and t.

The models are estimated with quarterly data from various issues of the International Monetary Fund's *International Financial Statistics* for the period from the first quarter of 1972 through the fourth quarter of 1983. The actual econometric regressions are performed with the Time Series Processor (TSP) software. The trade and balance of payments models are fitted by ordinary least squares with a Cochrane-Orcutt adjustment for autocorrelation. In addition, models are estimated with an Almon (1965) polynomial lag structure. Empirical models employing an Almon lag structure are theoretically appropriate as well as empirically revealing on both the theoretical and practical policy planes. Theoretically, it permits for a model specification with a lag structure with multiple coefficient signs for each parameter so that the intertemporal effect of each parameter is captured. Practically, adjustments to the international accounts do indeed take effect only after a period of time. In short, an Almon polynomial

Table 11.1
Balance of Trade Model

Parameter	M - M*	Y - Y*	i - i*	CR
Sum of coefficients	-36.770[a]	.139[b]	-1.330[a]	178E-03
	(10.630)	(.066)	(.205)	(.235E-03)
Mean lag	2.460	5.730	2.590	3.900
	(.721)	(2.390)	(.594)	(7426.070)

R^2 = .6312, DW = 1. 83, SSR = 30.51, SE = 1. 08, Constant = 11. 720 (6.440).

Note: Standard errors are in parentheses. All variables are defined in the chapter.
*Foreign parameter.
[a] Significant at the 1 percent level, one-tailed test; consistent with the Monetary approach (MA) to the trade balance.
[b] Significant at the 5 percent level, two-tailed test; consistent with the Monetary approach.

lag structure is an appropriate method to investigate the issues under study. The specific mechanics of the Almon technique can be found in Gujarati (1978).

For the trade balance model, an Almon specification is employed with the three domestic-foreign difference parameters of money, income, and interest rates, as well as a parameter referred to as the competitiveness ratio (CR). This last parameter is defined as a product of the German mark–dollar exchange rate and the ratio of the foreign to domestic price levels. The construction of this variable, given the small sample size, conserves on degrees of freedom as well as meaningfully introducing both the price level and the exchange rate into the model. The reported empirical specification of the trade balance model has an Almon polynomial of degree two, a lag of six quarters, a zero restriction on the head lag value, and a nonzero restriction on the tail value.

The reported results for the balance of payments model has an Almon specification with the three domestic-foreign difference parameters of money, income, price level and the nominal exchange rate, as well as the interest rate, which is included simply lagged two quarters. Further, this model has an Almon polynomial of degree two, with a lag of six quarters, as well as a nonzero restriction on the head lag value and a zero restriction on the tail value.

Empirical Results

Econometric results for the trade balance model are given in Table 11.1. The model explains about 63 percent of the variation in the balance of trade. Turning to an analysis of the individual parameters the results are as follows. A one-tailed test for the monetary and interest rate parameters show that they are statistically significant at the 1 percent level, both have negative signs, and they

Table 11.2
Balance of Payments Model

Parameter	M - M*	Y - Y*	P - P*	ER
Sum of coefficients	.240	- 1.200[a]	1.17[b]	.266[c]
	(.402)	(.850)	(.228)	(.188)
Mean lag	8.92	5.110	-3.590	-.360
	(3.72)	(2.920)	(2.040)	(2.500)

R^2 = .947, DW = 2.06, SSR = 256.40, SE = 3.20,
i = -.441[d] (.209), Constant = 56.88 (67.879).

Note: Standard errors are in parentheses. All variables are defined in the chapter.
*Foreign parameter.
[a] Significant at the 10 percent level, two-tailed test; consistent with the Keynesian approach to the balance of payments.
[b] Significant at the 1 percent level, two-tailed test; consistent with the Monetary approach.
[c] Significant at the 10 percent level, one-tailed test; consistent with the Keynesian and Monetary approaches.
[d] Significant at the 5 percent level, two-tailed test; consistent with the Monetary approach; *i* is the interest rate parameter lagged two quarters.

have mean lags of adjustment of 2.46 and 2.59 quarters, respectively; a two-tailed test for the income parameter indicates that it is statistically significant at the 5 percent level, has a positive sign, and has a mean lag of adjustment of 5.73 quarters; the competitiveness ratio, a composite of the price level and exchange rate parameters, is insignificant. These econometric results are consistent with the Monetary approach to the trade balance. Further, all the significant parameters have reasonable time horizons of adjustment.

Table 11.2 reports the findings for the balance of payments model. Although the regression model explains roughly 95 percent of the variation in international reserves, the results for the individual regression coefficients are elusive. The monetary parameter, for a one-tailed test, is insignificant, albeit it is positive and has a mean lag of 8.92 quarters; the income parameter, for a two-tailed test, is significant at the 10 percent level, with a negative sign and a mean lag of 5.11 quarters. The first result is not consistent with the Monetary approach, while the second finding agrees with the Keynesian approach to the balance of payments. The price level parameter is significant at the 1 percent level for a two-tailed test and has a positive sign, as predicted by the Monetary approach. In contrast, the exchange rate coefficient is positive and statistically significant at the 10 percent level with a one-tailed test, a finding consistent with both the Monetary and Traditional approaches. The interest rate coefficient, which is introduced into the model by lagging it by two quarterly periods, has the negative sign predicted by the Monetary approach and is statistically significant at the 5 percent level with a two-tailed test. Empirically speaking, the econometric evidence for the balance of payments model is more supportive of the Monetary approach than the Keynesian approach to international accounts adjustment.

Before closing this discussion, it is noteworthy to mention that the results reported in Tables 11.1 and 11.2 are the more robust findings from the extensive estimation of many alternatively specified models; even the transformation of the regressors to ratios between domestic and foreign variables and/or taking logarithms failed to improve the econometric findings.

CONCLUSIONS AND IMPLICATIONS

This research investigated whether Monetary or Keynesian parameters dominate international accounts adjustments for the large open economy of Germany. It concludes that the econometric evidence is consistent with the Monetary approach. Since monetary parameters are choice variables for policy makers, a target external adjustment may be achieved if successful parameter-specific fine-tuning is achieved. Under such a scenario, the country proactively affects its external competitive position. This is further supported by the parameters' empirical average lag-adjustment coefficients; the international accounts respond to the parameters within policy-planning horizons.

An important corollary conclusion is given by the theoretical presentation, which shows how elusive an endeavor, for policy makers and international financial analysts, it is to determine the path of the international accounts. International financial theory indicates several parameters with opposing effects on the accounts. Only if a correct differential diagnosis of the parameter disturbance is made and the shock is of sufficiently large magnitude can any meaningful external account path be extrapolated; even then, a country's external borrowing capacity can indeterminately delay any needed adjustments.

Finally, while this research reports heuristic evidence for Germany, the general relevance of these findings for large open economies is an empirical issue. A cross-sectional study encompassing several large open economies would indicate the general robustness of these findings.

REFERENCES

Almon, Shirley. "The Distributed Lag between Capital Appropriations and Expenditures." *Econometrica*, 33, no. 1 (1965): 178–196.

Bonitsis, Theologos Homer. "Dollar Exchange Rate Indices and U.S. Exports: Is There an Intertemporal Linkage?" *Journal of Business and Economic Studies*, 1, no. 2 (Fall/Winter 1991): 1–10.

Bonitsis, Theologos Homer, Krishna M. Kasibhatla and John Malindretos. "A Comparison of the Monetary and Traditional Approaches to International Competitive

Adjustment: The Case of South Korea." *Journal of International Economic Studies*, no. 9 (1995): 123–138.

Bonitsis, Theologos Homer, and Demetri Tsanacas. "Yen Appreciation, Hysteretic Effects, and Japanese Micro-Adjustments." *Detroit Business Journal*, 3, no. 1 (Spring 1990): 1–10.

Branson, William H. *Financial Capital Flows in the U.S. Balance of Payments*. Amsterdam: North Holland Publishing Company, 1968.

Dornbusch, Rudiger, and Paul Krugman. "Flexible Exchange Rates in the Short Run." *Brookings Papers on Economic Activity*, no. 3 (1976): 537–575.

Frenkel, Jacob A., Thorvaldur Gylfason and John F. Helliwell. "A Synthesis of Monetary and Keynesian Approaches to Short-Run Balance of Payments Theory." *Economic Journal*, 96 (September 1980): 582–592.

Frenkel, Jacob A., and Harry G. Johnson, eds. *The Monetary Approach to the Balance of Payments*. Toronto: University of Toronto Press, 1976.

Gujarati, Damodar. *Basic Econometrics*. New York: McGraw-Hill, 1978.

Houthakker, Hendrik S., and Stephen P. Magee. "Income and Price Elasticities in World Trade." *Review of Economics and Statistics*, 51, no. 2 (May 1969); 111–125.

International Monetary Fund. *International Financial Statistics*, various issues.

International Monetary Fund. *The Monetary Approach to the Balance of Payments*. Washington, D.C.: International Monetary Fund, 1977.

Johnson, Harry G. "The Monetary Theory of Balance-of-Payments Policies." In *The Monetary Approach to the Balance of Payments*, ed. Jacob A. Frenkel and H. G. Johnson. Toronto: University of Toronto Press, 1976, pp. 262–284.

Laffer, Arthur B. "Exchange Rates, the Terms of Trade, and the Trade Balance." In *The Effects of Exchange Rate Adjustments*, ed. Peter B. Clark, Dennis E. Logue and Richard J. Sweeney. Proceedings of a conference sponsored by OASIA Research, Department of the Treasury, 1974. Washington, D.C.: Department of the Treasury, 1977.

Magee, Stephen P. "The Empirical Evidence on the Monetary Approach to the Balance of Payments and Exchange Rates." *American Economic Review Papers and Proceedings*, 66, no. 2 (May 1976): 163–170.

Malindretos, John. "The Traditional and Monetary Approaches to the Balance of Payments: A Theoretical Comparison." *American Business Review*, 2 (June 1984): 31–42.

Malindretos, John. "An Examination of the Two Views of International Finance for an Advanced, Medium-Sized, Reserve Currency Country." In *Advances in Quantitative Analysis of Finance and Accounting*, vol. 1, part B, ed. Chen-Few Lee. Greenwich, Conn.: JAI Press, 1991, pp. 183–214.

Meese, Richard. "Currency Fluctuations in the Post–Bretton Woods Era." *Journal of Economic Perspectives*, 4 (Winter 1990): 117–134.

Miles, Marc A. *Devaluation, the Trade Balance and the Balance of Payments*. New York: Marcel Dekker, 1978.

Mundell, Robert A. *International Economics*. New York: Macmillan, 1968, pp. 111–133.

Mundell, Robert A. "Barter Theory and the Monetary Mechanism of Adjustment." In *Monetary Theory, Inflation, Interest Rates and Growth in the World Economy*. Pacific Palisades, Calif.: Goodyear Publishing, 1971, pp. 147–169.

Robinson, Joan. "The Foreign Exchanges." In *Essays in the Theory of Employment*. 2nd ed. Oxford, U.K.: Blackwell Publishing, 1947, pp. 213–228.

Whitman, Marina V. N. "Global Monetarism and the Monetary Approach to the Balance of Payments." *Brookings Papers on Economic Activity*, no. 3 (1975): 491–555.

Wilson, William, "J-Curve Effect and Exchange Rate Pass-Through: An Empirical Investigation of the United States." *International Trade Journal*, 7, no. 4 (Summer 1993): 463–483.

Zecher, Richard. "Monetary Equilibrium and International Reserve Flows in Australia." In *The Monetary Approach to the Balance of Payments*, ed. Jacob A. Frenkel and H. G. Johnson. Toronto: University of Toronto Press, 1976, pp. 287–297.

Chapter 12

The Role of Exogeneity, Causality and Exchange-Rate Volatility in the Modeling of U.S. Export-Demand Function: Some New Evidence

Augustine C. Arize

INTRODUCTION

In a number of empirical export-demand analyses (see, for example, Pozo, 1992; Thursby and Thursby, 1987; De Grauwe, 1988; Cushman, 1983) attempts have been made to examine the impact of exchange-rate volatility on export flows. These investigations have generally demonstrated that an exchange-rate volatility variable enters significantly into an otherwise conventional quarterly export-demand equation, with a negative sign. Investigations by Arize (1995; 1997) and Chowdhury (1993) have generally shown that there exists a long-run equilibrium relationship among real exports, foreign economic activity, relative prices and exchange-rate volatility. In addition, exchange-rate volatility is often reported to have a short-run effect on export demand. Nevertheless, as Granger (1988) points out, cointegration between two or more times series implies the presence of causality in at least one direction, and that one variable can be used to forecast another. Evidence suggesting that these variables are contemporaneously correlated in the long run does not imply that the causality is in the direction of volatility to real exports. The question as to the direction of causation is still an open one. In this chapter, we investigate empirically the direction of causation between exports and exchange-rate volatility, with quarterly data from the United States.

Previous empirical studies also have presumed that the volatility variable is weakly exogenous, in the sense of Engle, Hendry and Richard (1983).[1] This is a rather restrictive assumption, as a feedback from exchange-rate volatility to exports is likely because exchange-rate volatility is largely a function of macroeconomic fundamentals (Peree and Steinherr, 1989). Work by Koray and Lastrapes (1989, pp. 711–712) employed a vector autoregression (VAR) model and concluded that "shocks to the level of the macro variables can explain some of the instability in real exchange rates. This result suggests that exchange-rate volatility is not necessarily a purely exogenous source of macroeconomic instability." Invalid exogeneity assumptions may lead to inefficient or inconsistent inferences and result in misleading forecasts and policy simulations (Ericsson, 1992). It is possible that the inferences made in previous studies are biased because of the simultaneity between exchange-rate volatility and exports. Ignoring simultaneity may in part misrepresent the effects of volatility on exports. Therefore, another objective of this study is to examine the weak-exogeneity status of exchange-rate volatility in the export-demand equation.

Existing studies have also ignored the possibility that the cointegration model may experience parameter instability, as discussed in both Hansen (1992) and Hansen and Johansen (1993). Previous studies offer no persuasive evidence for this additional requirement. Therefore, it can be argued that the relevant parameters may not be suitable for policy analysis. In this study, we examine whether the cointegrating equation is statistically stable.

In sum, the contribution of this study to the literature on the effects of exchange-rate volatility on real exports is the extension of the analysis to: (a) an examination of the weak-exogeneity status of the risk variable; (b) an examination of the causal relationships between real exports and exchange-rate risk, and (c) a determination of the stability of the cointegration space.

Our approach differs from previous works in at least five important respects. First, we use a GARCH estimator to capture risk. The algorithm used is the Berndt-Hall-Hall-Hausman (BHHH) maximum likelihood procedure (1974). With the exception of Pozo (1992), none of the above studies has employed such a procedure. The recent work of Pagan and Ullah (1988) on constructed measures of uncertainty argues that this measure yields superior forecasts of volatility. Second, we present results employing the nominal effective exchange-rate volatility and the real effective exchange-rate volatility. Third, we examine unit-root properties of the data using univariate and multivariate tests. Fourth, we provide causality tests following the Sims, Stock and Watson (1990) procedure. These authors have argued that it may not be necessary to difference nonstationary variables before carrying out Granger causality tests. They suggest that the standard F-statistics for testing Granger causality in the level VAR have asymptotic F-distribution in spite of the fact that they are obtained within the framework of an I(1) system.

Finally, common factor restriction on prices and parameter stability of the cointegration space are examined using recent time-series procedures. These issues have been ignored in previous studies.

The rest of the chapter is structured as follows. The second section briefly examines the theory, while the third section discusses the regression results. Conclusions are drawn in the last section. The data are quarterly over the 1973: 2 through 1995:1 period. Details of the data definition and sources are presented in Appendix 12.1

THEORETICAL CONSIDERATIONS

A theoretical analysis of the relationship between higher exchange-rate volatility and international trade transactions has been conducted by Hooper and Kohlhagen (1978) and others. The argument is as follows: Higher exchange-rate volatility leads to higher cost for risk-averse traders and to less foreign trade. This is so because the exchange rate is agreed on at the time of the trade contract, but payment is not made until the future delivery actually takes place. If changes in exchange rates become unpredictable, this creates uncertainty about the profits to be made and, hence, reduces the benefits of international trade.

On the other hand, recent theoretical developments suggest that there are situations in which the volatility of the exchange rate could be expected to have negative or positive effects on trade volume. De Grauwe (1988) has stressed that the dominance of income effects over substitution effects can lead to a positive relationship between trade and exchange-rate volatility. This is because, if exporters are sufficiently risk averse, an increase in the exchange-rate variability raises the expected marginal utility of export revenue and therefore induces them to increase exports. He suggests that the effects of exchange-rate uncertainty on exports should depend on the degree of risk aversion. A very risk-averse exporter who worries about the decline in revenue may export more when risks are higher. On the other hand, a less risk-averse individual may not be concerned with the worst possible outcome and, considering the return on exports less attractive, may decide to export less when risks are higher.

TIME-SERIES PROPERTIES, MODELING STRATEGY AND EMPIRICAL RESULTS

The long-run equilibrium export-demand model to be examined is similar to Arize (1995):

$$x_t^d = \alpha_0 + \alpha_1 Aw_t + \alpha_2 P_t + \alpha_3 \sigma_t + \varepsilon_{1t} \tag{1}$$

where x_t denotes the logarithm of desired volume of a country's export goods; Aw_t is the logarithm of a scale variable which captures foreign economic activity conditions; P_t represents the logarithm of relative prices and is measured by the logarithm of $(P^x - eP^f)_t$, where P^x_t is the U.S. export price index; e_t is the effective nominal export-weighted exchange-rate index; P^f is the export-weighted foreign price index; σ_t stands for the logarithm of a risk variable [$\sigma(R)_t$ = real effective exchange-rate volatility and $\sigma(E)_t$ = nominal effective exchange-rate volatility. ε_{1t} is a disturbance term. It is expected that $\alpha_1 > 0$; $\alpha_2 < 0$ and $\alpha_3 = ?$

Table 12.1
The Volatility Measures

A. Estimation of real effective exchange rate variance as a GARCH process

R_t = 1.181R_{t-1} - 0.183R_{t-2}
　　　(10.1)　　　(1.56)

σ_t^2 = 1.186 + 0.213e_{t-1}^2 + 0.678σ_{t-1}^2
　　　(0.87)　　(1.33)　　　(3.42)

Log Likelihood = -223.10
LB(4) = 5.667 (0.23),　　LB(21) = 20.546 (0.49)

B. Estimation of nominal effective exchange rate variance as a GARCH process

E_t = 1.222E_{t-1} - 0.224E_{t-2}
　　　(11.0)　　　(2.01)

σ_t^2 = 2.243 + 0.145e_{t-1}^2 + 0.690σ_{t-1}^2
　　　(0.71)　　(12.3)　　　(2.27)

Log Likelihood = -241.32
LB(4) = 3.341 (0.50),　　LB(21) = 23.036 (0.34)

Notes: R is real effective exchange rate; E is nominal effective exchange rate; LB(4) is Ljung-Box test statistic with 4 degrees of freedom and LB(21) has 21 degrees of freedom.

Measuring Volatility

The estimated mean and conditional variance equations used to generate our proxy for exchange-rate uncertainty are reported in Panel A of Table 12.1.

Results (not reported here) using Engle's (1983) Lagrange multiplier (LM) test reveal an ARCH effect at various lags and therefore support our choice of the GARCH model. The predicted values of the conditional variance are interpreted as the uncertainty of the series because the effect of the mean equation is taken into account when the conditional variance is estimated. Following Davidian and Carroll (1987), we use the conditional standard deviation.

Unit-Root Tests

Recent work in econometrics has stressed the importance of time-series properties of the data, such as the degree of integration. As a preliminary step, we tested for the stationarity of the individual time series: X_t, Aw_t, P_t, $\sigma(R)_t$ and $\sigma(E)_t$. The common practice is to use the augmented Dickey-Fuller test and Stock's (1991) confidence intervals for the largest autoregressive root. The lag structures were determined as proposed by Ng and Perron (1995). The empirical results are in Appendix 12.2, and they suggest that it is likely that these series are integrated of order one, I(1). It may be objected that the I(1)-ness of the risk variables is not appropriate because of the low power of the unit-root tests.[2] However, following suggestions by a number of analysts (e.g., Schwert, 1989; Campbell and Perron, 1991; Hamilton, 1994; and Duffee, 1995), we assume that it is reasonable to carry out an empirical investigation predicated on integrated processes while keeping in mind that the results from models with unit-root identifying restrictions must be interpreted with some caution.

Multivariate Cointegration

A system-based cointegration procedure has been developed by Johansen (1992) and is used here to test for the presence or absence of long-run equilibria among the variables in equation (1). The test utilizes two likelihood-ratio (LR) test statistics for the number of cointegrating vectors: namely, the trace and the maximal eigenvalue (λ-max) statistics.

In implementing the system approach, two issues need to be addressed. The first is the setting of the appropriate lag length in the VAR model in order to ensure that the error terms in the VECM are Gaussian. In this paper, the appropriate lag length is determined by likelihood-ratio test statistics and multivariate Ljung-Box statistics for white-noise errors (see Arize, 1997, p. 243). For $\sigma(R)_t$ system, these tests indicate that a five-lag system adequately captures the dynamics of the system, whereas for $\sigma(E)_t$ system, it is six. However, there remain some outliers, and three dummies are used to eliminate them.[3] Our final VAR model, therefore, contains centered seasonal dummy variables and three impulse dummy variables. The first dummy is D_1, which is coded one in 1975:1 and minus one in 1975:4. The second dummy is D_2 (coded one in 1979:1 and minus one in 1979:2) and D_3 (coded one in 1975:4 and minus one in 1979:1). The above imposed dummies were included unrestrictedly in the analysis. Similar dummies are included in the studies by Johansen (1992) and Hendry and Doornik (1994, pp. 11–13).

The second issue to be addressed is whether deterministic variables such as an intercept and trend should enter into the long-run cointegrating space or the short-run model. To determine the most appropriate deterministic specification, we followed the Pantula principle suggested in Johansen (1992) and chose the unrestricted intercept model that allows trending variables, with trend in the DGP.

Table 12.2 assembles the estimated λ-max and trace test statistics and their attendant critical values. The results for the system $(X_t, Aw_t, P_t, \sigma(R)_t)$ are reported in Panel A, whereas for system $(X_t, Aw_t, P_t, \sigma(E)_t)$, the results are in Panel B.

Starting with the λ-max test results, the null hypothesis of non-cointegration, $r = 0$, is rejected in favor of $r = 1$ in Panels A to C at the conventional levels. The calculated test statistics are 31.84 and 35.04 for real exchange-rate volatility, $\sigma(R)_t$, and nominal exchange-rate volatility, $(\sigma(E)_t)$ systems, respectively. The values are greater than the critical values of 27.07 and 24.73 from Osterwald-

Table 12.2
Cointegration Test Results

Cointegration Test Results: The Johansen Approach

A. Multivariate System [X, Aw, P, σ(R)]

Null Hypothesis	Alternative Hypothesis	λ-Max Test Statistics	Critical Values (95%)	(90%)	Alternative Hypothesis	Trace Test Statistics	Critical Values (95%)	(90%)
r = 0	r = 1	31.84	27.07	24.73	r ≥ 1	49.85	47.21	43.95
r ≤ 1	r = 2	10.67	20.97	18.60	r ≥ 2	18.01	29.68	26.79
r ≤ 2	r = 3	4.93	14.07	12.07	r ≥ 3	7.35	15.41	13.33
r ≤ 3	r = 4	2.42	3.76	2.69	r ≥ 4	2.42	3.76	2.69

Stationary Cointegrating Vector (Normalized on X)

X	Aw	P	σ(R)
(-1.00)	1.79	-0.95	-0.61

Cointegration Hypotheses Tests

	Stationarity Test	Long-run Exclusion Test	Weak-Exogeneity Test
X	27.81**	9.91**	5.29**
Aw	30.76***	12.26***	2.39
P	19.26***	5.42**	2.41
σ(R)	26.28***	14.23***	8.09***
C.V.(5%)	7.81	3.84	3.84

B. Multivariate System [X, Aw, P, $\sigma(E)$]

r = 0	r = 1	35.04	27.07	24.73		59.55	47.21	43.95	r ≥ 1
r ≤ 1	r = 2	17.42	20.97	18.60		24.51	29.68	26.79	r ≥ 2
r ≤ 2	r = 3	4.94	14.07	12.07		7.10	15.41	13.33	r ≥ 3
r ≤ 3	r = 4	2.15	3.76	2.69		2.16	3.76	2.69	r ≥ 4

Stationary Cointegrating Vector (Normalized on X)

X	Aw	P	$\sigma(E)$
-1.00	1.96	-0.70	-0.98

Cointegration Hypotheses Tests

	Stationarity Test	Long-run Exclusion Test	Weak-Exogeneity Test
X	18.40**	6.86**	4.10**
Aw	24.33**	9.45**	2.22
P	12.65**	3.76*	1.12
$\sigma(E)$	28.16**	11.90***	9.69***
C.V.(5%)	7.81	3.84	3.84

Notes: ** and * indicate rejection of the corresponding null hypotheses at the 5 percent and 10 percent levels, respectively. The stationarity tests areas are distributed as a χ^2 with d.f. = 3. The Long-run Exclusion and Weak-Exogeneity tests are distributed as χ^2 with d.f. = 1. For Panels A and B, the VAR order are five and six, respectively.

Lenum (1992). Furthermore, the null hypotheses of $r \leqslant 1$, $r \leqslant 2$ and $r \leqslant 3$ cannot be rejected in favor of $r = 2$, $r = 3$ and $r = 4$, respectively. These findings indicate the presence of a cointegrating relationship in each panel. Taken together, the results suggest that there is a long-run equilibrium path at which real exports and its determinants converge.

Long-Run Equilibrium Estimates and Hypotheses

As discussed above, there is evidence of one cointegrating relationship in each panel, and the results from testing various hypotheses regarding the cointegrating relationship are reported at the bottom of each panel. First, we apply a multivariate stationarity test, and the results are at the bottom of each Panel in Table 12.2. Under the assumption that $r = 1$, it was tested for each variable if the cointegrating vector is unity for the respective variable and zero elsewhere, under the null that the respective variable is I(0) and the alternative is a unit root. This was rejected for all variables and is in line with conclusions drawn in Appendix 12.2.

The long-run exclusion test results of the variables in the cointegration space are also reported in each panel of Table 12.2, which presents the long-run elasticities obtained from the normalized equations, including the hypothesis test results regarding these cointegrating relationships.[4] Consistent with the objectives of the study, an appealing aspect of the results is that the real exchange-rate volatility effects are comparable to those of the exchange-rate volatility on export volume. For example, the estimated coefficient for the real exchange-rate volatility is -0.61 in Panel A, and the test statistic of excluding the variable from the cointegrating space yielded a $\chi^2(1)$ test statistic of 14.23, which is significant at the 5 percent level. On the other hand, the estimated exchange-rate volatility of -0.98 in Panel B proves to be very significant, with $\chi^2(1)$ test statistic of 11.90. Observe that foreign economic activity and relative prices have the correct signs and are significantly different from zero at the 5 percent level in each case.

Tests for weak exogeneity reported in the last column of each panel suggest that the cointegrating relationship enters not only the real exports equation. In Panel A, the null hypothesis of weak exogeneity is rejected for real exports and the real exchange-rate volatility, and the test statistics are 5.29 and 8.09, respectively. The critical value is 3.84 at the 5 percent level. A similar result is reported in Panel B for nominal exchange-rate volatility. These results provide new evidence that exchange-rate volatility is not weakly exogenous. This evidence complements the results in Koray and Lastrapes (1989).

Granger-causality tests (five lags) for feedbacks from ΔX_t are reported in Table 12.3. As Sims et al. (1990) suggested, given the existence of a long-run equilibrium relationship among real exports, foreign economic activity, relative prices and real exchange-rate volatility, Granger causality can also be tested within the complete VAR model in I(1) space. Following Watson (1994) and

Table 12.3
Multivariate Granger-Causality and Stability Tests

Panel A. Granger-Causality Tests

Variable z_i, $i=1,\ldots,5$	Test statistic	Aw_t	p_t	$\sigma(R)_t$
H_0: Granger-causality; tested individually or jointly				
Δx_t Granger-causes $\Delta z_{i,t}$ individually in bivariate systems	$F(5, 68)$	1.44 [0.22]	1.27 [0.29]	0.98 [0.44]
x_t Granger-causes $z_{i,t}$; individually in VAR	$\chi^2(5)$	10.37 [0.07]	6.05 [0.30]	5.97 [0.31]
x_t Granger-causes $z_{i,t}$; jointly in VAR	$\chi^2(15)$		20.81 [0.14]	
$\sigma(R)_t$ Granger-causes x_t; ; individually in VAR	$\chi^2(5)=11.04$			

Panel B. Johansen Stability Test

Cointegration results to test constancy of the cointegrating space

Test Statistics	Full Period	1994				1993				1992			
		QI	QII	QIII	QIV	QI	QII	QIII	QIV	QI	QII	QIII	QIV
#Cointegrating vectors	1	1	1	1	1	1	1	1	1	1	1	1	1
Eigenvalues	0.3218	0.3218	0.3219	0.3228	0.3233	0.3226	0.3226	0.3296	0.3385	0.3708	0.3816	0.3817	0.3743
HJ Statistic	-	-0.012	-0.120	-0.185	-0.102	-0.104	-0.957	-1.850	-2.057	-6.157	-7.566	-7.586	-6.604

Notes: The test statistics are LR tests distributed as $\chi^2(3)$ in all cases.

Beyer (1998), the test statistics for excluding coefficients of lagged χ_t having a limiting χ^2_p distribution.

The results reported in Table 12.3 for the test statistics F(5, 68) and $\chi^2(5)$ for individual and $\chi^2(15)$ for the joint tests show that Granger noncausality is accepted for real exports. The test statistic of $\chi^2(5) = 11.04$ suggests that Granger noncausality is rejected for exchange-rate volatility, implying that real exports do not Granger-cause volatility. Mention should be made that Granger noncausality is also accepted for real exports when examined using the block causation under the ECM format. The LR test of block noncausality is $\chi^2(15) = 20.51$, with a probability value of 0.153. On the other hand, Granger noncausality is rejected for real exchange-rate volatility. The LR test of block noncausality is $\chi^2(15) = 41.05$, with a probability of 0.0001. These results indicate that volatility does Granger-cause real exports.

Finally, the significance of the error-correction term reflects long-run causality. The LR test for Granger noncausality is rejected for the error-correction term. The LR test statistic is $\chi^2(1) = 6.69$, with a probability of 0.01.

A possible problem with the results reported in Table 12.2A stems from the fact that the tests of the structural stability in the VAR model were of each variable individually, instead of jointly. As an additional test of the constancy of the long-run parameters or the constancy of the cointegrating space, we employ the Hansen and Johansen (HJ) (1993, 8) test. For a given (and fixed) cointegrating rank, a sequence of likelihood ratio tests is performed, using the largest eigenvalue estimates of the full sample and the largest recursive eigenvalue estimates of the restricted sample. For our purpose, we not only apply the Johansen system procedure for the full sample ending in the first quarter of 1995, but also for subsamples in the fourth quarter of 1994, the third quarter of 1994, and so on, as the sample period is updated recursively. As can be seen from Table 12.3B, the calculated HJ statistics (in absolute terms) are all below the critical value of $\chi^2(4) = 9.49$ at the 5 percent level. Further, in all subsamples and the whole sample, the number of cointegrating vectors remained at one (r = 1). These results indicate that we cannot reject the constancy of the cointegrating space or the constancy of the estimated parameters. Note that Hansen's (Sup-F) test for the stability of FM-OLS cointegrating estimates yields a Sup-F value of 7.13, which has a p-value of more than 0.20, thus reinforcing the above conclusion about stability.

Another possible problem with the results reported so far is that our empirical analysis imposes the ''common factor restriction'' because domestic and foreign prices are entered in ratio format in equation (1). This is a restriction that is frequently imposed but rarely tested in empirical demand studies (see Kremers et al., 1992). In the interests of brevity, we report the test of the possible common factor restriction problem for only the data in Table 12.2A. A formal test yields $\chi^2(1)$ statistics of 0.64, 2.65 and 3.1, using the Johansen, the dynamic ordinary least squares (DOLS) and the fully modified ordinary least squares

(FM-OLS) estimators, respectively. The critical value is 3.84 at the 5 percent level. Therefore, the common factor restriction is convincingly accepted.

CONCLUDING REMARKS

This chapter reexamines empirically the conventional proposition that volatile exchange rates have deterred U.S. exports. It should be stressed that the empirical analysis in the present paper was characterized by several important elements; namely, the GARCH estimator was used to obtain measures of risk as suggested by Pagan and Ullah (1988); the unit-root features of the variables were examined using univariate and multivariate tests; Granger causality was examined using both the level VARs and the ECM representation (see Sims et al., 1990); parameter stability was examined using both the conventional tests and the recent tests for nonstationary data (i.e., Sup-F and HJ statistics suggested by Hansen (1992) and Hansen and Johansen (1993), respectively); and the common factor restriction was tested as suggested by Kremers et al. (1992). These are in contrast to studies mentioned in the first section of this chapter, since none examined or employed any of these elements. It is possible that their analyses may have been limited by the lack of attention to these issues. The empirical results suggest the following conclusions.

First, the trend properties of real exports, relative prices, foreign activity and exchange-rate risk may be characterized as single unit-root processes. Use of econometric techniques that exploit this unit-root feature of the data will serve to minimize spurious inferences (i.e., a Type II error).

Second, there is a unique, statistically significant long-run relationship among the variables in estimating equation. Also, the empirical results suggest that real exchange-rate risk has effects comparable to those of the nominal exchange-rate volatility. These results imply that exchange-rate volatility may have significant effects on the allocation of resources as market participants attempt to minimize exposure to the effects of exchange risk.

Third, the hypothesis that exchange-rate volatility is a weakly exogenous variable is soundly rejected. Endogeneity of exchange-rate volatility suggests that inference based on a single-equation conditional framework is less straightforward than in the case where the variables are weakly exogenous. This raises some concern about previous studies dealing with trade models. It is possible that the surprisingly weak relationship between exchange-rate volatility and trade flows reported in several previous studies is due to insufficient attention to the endogeneity of the variable. The results also indicate that the direction of causation between real exports and exchange-rate volatility is unidirectional. Real exports do not Granger-cause exchange-rate volatility, whereas exchange-rate volatility Granger-causes real exports. Finally, parameter stability of the cointegration space and the common factor restriction are supported.

Appendix 12.1
Data, Definition and Sources

This appendix describes the raw data, sources and construction of variables used in the empirical tests. All data (1973:2–1995:1) were obtained from the International Monetary Fund's (IMF) *International Financial Statistics* (*IFS*), IMF's Central Statistics Office and Directions of Trade.

x_i^d—Real exports.

Index of the volume of exports, 1990 = 1.0.

Source for export volume: IFS, line 74.

Aw_t—Foreign economic activity.

It is proxied by a geometric exports-weighted average of industrial production across sixteen countries. The countries used are Austria, Belgium, Canada, Germany, Spain, France, Japan, the Netherlands, Norway, Sweden, Italy, the United Kingdom, Finland, Ireland, Singapore and Korea.

Source for industrial production: For the first twelve countries the data are taken from the Organization of Economic Cooperation and Development's (OECD) *Main Economic Indicators*. For Finland, Ireland, Singapore and Korea, the data are taken from the IMF's *IFS*.

P^x—The U.S. export price index, 1990 = 1.0.

Source for export volume: IMF's *IFS*.

P^f—The export-weighted foreign price index.

This is measured as a geometric-weighted mean of export prices indices of sixteen U.S. trading partners. The foreign price index in quarter t is calculated as:

$$P_t^f = EXP\ [\Sigma_i w_i \ln PX_{i,t}]$$

where $\Sigma_i w_i = 1$ and w_i is the share of country i in the United States' exports: i.e.,

w_i = (Export of the U.S. to country i) / (Total exports of the United States)

i = 1 . . . n denotes the trading partners of the United States in the sample. The base period for w_i is 1990 = 100. PX is an index of unit value of exports.

Ex—Exchange rate.

$R_t = \exp\{\Sigma(w_i \ln r_{i,t} + w_i \ln CPI_{U.S.,t} - w_i \ln CPI_{i,t})\}$ and $e_i = \exp \{\Sigma(w_i \ln R_{i,t})\}$ where ln represents natural logarithm; exp is exponent; n = 16 currencies in the index; $R_{i,t}$ is the period average bilateral exchange rate (units of foreign currency per dollar) in the index form (1990 = 1.0) for country i in quarter t; $CPI_{U.S.,t}$ is the consumer price index (1990 = 1.0) of the United States in quarter t; and $CPI_{i,t}$ is the consumer price index (1990 = 1.0).

Appendix 12.2
Augmented Dickey-Fuller Tests and Confidence Intervals for the Largest
Autoregressive Root

Variable	N	Lags	ADF Level	BG	90% Confidence Interval	ADF TWO UNIT ROOTS
P	84	4	-1.90	0.74	(0.884, 1.048)	-4.58
Yw	79	8	-2.77	0.15	(0.735, 1.036)	-4.57
X	80	8	-2.11	0.79	(0.850, 1.048)	-4.10
σ(R)	83	3	-2.80	1.18	(0.748, 1.034)	-4.70
σ(E)	83	3	-2.78	0.28	(0.748, 1.034)	-4.94

Notes: All variables are in logarithm. The Dickey-Fuller regression includes a constant and a time trend. N denotes the number of observations. Lags denotes the included augmentation lags. ADF is the augmented Dickey-Fuller test. The critical value for ADF is approximately -3.53. Our confidence interval estimates of the largest autoregressive root (p_1) show that, while it is reasonable to carry out cointegration tests, our results should be interpreted with caution. For example, the data for foreign economic activity and volatility of real or nominal exchange rates are consistent with the hypothesis that the process is I(1), but also are consistent with the hypothesis that the data are trend stationary with autoregressive process of 0.74. However, note that the estimated interval contains that value $p_1 = 1$. Keep in mind that it is difficult to discriminate between trend stationary and simple I(1) processes; we prefer to operate under the assumption of a stochastic trend in the series.

NOTES

The author would like to thank Ed Manton, Keith McFarland and Lee Schmidt for helpful comments on an earlier draft. Special thanks go to Kathleen Smith for excellent research assistance.

1. Pozo (1992) finds an inverse relationship between real exchange-rate uncertainty and trade flows between the United States and Great Britain, using annual data for the period 1990–1940.

2. The GARCH process for conditional standard deviation is a nonlinear transformation and may not be subject to unit-root tests designed for linear stochastic processes. Entering the GARCH variable in logarithmic format as performed in this study minimizes these nonlinear effects (Ramanathan, 1993). Second, one should keep in mind that Campbell and Perron (1991) have noted that it would be advantageous to econometrically treat a stationary variable with great persistence as a nonstationary one. Third, even if the series is nonetheless I(O), its coefficient has the usual properties of an OLS estimator (Banerjee et al., 1993, p. 158). Finally, preliminary examination using two recent procedures that do not require one to know the integration properties of the variables suggests that exchange-rate risk has a negative effect on export flows. The procedures are in GAUSS application COINT 2.0 by Ouliaris and Phillips (1995, p. 37) and MICROFIT 4.0 by Pesaran and Pesaran (1997, p. 308).

3. These dummies are not assumed to have a long-run effect, so they enter the system unrestrictedly and have only short-run effects. The shift dummy was identified from the

inspection of the studentized residuals. The studentized residual of observation j, e_j^*, is defined as $e_j^* = e_j/[s(j)(1-h_j)^{1/2}]$, where e_j is the residual from the original regression, s_j is the estimated standard error of the residual from a regression where the jth row of the matrix of explanatory variables X and the vector of dependent variables Y have been deleted, and $h_j = x_j(X'X)^{-1}x_j$, where x_j is the jth row vector from the X matrix. The studentized residual has an interesting interpretation, since it can be shown that it is the t-value one would obtain for a dummy variable taking the value 1 for the jth observation and 0 otherwise in the original regression (Belsley et al, 1980). See Lloyd (1994, p. 217) for the procedure followed in testing parameter stability in the VAR and Arize and Darrat (1994, p. 575) for the tests employed.

4. We normalize all models on the real exports, X_t by setting the coefficient at minus one. The resulting values are long-run elasticities.

REFERENCES

Arize, A. C. "The Effect of Exchange-Rate Volatility on U.S. Export: An Empirical Investigation." *Southern Economic Journal*, 62 (July 1995): 34–43.

Arize, A. C. "Conditional Exchange-Rate Volatility and the Volume of Foreign Trade: Evidence from Seven Industrialized Countries." *Southern Economic Journal*, 64 (July 1997): 235–254.

Arize, A. C., and A. F. Darrat. "The Value of Time and Recent U.S. Money Demand Instability." *Southern Economic Journal*, 60 (January 1994): 546–578.

Banerjee, A., J. J. Dolado, J. W. Galbraith and D. F. Hendry. *Cointegration, Error Correction and the Econometric Analysis of Non-Stationary Data*. New York: Oxford University Press, 1993.

Belsley, David A., Edwin Kuh and Roy E. Welsch. *Regression Diagnostics*. New York: Wiley, 1980.

Berndt, E. R., B. H. Hall, R. R. Hall and J. A. Hausman. "Estimation and Inference in Nonlinear Structural Models." *Annals of Economics and Social Measurement*, 3 (1974): 653–655.

Beyer, Andreas. "Modelling Money Demand in Germany." *Journal of Applied Econometrics*, 13 (1998): 57–76.

Campbell, J. Y., and P. Perron. "Pitfalls and Opportunities: What Macroeconomists Should Know about Unit Roots." *NBER Macroeconomics Annual*. Cambridge, Mass.: MIT Press, 1991.

Chowdhury, Abdur R. "Does Exchange Rate Volatility Depress Trade Flows? Evidence from Error-Correction Model." *The Review of Economics and Statistics*, 75 (November 1993): 700–706.

Cushman, D. O. "The Effects of Real Exchange Rate Risk on International Trade." *Journal of International Economics*, 15 (August 1983): 45–63.

Davidian, M., and R. J. Carroll. "Variance Function Estimation." *Journal of the American Statistical Association*, 82 (1987): 1079–1091.

De Grauwe, P. "Exchange Rate Variability and the Slowdown in Growth of International Trade." *IMF Staff Papers*, 35 (March 1988): 63–84.

Duffee, Gregory R. "Stock Returns and Volatility: A Firm-Level of Analysis." *Journal of Financial Economics*, 37 (1995): 399–420.

Engle, R. F. "Estimate of the Variance of U.S. Inflation Based upon the ARCH Model." *Journal of Money, Credit, and Banking* (August 1983): 286–301.

Engle, R. F., David F. Hendry and Jean-Francois Richard. "Exogeneity." *Econometrica*, 51 (March 1983): 277–304.

Ericsson N. R. "Cointegration, Exogeneity and Policy Analysis: An Overview." *Journal of Policy Modeling*, 14, (1992): 251–80.

Granger, C. W. J. "Some Recent Developments in a Concept of Causality." *Journal of Econometrics*, 39 (September/October 1988): 199–211.

Hamilton, J. D. *Time Series Analysis.* Princeton, N.J.: Princeton University Press, 1994.

Hansen, B. E. "Tests for Parameter Stability in Regressions with I(1) Processes." *Journal of Business and Economic Statistics*, 10 (1992): 321–335.

Hansen, H., and S. Johansen. "Recursive Estimation in Cointegrated VAR-Models." Institute of Mathematical Statistics, Preprint 1, January 1993 (Copenhagen: University of Copenhagen).

Hendry, David D. F., and Jurgen A. Doornik. "Modeling Linear Dynamic Econometric Systems." *Scottish Journal of Political Economy*, 45 (1994): 1–33.

Hooper, P., and S. W. Kohlhagen. "The Effect of Exchange Rate Uncertainty on the Prices and Volume of International Trade." *Journal of International Economics*, 8 (November 1978): 483–511.

Johansen, Søren. "Determination of Cointegration Rank in the Presence of a Linear Trend." *Oxford Bulletin of Economics and Statistics*, 54 (1992): 383–397.

Koray, F., and William D. Lastrapes. "Real Exchange Rate Volatility and U.S. Bilateral Trade: A VAR Approach." *Review of Economics and Statistics*, 71 (November 1989): 708–712.

Kremers, Jeroen J. M., Neil R. Ericsson and Juan J. Dolado. "The Power of Cointegration Tests." *Oxford Bulletin of Economics and Statistics* (August 1992): 325–348.

Lloyd, Tim. "Testing a Present Value Model of Agricultural Land Values." *Oxford Bulletin of Economics and Statistics*, 56 (1994): 209–223.

Ng, Serena, and Pierre Perron. "Unit Root Tests in ARMA Models with Data-Dependent Methods for the Selection of the Truncation Lag." *Journal of the American Statistical Association* (March 1995): 268–281.

Osterwald-Lenum, M. "A Note with Quantiles of the Asymptotic Distributions of the Maximum Likelihood Cointegration Ranks Test Statistics: Four Cases." *Oxford Bulletin of Economics and Statistics* (August 1992): 461–472.

Ouliaris, Sam, and Peter C. B. Phillips. *Coint 2.0$_a$ Gauss Procedures for Cointegrated Regressions.* Aptech Systems Inc., USA, 1995.

Pagan, Adrian, and Aman Ullah. "The Econometric Analysis of Models with Risk Terms." *Journal of Applied Econometrics* (April 1988): 221–247.

Peree, E., and A. Steinherr. "Exchange Rate Uncertainty and Foreign Trade." *European Economic Review*, 33 (1989): 1244–1264.

Pesaran, H. H., and B. Pesaran. *Working with Microfit 4.0: Interactive Econometric Analysis.* Camfit Data Ltd., England, 1997.

Pozo, Susan. "Conditional Exchange-Rate Volatility and the Volume of International Trade: Evidence from the Early 1900s." *Review of Economics and Statistics* (May 1992): 325–329.

Ramanathan, Ramu. *Statistical Methods in Econometrics.* New York: Academic Press Inc., 1993.

Schwert, G. W. "Why Does Stock Market Volatility Change Over Time?" *The Journal of Finance*, 44 (1989): 1115–1153.

Sims, C. A., J. H. Stock and M. Watson. "Inference in Linear Time Series with Some Unit Roots." *Econometrica*, 58 (1990): 113–144.

Stock, James. "Confidence Intervals for the Largest Autoregressive Root in U.S. Macroeconomic Time Series." *Journal of Monetary Economics*, 28 (December 1991): 435–459.

Thursby, Marie C., and Jerry G. Thursby. "Bilateral Trade Flows, Linders Hypothesis, and Exchange Risk." *Review of Economics and Statistics* (August 1987): 488–495.

Watson, M. "Vector Autoregressions and Cointegration." In *The Handbook of Econometrics*, 6, ed. R. F. Engle and D. L. MacFadden, ch. 47. Amsterdam: Elsevier, 1994.

Part VI

A Review of the Theoretical Literature on Exchange Rate Determination

Chapter 13

The Traditional Approach to Balance of Payments Adjustment under Flexible Exchange Rates

Augustine C. Arize, Elias C. Grivoyannis,
Ioannis N. Kallianiotis and Valerie Englander

INTRODUCTION

The objective of this chapter is to define, determine, and analyze the Keynesian (Traditional) approach to exchange rate theory. This exchange rate theory focuses on the theory of exchange rate determination under flexible exchange rates, the determinants of the balance of payments under fixed exchange rates, and the role of the exchange rate under exchange rate control.[1] By 1973, a large part of that theory centered on exchange rate determination under flexible exchange rates versus changes in quantities under fixed exchange rates, as had been emphasized earlier. This theory was developed by James E. Meade, Fritz Machlup, Joan Robinson, and Sidney Alexander, who emphasized the current account of the balance of payments.

The Keynesian (Traditional) approach to the balance of payments is effectively a view of one particular component of the balance of payments, the trade account (merchandise exports minus imports). For the most part, the Traditional model attempts to describe the explanatory variables of the trade balance. It has relied heavily on basic economic theory (both macro and micro) for its tools of analysis by drawing on both branches and utilizing the one that best fits the problem at hand.

Exchange rate policy cannot permanently alter the balance of payments nor can monetary policy lastingly affect the domestic economy, but a change in the exchange rate (through a government intervention) will have a direct impact on the domestic price level, and monetary policy will have a direct effect on the country's payments position (measured by the change in its reserves under a fixed exchange rate system, by the movement in its exchange rate under freely flexible rates, and by a combination of the two under managed flexibility).

The Traditional approach is almost 300 years old. The evolution started from the mercantilist preoccupation with achieving a surplus on the trade account. Then, it was continued by David Hume (1711–1776), with the price specie flow mechanism; Adam Smith (1723–1790), with the concept of absolute advantage, and David Ricardo (1772–1823), with his introduction of comparative advantage. It was further developed by John Maynard Keynes (1883–1946) and formalized after the 1950s by the other economists already mentioned. Our focus will be on determination of the balance of payments under a fixed exchange-rate regime and the exchange rate under a floating exchange-rate regime.

The main body of this chapter is divided into five parts. The first part treats the fixed exchange-rate models with a discussion of two different models, the single equation and the simultaneous equation. The second part covers the flexible exchange rate models in two sections; the first, on international parity conditions, deals with purchasing power parity (PPP), interest rate parity (IRP), the Fisher Parity condition (FPC), the International Fisher effect (IFE), the balance of payments view (BPV), the speculative run view (SRV), the unbiased forward-rate hypothesis (UFRH), and real interest rate parity (RIRP); the second section deals with capital account models. The remainder of the chapter debates the Mundell-Fleming Model and empirical regularities of exchange-rate movements; it ends with some concluding remarks and a general summary of the different theoretical perspectives.

FIXED EXCHANGE RATE MODELS

The fixed exchange-rate models deal with the analysis of the current account theory and begin by making two simplifying assumptions: (1) there are no capital movements and (2) the exchange rates are fixed by the actions of the central banks. In practice, it is impossible to tell whether government actions were undertaken for normal purposes or for balance of payments reasons, but usually an effort is made to identify the deficit in the current account (under fixed rates) with the amount of government intervention. If a central bank intervenes in the market to affect the exchange rate, it is regarded as being in surplus if it is buying more foreign currencies than it sells (i.e., it is accumulating foreign assets or paying off liabilities to foreigners), and in deficit if it is selling foreign assets (or borrowing from abroad).

Under the gold standard (fixed exchange-rate regime), there was a trade adjustment mechanism called the price specie flow mechanism. Under that system, countries fix the values of their currencies in terms of gold, settle their trade surpluses and deficits by transferring gold, and refrain from altering the effects of those gold flows on their money supplies. The basic idea of the gold standard adjustment mechanism was as follows. A country with a trade deficit had to pay with foreign assets or gold, which caused a loss of its reserves and a reduction of its money supply. This decrease in money supply lowered the price level and made the home country's goods more competitive. Exports were stimulated and imports were reduced; thus, the balance of trade account was improved. Moreover, this process would continue until the deficit was eliminated.

Single Equation Models

Many empirical studies have been done using the single equation model and determined price and income elasticities. Tests have also been made of the Marshall-Lerner condition ($|\varepsilon_p| + |\varepsilon^*_p| > 1$); where ε_p is the domestic price elasticity of demand for imports, and ε^*_p is the foreign price elasticity of demand for a foreign country's imports (domestic exports).[2] In particular, see Houthakker and Magee (1969), Houthakker and Taylor (1970), Magee (1975), Dornbusch and Krugman (1976), Murray and Ginman (1976), and Kallianiotis and Patel (1990).

A current account deficit can be corrected but will negatively affect production. In a Keynesian view, the effect will be as follows: The deficit in the current account will cause a loss of reserves, which will lead the central bank to raise its interest rates to attract a capital inflow and stem the fall in the money supply. These high interest rates will lead to a decline in aggregate demand, a drop in income, a recession, and a fall in imports. The balance of the current account will indeed improved, but at the cost of a loss of output.

Throughout the entire chapter, we have borrowed most of the models from the existing literature and then made minor modifications and additions for uniformity, clarity, or improvement. An asterisk indicates variables for the foreign country, a dot indicates rate of change, and the lower-case letters are the natural logarithms of the upper-case counterparts.[3] The traditional approach proposes the following single equation model for the trade account.[4]

$$\dot{T}A_t = \alpha_0 + \alpha_1(\dot{Y}_t - \dot{Y}^w_t) + \alpha_2\dot{Q}_t + \alpha_3\dot{E}_t \qquad (1)$$
$$+ \; \varepsilon_{1t}; \; \alpha_1 < 0, \; \alpha_2 > 0, \; \alpha_3 < 0,$$

where TA is the trade account ($TA = X - M$); X and M are merchandise exports and imports; respectively; Y is domestic real income; Y^w is global real income; Q is the terms of trade ($Q = \dfrac{P_M}{P_x} = \dfrac{SP^*}{P}$); P_M is the price of imports; P_X is the price of exports; S is the spot exchange rate in direct quotes (i.e. dollar/mark); P is the price level (a price index in this case, i.e., CPI); E is the effective exchange rate ($\dfrac{\sum_{i=1}^{n} FC_i}{\$}$); FC is foreign currency units; and ε is the error term.[5]

Equation (1) may be written differently, as in (2):

$$\dot{T}A_t = \beta_0 + \beta_1\dot{Y}_t + \beta_2\dot{Y}^w_t + \beta_3\dot{P}_{Mt} + \beta_4\dot{P}_{xt} + \beta_5\dot{P}_t + \sum_{i=0}^{n}\beta_i\dot{E}_{t-i} \qquad (2)$$
$$+ \; \varepsilon_{2t}; \; \beta_1 < 0, \; \beta_2 > 0, \; \beta_3 > 0, \; \beta_4 < 0, \; \beta_5 < 0, \; \beta_i < 0.$$

In equation (2) we included P_M and P_X as two separate, independent variables; we added current and lagged values of E; and we could include another price variable as the price of the commodities consumed in the focus nation (P).[6] We made these changes because we feel that domestic goods compete with a nation's exports. Thus, we want to examine the price level of the nation's goods relatively to the price level of its exports.

When using this single equation model, there are three important areas to examine as far as price—that is, terms of trade (TOT)—is concerned. The areas are: (1) size and sign of the price elasticity of demand, (2) stability of the coefficient of price elasticity of demand, and (3) speed of adjustment of quantity responses to a change in price.

Another single equation model is the absorption approach, which takes from the national income-accounting system the relationship between current account (CA) and national income (Y) and domestic expenditures or absorption (A) and points out that as policy changes, such a devaluation can improve the current account only if they increase income by more than they increase expenditures.

Alexander (1952) started from the identity that the foreign balance (B) is equal to the difference between the total production of goods and services (Y) and the total absorption of goods and services (A),

$$B = CA = Y - A = Y - (C + I + G), \tag{3}$$

where C is personal consumption expenditures; I is gross, private, domestic fixed investment; and G is government purchases of goods and services.

The central question in equation (3) is how devaluation might change the relationship between expenditures (absorption) and income. This is calculated in both nominal and real terms because the identity holds both ways. In 1960s and 1970s, economists focused on the exchange rates role in the determination of the relative prices of tradable and home goods, its effect on real balances, and its impact on the intertemporal allocation of expenditures relative to income (expenditure-switching effects in favor of domestic or foreign goods).

In general, it is not evident how devaluation lowers expenditures relative to income, but one scenario might be as follows. A devaluation raises the terms of trade (and therefore the nominal price) of tradables. Consumers tend to switch expenditures toward home goods (law of demand), thus driving up their nominal prices. The nation's monetary and fiscal authorities are then obliged to levy an income tax to reduce the demand for home goods sufficiently to prevent their prices from rising further. Such increased tax receipts constitute the source of the expenditure reduction accompanying devaluation (in this case, of course, the net increases in taxes must be equal to the improvement in the current account).

Simultaneous Equation Models

Quite frequently in economic modeling the process under study can best be represented by a series of simultaneous, interdependent equations. In these systems, all the endogenous variables are random variables. Moreover, a change in any disturbance term changes all the endogenous variables because they were determined simultaneously.

The simultaneous equations model for the open economy arguments seems to be a prominent one, especially because prices and quantities are determined by both supply and demand. Stephen Magee (1975) and Peter Hooper (1972) used the following model to determine imports demand and exports supply:[7]

$$Q_{M_j}^{\ d} = f_1(Y_j, P_{m_j}^{\ d}, P_j), \tag{4}$$

$$Q_{x_i}^{\ s} = f_2(Y_i, P_{x_i}^{\ s}, P_i), \tag{5}$$

$$Q_{M_j}^{\ d} = Q_{x_i}^{\ s}, \tag{6}$$

$$P_{M_j}^{\ d} = S_{ij}(1 + T_j)P_{x_i}^{\ s}. \tag{7}$$

where $Q_{M_j}^{\ d}$ is the quantity of imports demanded in country j; Y_j is the real income in country j; $P_{M_j}^{\ d}$ is the price of imports in country j; P_j is the price of goods whose production occurs in country j; $Q_{x_i}^{\ s}$ is the quantity of exports supplied to country i; Y_i is the real income in country i; $P_{x_i}^{\ s}$ is the price of exports to country i; P_i is the price of all goods produced in country i; S_{ij} is the spot exchange rate between i and j, and T_j is the proportional tariff rate in economy j.

The trade balance (TA), measured in terms of domestic currency, is equal to the excess of exports over the value of imports:

$$TA_j = Q_{x_i}^{\ s}P_{x_i}^{\ s} - Q_{m_j}^{\ d}P_{M_j}^{\ d} \tag{8}$$

By substituting the equivalent from equations (4) and (5) into equation (8), we obtain:

$$TA_j = X_j(Y_i, P_{x_i}^{\ s}, P_i) - \frac{P_{M_j}^{\ d}}{P_{x_i}^{\ s}}M_j(Y_j, P_{M_j}^{\ d}, P_j) \tag{9}$$

Equation (9) gives the trade balance as a function of incomes and relative prices. The important point to note, however, is that an increase in the relative price of imports may not necessarily improve the trade balance. Although it is true that as the nation becomes more competitive, exports rise and imports decline, it is also true that the country will pay more per unit for imports. This cost effect will dominate unless the exports and imports are sufficiently price elastic. This point is formalized in the Marshall-Lerner condition.

Differentiating (9) with respect to the terms of trade, we obtain:[8]

$$\frac{d\,TA}{d\,Q} = M(\varepsilon_p^* + \varepsilon_p - 1), \tag{10}$$

where ε_p and ε_p^* are the price elasticities of domestic and foreign demand for imports.[9]

For a devaluation to have a positive (direct) effect on the trade balance, it must be true that $\varepsilon_p^* + \varepsilon_p - 1 > 0$, or equivalently:

$$|\varepsilon_p^*| + |\varepsilon_p| > 1 \tag{11}$$

The inequality in equation (11) is the so-called Marshall-Lerner condition, which states that the direct effect of a devaluation on the trade balance will be positive when the sum (in absolute terms) of the price elasticities of domestic exports and imports exceeds unity. Sufficiently low elasticities might cause the trade account balance to fail to improve consequent to devaluation. This is a Keynesian analysis of devaluation called the simple elasticities approach, which is clearly a microeconomic, partial equilibrium approach. Modern theory is a little skeptical about this approach.

"It is frequently difficult to draw the line—to tell where the 'soft monetarists' leave off and the 'eclectic Keynesians' begin," as Whitman (1975, p. 510) mentioned. However, the elasticities approach to balance of payments analysis is clearly Keynesian because only under Keynesian assumptions of unemployment and wage-price rigidity in domestic markets can it be assumed that "a devaluation would change the real prices of domestic goods relative to foreign goods in the foreign and domestic markets, thereby promoting substitution in production and consumption," and that "any repercussions of these substitutions on the demand for domestic output could be assumed to be met by variations in output and employment" (Whitman, 1975, p. 510).

Emphasis has shifted from asking how quantities change under fixed exchange rates to querying how prices change under flexible exchange rates, but the two questions are very closely related. As suggested in the following quotation, exchange-rate theories rely today somewhat more on Monetary theory (the modern asset view divided into the Portfolio Balance approach and the Monetary approach) and have moved further away from the theory of commercial policy that was espoused earlier.

Questions have also been raised about the short-term effects of exchange-rate changes on the current account. It is quite possible that flows of goods and services respond only with time lags to changes in the exchange rate. This proposition is termed the J-curve effect.

This type of pattern emanates from the observation that at the time when an exchange rate change occurs, goods already in transit and under contract have been purchased and the completion of those transactions will dominate the short-term change in the current account balance. The term J-curve is used to describe the movement over time of the current account balance, which may deteriorate at first as exports denominated in domestic currency in shipping contracts earn less foreign exchange while imports are paid for in foreign exchange. The initial impact of a depreciation of exchange rate could therefore be that foreign exchange expenditures would remain unaltered while foreign exchange receipts would decline. Magee (1973) characterized the phenomenon as consisting of a period during which contracts already in force in specified currencies dominate the determinants of the current account (the currency contract period). Over time, new contracts made after the exchange-rate depreciation begin to dominate, and the "pass-through" of the devaluation (or depreciation under the flexible exchange-rate system) affects the current account.

The extent to which there is a J-curve effect depends on the extent to which trade takes place under preexisting contracts (as contrasted with spot-market transactions), the degree to which there may be an asymmetric use of domestic and foreign currency in making contracts, and the length of the lags in contract execution. In some countries there may be no negatively sloped behavior of the current account over time in response to exchange-rate changes, whereas in others there may be particularly prolonged periods of negative response.[10] Although the validity of the J-curve effect rests largely on the empirical considerations associated with time lags and the currency denomination of contracts, it assumes importance for the modeling of exchange-rate determination because its existence would imply that in the short run, in the absence of capital mobility the foreign exchange market might be unstable.

FLEXIBLE EXCHANGE RATE MODELS

A freely flexible (or free-floating) exchange-rate regime exists whenever exchange rates (currency prices) are freely determined by the demand for, and supply of, foreign currencies by private parties. This regime assumes the absence of any systematic government intervention in the foreign exchange market, thus, the exchange rate moves freely in response to market forces. In contrast to the free-floating regime, what actually exits today is a managed or controlled-floating regime, where governments intervene in the foreign exchange market in order to influence the exchange rate.

The Keynesian approach perceives government intervention as necessary and sees the government as a stabilizer of fluctuations in the private sector. It views equilibrium as a state to be achieved by deliberate policy intervention rather than through the operation of automatic market forces alone, and it views collective goods as an important component of the social welfare function. Those who take this view tend to base their concern with explicit balance of payments policies in a fixed-rate world and their frequent preference for managed flexibility on the need to insulate the domestic economy from foreign disturbances and permit national governments to pursue independent macro-stabilization policies in a world of integrated markets, like the world we live in today. Fundamentally, this view regards exchange rate policy as one instrument by which governments may preserve some independence in the policy sphere with a minimum of disruption to the benefits of market integration in the private sphere.

International Parity Conditions

A conventional approach to explaining the observed international parity conditions is to regard the exchange rate as an asset price—as the relative price of two national currencies. From this perspective the exchange rate is determined by the framework applicable to other asset prices, and particularly by the efficient market hypothesis.[11] Consequently asset prices are said to depend primarily on expectations, conditional on available information, that are formed concerning the future behavior of the relevant variables. Rapid market adjustment to new information immediately eliminates any unusual profit opportunities for investors.

The balance of payments of a country records all the economic transactions that have taken place, during a given period, between the country's residents and the rest of the world. The components (current account, capital account, and official settlements account) of the balance of payments involve transactions in commodities, services, and assets. These transactions are the results of decisions by traders shipping goods across countries, capital movements among countries, manipulation of international funds by interest arbitragers, and speculators (due to changes in their expectations, and to attitudes and actions in regard to risk). The principles that dictate these international trade flows and capital movements among countries are examined here as the international parity conditions. Even though the Keynesian theory of exchange-rate determination concentrates more on the determinants of the current account and less on the capital account, it has some variants that deal with all the components of the balance of payments.

Purchasing Power Parity (PPP)

The purchasing power parity (PPP) theory was first delineated by Gustav Cassel (1916, 1918, 1921) to answer the question of what the new exchange-rate parities should be following the disruption of the fixed exchange-rate system by World War I. The theory states that if an identical product or service can be sold in two different markets and there are no restrictions on its sale or the transportation costs of moving it between markets, the price should be the same in both markets. This is also called the law of one price:[12]

$$P(\$/\text{unit}) = S(\frac{\$}{\text{DM}}) \times P^*(\text{DM/unit}), \tag{12}$$

where P is the price of the product in $ per unit, S is the spot exchange rate in $ per DM, and P* is the price of the product in foreign currency (DM per unit).

By solving equation (12) for S, we can determine the exchange rate as the relative prices of the two products. Alternately, by using two identical price indices for the United States and for Germany, the "absolute" version of the PPP can be determined:

$$S = \frac{P}{P*} \qquad (13)$$

where P is the consumer price index (CPI) in the United States, and P* is the CPI in Germany.

Because price levels are never directly comparable across countries, what are usually observed are price indices. In this form, it makes a significant difference whether a cost of living price index, a wholesale price index, an index of home-goods prices (this is almost never available), or some other measure of the price level is used.

Another version of the PPP is the "relative" theory of PPP, which states that if the spot exchange rate between two countries starts in equilibrium, any change in the differential rate of inflation between the two tends to be offset over the long run by an equal, but opposite change in the spot exchange rate.[13] The ex post version is given in equation (14), and the ex ante version, in equation (15):

$$\Delta s_t = \pi_t - \pi_t^*, \qquad (14)$$

$$\Delta s_t^e = \Delta p_t^e - \Delta p_t^{*e} \qquad (15)$$

where π_t is the inflation rate, Δs_t^e is the expected change in the spot exchange rate, Δp_t^e is the expected inflation rate domestically, and Δp_t^{*e} is the expected foreign inflation rate.[14]

"Absolute" PPP has been interpreted to mean that price levels are equated between countries, whereas "relative" PPP is the prediction that the proportionate change in the home country's price level will equal the proportionate change in the product of the foreign price level and the exchange rate. Either version can be interpreted: (1) as a prediction of exchange-rate movements, given the rates of inflation, (2) as an equilibrium condition, or (3) as an identity holding for tradable goods and services.[15]

It should be noted that absolute PPP can hold even in the presence of home goods. This occurs if home and tradable goods are sufficiently close substitutes in production or if trade assures factor price equalization and that the production technologies used for both goods are identical. There are two possible time horizons for which PPP might hold: (1) the long run, during which the short-run exchange rate tends toward a long-run equilibrium representing PPP; (2) the short run, during which fluctuations in the exchange rate can occur for a variety of reasons (presumably as a function of disturbances in the underlying parameters of the system), but once a disturbance has occurred, the exchange rate will eventually return to its long-run PPP rate. The alternative, stricter version is that PPP must always hold, even in the short run.

Sometimes, we may see a deviation from the PPP theory version as follows:[16]

$$s_t - s_{t-1} = \Theta(p_t - p_t^* - s_{t-1}), \tag{16}$$

where θ is the speed of price adjustment after a monetary shock. Financial markets adjust instantaneously (and sometimes overadjust or overshoot) after a monetary shock, whereas goods markets adjust only gradually.[17]

In the simple Keynesian models, the price of domestic output or level of the money wage rate is given, and the level of output is determined by aggregate demand. The PPP theorem essentially asserts that prices in one country must, when expressed in a common currency, equal those in any other country. PPP can hold because exchange rates determine prices, or conversely. PPP can be assumed to hold through arbitrage or can be a theory of exchange rate or price level determination.

In a one-commodity model, one could invoke arbitrage and either a zero-transport-cost assumption or a constant-transport-cost (with no time lags) assumption to ensure that equation (12) would always hold. However, the meaning of PPP as a theory of exchange-rate determination is not at all clear. There are questions as to whether PPP should be interpreted as either a short-run or long-run equilibrium condition or alternately, as an identity. Much of the analysis takes on the appearance of a phenomenon in search of a theory, as authors either have found reasons why PPP fails to hold (poor data, wrong measures, etc.) or developed alternative versions. Some authors conclude that PPP did not work well in either the short or the long run.[18]

In general, there are sound analytical reasons for skepticism about the proposition that PPP must hold, in either its absolute or relative form, without qualification. McKinnon (1979, p. 136) is typical when he concluded that "until a more robust theory replaces it, I shall assume that purchasing power parity among tradable goods tends to hold in the long run in the absence of overt impediments to trade and among countries with convertible currencies."

There is a very extensive literature testing the absolute, relative, and deviation versions of the PPP and evaluating the law of one price.[19] The test have, for the most part, not proven accurate in their estimates of future exchange rates.[20] Goods and services do not in reality move at zero cost between countries, and in fact, many goods are not tradable. Moreover, many goods and services are not the same quality across countries, reflecting the differences in tastes and resources of the countries of their manufacture and consumption. The empirical results generally conclude that PPP holds up well over the very long run but poorly for shorter time periods and that the theory holds better for countries with relatively high rates of inflation and underdeveloped capital markets.

To conduct the empirical tests of PPP, it is convenient to write equations (13), (14), and (16) in natural logarithm form as follows:

$$s_t = \gamma_0 + \gamma_1(p_t - p_t^*) + \varepsilon_{17t}, \tag{17}$$

$$\Delta s_t = \delta_0 + \delta_1(\pi_t - \pi_t^*) + \varepsilon_{18t}, \tag{18}$$

$$\Delta s_t = s_t - s_{t-1} = \Theta_0 + \Theta_1(p_t - p_t^* - s_{t-1}) + \varepsilon_{19t}, \tag{19}$$

where γ_0, δ_0, and θ_0 are the constants: γ_1, δ_1, and θ_1 are the parameters; and ε_t is the error term.

The empirical verification of PPP involves a test of the null hypothesis—that $\gamma_0 = \delta_0 = \theta_0 = 0$ and $\gamma_1 = \delta_1 = \theta_1 = 1$. The significance tests usually consist of individual tests using the t statistic and a joint test using the F statistic or the log likelihood ratio statistic.

The departure from PPP in the 1970s and 1980s leads us to inquire about the factors that contributed to its rejection. The factors that may account for the failure of PPP are the existence of transaction costs and impediments to trade, changes of relative prices, intervention in foreign exchange markets, sluggishness in the price adjustment, lack of information or high opportunity cost of acquiring information, and the multivariate and simultaneity problems.

Interest Rate Parity (IRP)

The theory of forward exchange rates (also sometimes referred to as interest rate parity) is based on the proposition that in the absence of transaction costs, the forward premium (i.e., the proportionate differential between the forward and spot exchange rates) must equal the interest rate differential (measured over the same time interval). The reason is that one could, without exchange-rate risk, buy foreign bonds and sell foreign exchange forward by borrowing from the domestic market if the interest differential in the two countries were less than the forward premium.

If a corporation were to invest in U.S. Treasury bills, it would receive $\$R_{U.S.}$ back after one year per dollar invested, where:

$$\$R_{U.S.} = 1 + i_t. \tag{20}$$

The alternative investment involves German Treasury bills, which yield an interest return per DM in one year of:

$$DM\ R_G = 1 + i_t^* \tag{21}$$

This covered investment strategy, then, involves the following simultaneous steps: (1) You buy DM in the spot market at a spot exchange rate of S ($/DM) and obtain $\$1/S(\$/DM) = DM1/S$ for each $ invested. (2) You invest the DM in one-year German Treasury bills. This will give you DM $(1/S\ [1 + i^*])$ at the end of the first year. (3) You sell forward the future DM proceeds from the investment at a forward exchange rate F($/DM). You will then receive $ ([1/S {1 + i*}] F) one year from now.

The proceeds from the covered investment strategy, in terms of the dollars you end up accumulating—after a period of one year—per dollar initially invested abroad are represented by R_G are given by:

$$\$R_G = \frac{F_t}{S_t}(1 + i^*_t) \tag{22}$$

Note that this covered investment strategy avoids both default and exchange rate risk. This was achieved, first, by investing in a risk-free asset (Treasury bills), and second, by selling forward the future DM proceeds so that exchange-rate risk would be eliminated.

When investment alternatives are similar in terms of maturity and the explicit objective is to minimize risk, a return-maximizing investor will choose whatever investment provides the highest dollar return after one year. As long as $R_{U.S.} > R_G$, you should invest in the United States; if $R_{U.S.} < R_G$, you should invest in Germany; and if $R_{U.S.} = R_G$, the options are equally attractive.

The existence of incentives to invest in one or the other country is, therefore, measured by the differential between $R_{U.S.}$ and R_G, which is called the covered interest differential or Covered Interest Arbitrage (CIA).

$$CIA = R_G - R_{U.S.} = \frac{F_t}{S_t}(1 + i^*_t) - (1 + i_t), \text{ or} \tag{23}$$

$$CIA = \frac{F_t - S_t}{S_t} - i_t + i^*_t + \frac{F_t - S_t}{S_t}i^*_t \tag{24}$$

By setting CIA = 0, parity exists, and we have:

$$\frac{i_t - i^*_t}{1 + i^*_t} = \frac{F_t - S_t}{S_t} \tag{25}$$

Equation (25) is known as the Covered Interest Parity (CIP) condition. The term $(\frac{F_t - S_t}{S_t}i_t)$ in equation (24) can be ignored because it is a very small number, especially if investments last only a few days. By putting this term equal to zero, we have, from equation (24), an approximation of the CIP that is used much more often to represent the Interest Rate Parity (IRP).

$$i_t - i^*_t = \frac{F_t - S_t}{S_t} \tag{26}$$

The theory of interest rate parity provides the linkage between the foreign exchange and international money markets. It states that the interest rate differential between two countries will be matched by the forward premium (fp) or forward discount (fd) of the exchange rate:[21]

$$i_t - i^*_t = f_t - s_t, \tag{27}$$

where f_t is the $\ln(F)$ of the forward exchange rate (F).

This relation holds due to the efficient arbitrage involved in risk-free assets. It can be applied to international investments as well as to international lending. The theory is applicable only to securities with maturities of one year or less, since forward contracts are not routinely available for periods of longer than one year.

This formula tells us that interest rates and exchange rates are determined simultaneously. However, we can test causality here, too. The theory means that there are no profit opportunities to be had in foreign exchange markets, since arbitrators and hedgers will see to them and equalize the interest differential with the forward discount or premium.[22]

The spot and the forward exchange markets are not, however, constantly in the state of equilibrium described by the interest rate parity. When the market is not in equilibrium, the potential for "riskless" or arbitrage profit exists. The arbitrager who recognizes such an imbalance will move to take advantage of the disequilibrium by investing in whichever country and currency that offer the higher return on a covered basis. This is what we called above the covered interest arbitrage (CIA).

If transaction costs are negligible and political and default risks are ignored, arbitragers can earn an arbitrage profit and create an equilibrium in the foreign exchange and money markets whenever equation (27) is not satisfied. As it stands, equation (27) is an equilibrium condition stating a relationship that must hold between interest rate differentials and spot and forward exchange rates. It indicates nothing about the determinants of any particular variable until more variables are placed on the model, although it does serve as a useful reminder that countries' monetary authorities cannot follow interest-rate targets and simultaneously attempt to regulate the forward exchange rate under a fixed exchange-rate system. Intervention in the forward market can be equivalent to domestic open-market operations for small countries because it can alter the domestic rate of interest.[23]

Fisher Parity Condition (FPC)

The Fisher Parity Condition (FPC) or Fisher Effect (named after the American economist Irving Fisher) states that nominal interest rates in each country are equal to the required real rate of interest plus an inflation premium for compensation due to the expected inflation.

$$i_t = r_t + \pi^e_{t+1}, \tag{28}$$

$$i^*_t = r^*_t + \pi^{*e}_{t+1}, \tag{29}$$

where i is the nominal rate of interest, r is the real rate of interest, and π^e is the expected inflation rate over the period of time for which funds are to be lent.

Subtracting equation (29) from equation (28) and assuming that $r_t = r^*_t$, we get:

$$i_t - i^*_t = \pi^e_{t+1} - \pi^{*e}_{t+1} = \Delta p^e_t - \Delta p^{*e}_t \tag{30}$$

Equation (30) represents the Fisher effect between the two countries. If this Fisher equation holds true and the real interest rates are equal in the two countries, the nominal interest rate differential will reflect the expected inflation differential. It should be noted that this relationship requires a forecast of the future rate of inflation in both countries. Predicting the future can be difficult, but the condition is more applicable in cases of high inflation. Empirical tests by Cumby and Obstfeld (1981) and Kallianiotis (1985) using ex post national inflation rates have shown the Fisher effect to exist particularly for short maturity government securities.

International Fisher Effect (IFE)

The relationship between the percentage change in the spot exchange rate over time and the differential between comparable interest rates in two countries is known as the International Fisher effect (IFE), or International Fisher Parity, or "Fisher-open." It states that the spot exchange rate should change in an equal amount, but in the opposite direction, to the difference in interest rates between two countries.

$$s^e_{t+1} - s_t = i_t - i^*_t, \tag{31}$$

where s is the spot exchange rate and i is the nominal interest rate.

If the interest rate differential between two countries is −2 percent, this condition can be used to predict that the domestic currency will appreciate by 2 percent. Empirical tests lend some support to the relationship postulated by the international Fisher effect, although considerable short-run deviations occur.[24]

Balance of Payments View (BPV)

The balance of payments view (BPV) or trade balance view of exchange-rate determination states that the trade account surplus or deficit will induce the spot exchange rate to decrease (appreciation of the dollar) or increase (depreciation of the dollar). The reason is that if there is a trade account surplus, there will be excess demand for dollars which will strengthen the domestic currency (spot rate will fall).

$$S_t = f(TA_t, \ldots); \frac{\delta S_t}{\delta TA_t} < 0 \tag{32}$$

There are some weaknesses to this view, and the most important of which involves asserting causality between the trade account and exchange rate to find the direction of the effect.[25] Another point is that the exchange rate is determined by many other independent variables, and not only from the trade account.

Speculative Run View (SRV)

In developing this view, Grubel (1966) and Malindretos (1988) referred to a group of market participants in the foreign exchange market, which does not cover its position by using forward contracts. These are speculators which take an open forward exchange rate position (they stay uncovered). The result of the actions of speculators is that interest rate parity theory does not hold and they can take advantage of this arbitrage.

The speculators are motivated by two variables. The expected spot rate next period (S^e_{t+1}) and the forward exchange rate (F_t). The speculator will sell forward DM if:

$$F_t > S^e_{t+1} \tag{33}$$

Unbiased Forward Rate Hypothesis (UFRH)

Some economists believe that for the major freely floating currencies, foreign exchange markets are efficient and forward exchange rates are unbiased predictors of future spot exchange rates.[26] This is a hypothesis that emphasizes effective use of information in the forward exchange rate to predict the future spot rate. The Unbiased Forward Rate Hypothesis (UFRH) claims that market expectations of the economic fundamentals that determine exchange rates are reflected in the forward exchange rate. Then, on the average, the forward rate is approximately equal to the future spot exchange rate.

$$F_t = S^e_{t+1}, \text{ or} \tag{34}$$

$$E(s_{t+1} - f_t|I_t) = 0 \tag{35}$$

where I_t is the information available at time t.

The rationale for equations (34) and (35) is based on the hypothesis that the foreign exchange market is reasonably efficient. Market efficiency assumes that: (1) all relevant information is quickly reflected in both the spot and forward exchange markets; (2) transaction costs are low; (3) instruments denominated in different currencies are perfect substitutes for one another; and (4) investors are risk neutral.

We can conduct significance tests for the efficient market hypothesis by testing spot market efficiency that involves a test of the joint hypothesis of $\alpha_0 = 0$ and $\alpha_1 = 1$:

$$s_{t+1} = \alpha_0 + \alpha_1 s_t + \varepsilon_{t+1}; \tag{36}$$

by testing forward market efficiency that $\beta_0 = 0$ and $\beta_1 = 1$:

$$s_{t+1} = \beta_0 + \beta_1 f_t + \varepsilon_{t+1}; \tag{37}$$

and by testing composite market efficiency, that is, $\gamma_0 = 0$ and $\gamma_1 + \gamma_2 = 1$,

$$s_{t+1} = \gamma_0 + \gamma_1 s_t + \gamma_2 f_t + \varepsilon_{t+1} \tag{38}$$

Empirical studies of the efficient foreign exchange market hypothesis have yielded conflicting results. Nevertheless, a consensus is developing that rejects the efficient market hypothesis. It appears that the forward rate is not an unbiased predictor of the future spot rate and that it does pay to use resources to attempt to forecast exchange rates and to hedge in the forward market. The sources of rejection of the efficient market may be attributable to nonnegligible transaction cost associated with arbitrage, a risk premium if investors are not risk neutral, governments' interventions, or a specification error (if the model is not well specified).

Real Interest Rate Parity (RIRP)

Sometimes, researchers are concerned not only with the nominal relationship but also with the real relationship between the exchange rate and the interest rate differential.[27] Thus, it is appropriate to express the international Fisher parity condition in real terms.

$$\Delta s_t^e + \pi_t^{*e} - \pi_t^e = (i_t - \pi_t^e) - (i_t^* - \pi_t^{*e}) = r_t - r_t^* \tag{39}$$

Equation (39) is called real interest rate parity (RIRP) and states that the expected change in real exchange rates equals the real interest rate differential.

Finally, we can go one step further to determine an international parity identity.[28] By subtracting equation (29) from equation (28) and adding and subtracting the terms fd_t and Δs_t^e on the right-hand side of the new equation, we have:

$$i_t - i_t^* = r_t - r_t^* + fd_t - fd_t + \Delta s_t^e - \Delta s_t^e + \pi_t^e - \pi_t^{*e} \tag{40}$$

Now, we rearrange the terms in equation (40), and the equation becomes :

$$(\Delta s_t^e + \pi_t^{*e} - \pi_t^e) \equiv (r_t - r_t^*) - (i_t - i_t^* - fd_t) - (fd_t - \Delta s_t^e) \tag{41}$$

The left-hand side term in equation (41) is the expected real exchange rate (Δq_t^e)—the expected real depreciation of the currency, terms of trade, or PPP.

The first term on the right-hand side of equation (41) is the real interest differential between the two countries (RID) or real interest rate parity (RIRP). The second term is the covered interest rate parity (CIP), and the last term involves the foreign exchange market surprises (FXMS).

Equation (41) must hold as an identity. If $r_t - r_t^* = 0$, it means that financial markets are integrated, or that perfect capital mobility exists across countries. If $i_t - i_t^* - fd_t = 0$, it means that the bond market is efficient and a nominal interest differential exists between countries because of the expected depreciation of the currency of the country with higher interest rate, which is exactly equal to the interest differential. If $fd_t - \Delta S_t^e = 0$, it means that currencies are perfect substitutes and the foreign exchange market is efficient. Based on these hypotheses, equation (41) becomes $\Delta q_t^e = 0$, which means that the goods markets are integrated and the law of one price (PPP) holds.

Capital Account Models

The capital account (KA) measures the flows of financial assets across national borders. These flows may be associated with the international trade of goods and services or with portfolio shifts entailing foreign stocks, bonds, direct investments, and other financial transactions. Today goods and services are not traded directly through a barter system; each international transaction that entails a current account entry also yields an offsetting capital account entry.[29]

The most important characteristic of the Traditional approach models was that they dealt with the trade or the current account of the balance of payments. This view changed in the 1960s and into 1970s when some studies on the factors determining capital flows appeared. In 1940s and 1950s the capital account was not important because of its small size (due to capital controls) and because only real variables and not monetary ones were considered as important.

James Tobin (1958, 1963) developed the portfolio distribution model, which states that changes in the rates of return will change the allocation of capital (capital flows among countries). He foreshadowed the Monetary approach to the balance of payments by stating that the capital account will be affected by an interest rate differential between two countries. Mundell's (1960) and Kenen's (1963) writings also show how capital flows are affected by the differences in interest rates among countries:

$$KA_t = f(i_t - i_t^*, ...); \frac{\partial KA_t}{\partial(_t - i_t^*)} > 0, \qquad (42)$$

where KA is the capital account balance, and $i - i^*$ is the interest differential.

Branson and Hill (1971) undertook an analysis of determinants of the capital account for the United States and a few other OECD nations. They took as independent variables the domestic and foreign interest rates ($i - i^*$), changes in interest rates $\Delta(i - i^*)$, the domestic and foreign wealth ($W - W^*$), the trade balance (TA), the velocity of money (V − V*), and a credit rationing variable (CRV):

$$KA_t = f[i_t - i_t^*, \Delta(i_t - i_t^*), W - W^*, TA, V - V^*, CRV];$$ (43)

$$f_i > 0,\ f_{i^*} < 0,\ f_{TA} < 0,\ f_V > 0,\ f_{V^*} < 0,\ f_{CRV} > 0.$$

Three of those variables—the domestic interest rate, the credit rationing index, and the velocity of money—are monetary variables, which indicate the basic policy of the monetary authority of the focus country.[30]

THE MUNDELL-FLEMING MODEL

In the 1950s, Meade focused on the possibility of incompatibility between the goals of external and internal balance. Fleming (1962), Mundell (1963), Polak (1977), and others developed a Keynesian-type model in which the net current account balance is a function of real income and the exchange rate (assuming Keynesian underemployment at a constant domestic price level), whereas the net capital account balance is a function of the differential in interest rates between the home country and the rest of the world. Real income, in turn, is a function of monetary and fiscal policy variables, which increases (through the multiplier) with increases in government expenditures and decreases with the interest rate.

This model is set in the context of a macroeconomic model with the following assumptions: (1) the aggregate supply curve is flat, (2) PPP does not hold, even in the long run; instead, the size of the current account surplus depends positively on the (real) exchange rate and negatively on (real) income; (3) exchange rate expectations are static; and (4) capital mobility is less than perfect.

With two instruments—monetary and fiscal policy, two targets—the balance of payments (not the current account balance) and the level of real income, and an appropriate combination of monetary and fiscal instruments, a country could achieve both targets. Apparently, therefore, the potential conflicts between external and internal balance under fixed exchange rates might be resolved if the appropriate assignments of instruments to targets were made.

Finally, according to today's standards, the model is pretty elementary. For simplicity, the small country case is set forth here, although extension to a two-country world is straightforward.[31] The small-country assumption permits taking the world interest rate and prices as given. Hence,

$$NCA = X(Y, E) - M(Y, E);\ \frac{\partial X}{\partial Y} < 0,\ \frac{\partial X}{\partial E} > 0,\ \frac{\partial M}{\partial Y} > 0,\ \frac{\partial M}{\partial E} < 0$$ (44)

$$I = I(i);\ \frac{\partial I}{\partial i} > 0$$ (45)

$$B \equiv NCA + I; \tag{46}$$

$$Y = Y(G, i, E, Y^*); \frac{\partial Y}{\partial G} > 0, \frac{\partial Y}{\partial i} < 0, \frac{\partial Y}{\partial E} > 0, \frac{\partial Y}{\partial Y^*} > 0, \tag{47}$$

where NCA is the net current account balance; X and M are exports and imports (a function of Y, nominal income, and E, the price of foreign exchange); and the partial derivatives are as indicated. The fact that no domestic price level appears in the model reflects the implicit assumption of an underemployment equilibrium of the type in which an increase in aggregate demand can increase real income without any accompanying increase in domestic prices. The symbol I is the net capital inflow to the country (which might be positive or negative); B is the balance of payments; G is government expenditures (or tax receipts, with opposite signs on all derivatives); i is the rate of interest; and Y* is the foreign output or nominal income. Equation (47) is a reduced form because real income increases with aggregate demand, which is positively related to government expenditures, exchange rate, and foreign income and negatively related to the interest rate.

Differentiating totally equation (46) with respect to the exogenous variables G, i, and Y*; holding the exchange rate constant; and substituting equations (44), (45), and (47) into equation (46) yields:

$$dB = (\frac{\partial X}{\partial Y} - \frac{\partial M}{\partial Y})(\frac{\partial Y}{\partial G}dG + \frac{\partial Y}{\partial i}di + \frac{\partial Y}{\partial Y^*}dY^*) + \frac{\partial I}{\partial i}di \tag{48}$$

As can be seen, any combination of income and balance of payments targets may be compatible. For a given real income, the balance of payments can always be improved by raising both the interest rate and the level of government expenditures (or lowering taxes) or by any increase in foreign income. For a given balance of payments, real income can always be increased by raising both government expenditures and foreign income or by reducing the interest rate. The role of interest rates is absolutely central to the Mundell-Fleming model. In general, international interest rate differentials are assumed to provoke finite flows into or out of the country.

The Mundell-Fleming model's contribution was to call economists' attention to the important fact that the balance of payments consists of both current and capital account transactions. Thus any satisfactory analysis of exchange rate determination and of the balance of payments must also take into account capital flows.

EMPIRICAL REGULARITIES OF EXCHANGE-RATE MOVEMENTS

The Keynesian approach focuses on the balance of goods and services, which corresponds to the "net exports" sector in the national income and product accounts. When the Keynesian (Traditional) approach is expanded to incorporate a flow theory of international capital movements, the corresponding accounting framework will logically include a balance on goods and services (the remaining item in the balance on current account, unilateral transfers, is something of an anomaly, which does not fit easily into any sectoral analytical framework); a balance on securities (the capital account); and a residual and offsetting reserve balance, which includes the means of payment to finance the other two accounts. Keynesians, in other words, analyze the balance of payments ''from the top down.''

On the other hand, under an asset-market approach involving flexible rates, the exchange rate is determined in the short run by the requirements of asset-market equilibrium. The exchange rate then influences the current account, after a lag. Since rates are flexible, the capital account balance is the negative of the current account, so the current account balance also is the rate of change of net foreign asset holdings.[32] Thus, the current account balance feeds holdings of net foreign assets and moves the exchange rate. The system works as follows:

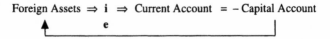

Here, i is the vector of interest rates and e is the vector of exchange rates. This system comes into full equilibrium (stationary or growing) when all stocks (assets) reach equilibrium values. The important aspect of the current account here is its role as the foreign net worth account; it gives the rate of net foreign investment. The consistency of this mechanism with long-run purchasing power parity (PPP) can be illustrated as follows. If, from an initial equilibrium, the home government starts running a budget deficit, thus increasing the rate of growth of supply of home-denominated assets (money or debt), the exchange rate will rise (currency will be depreciated). This stimulates net exports and aggregate demand, pulling up the price level. Eventually, the price increase brings the system back to PPP, but with a higher exchange rate. The analogy to the Tobin view of the relationship between equity prices and investment should be obvious.[33]

In the short run, exchange rates may be determined substantially, and even primarily, by stock equilibrium in asset markets rather than by the current account. The interactions, in a regime of flexible rates, traded goods and services, really establish a long-run supply price for a currency; while the floating exchange rate clears the asset market in the short run, thereby triggering quantity adjustments in the current account that restore long-term asset equilibrium. In such a system, the exchange rate will overshoot its long-run equilibrium in response to many (though not all) disturbances. That overshooting can impose important social costs in the presence of market imperfections or discontinuities, such as dependence on internal financing, bankruptcy, or asymmetrical responses of domestic prices to appreciation and depreciation. These, in turn, make the volatility of exchange rates a proper concern of public policy.[34]

Under the new exchange-rate regime (the introduction of a floating system in industrial countries in March 1973), exchange rates have tended to exhibit several empirical regularities. An examination of these regularities will help us to understand the fundamental characteristics of exchange-rate behavior.

First, levels of exchange rates may display some degree of persistence; that is, there may be a tendency toward continual appreciation or depreciation over a period of time. However, when we look at the rate of change of the spot rate on a week-to-week or month-to-month basis, it appears to be random, and the process can be best described as a random walk.

$$E(s_{t + 1}) = s_t + \varepsilon_{t + 1}; \varepsilon_{t + 1} \sim N(0, \sigma^2) \tag{49}$$

Second, the spot rate and the forward rate tend to move together, or covary, over time. The forward rate (F) can, under certain selective assumptions, be viewed as the market's expectation of the future spot rate ($S^e_{t + 1}$). The evidence concerning whether the forward rate is an unbiased predictor of the future spot rate is mixed. The forward rate does not, in any event, constitute a good predictor of the future spot rate. This can be explained by the arrival of unanticipated shocks (news), which alter the market's expectations of the future spot rate.

Third, since the introduction of the floating exchange-rate regime, exchange rates have tended to be highly volatile or turbulent. With the exception of interest-rate differentials, exchange rates have been more volatile than the fundamental factors on which they depend, including domestic and foreign money supplies, real incomes, price levels, and the balance of payments.[35]

Fourth, exchange rate movements essentially display an asset behavior. In the short run, the spot exchange rate is sensitive to economic news and political events. However, in the long run it is functionally related to economic fundamentals, which are reflected in a set of relationships known as the international parity conditions. Survey data also show that expectations for short horizons seem to exhibit "bandwagon" effects, which are destabilizing while expectations for long horizons appear to be regressive, and thus stabilizing.[36]

Fifth, in a short time horizon, no model can outperform the random walk hypothesis. In particular, no other variables can predict the future spot rate better than the current spot rate.

Sixth, short-term forecasts are typically motivated by a desire to hedge a receivable, payable, or dividend for, perhaps, a period of three months or less. In this case, the long-run economic fundamentals may not be as important as technical or speculative factors in the marketplace, or government intervention, or news, and the whims of traders and investors. Accuracy of the forecast is critical, since most of the exchange-rate changes are relatively small, even when day-to-day volatility is high.

Seventh, under conditions of freely floating rates, the expected rate of change in the spot exchange rate, differential rates of national inflation and interest, and the forward discount or premium are all directly proportional to each other and mutually determined. Thus, a change in one of these variables has a tendency to change them, all with a feedback on the variable that changes first. However, there has rarely been a time period in which at least some government interference in the trade process did not exist, causing international parity conditions to be disturbed.

These empirical regularities suggest that, in part, exchange-rate movements can be explained by economic variables. In this case, investors can make use of these variables to predict exchange-rate behavior and engage in profitable trading. However, the volatility of exchange rates also implies that they are largely unpredictable by any observable economic reasoning, and that they exhibit random behavior. The consequence is that no particular trading rule can be developed to allow investors to realize excess profits in the currency markets.

SUMMARY AND CONCLUSIONS

The traditional (Keynesian) framework views the achievement of equilibrium—both internal and external—as a specific objective of deliberate government policy rather than the automatic result of the operation of market forces.

A fixed exchange-rate system is a convertible currency system in which individuals are free to undertake their desired transactions at prevailing prices and the government buys and sells foreign exchange in order to maintain the exchange rate.

A flexible exchange-rate system is a convertible currency system in which the exchange rate is market determined and there can be no deficit. In practice, governments intervene under flexible exchange rates.

A managed float- (or "dirty" float) exchange-rate system is a convertible currency system that still relies on market conditions for day-to-day exchange rate determination but whereby countries often find it necessary to take actions to maintain their desired exchange values by intervening in the foreign exchange market.

An exchange control system is one in which the government sets the exchange rate and does not necessarily let individuals carry out their desired transactions. Foreign exchange is sold only under certain conditions, and individuals generally are required to sell any foreign exchange they may have to the government. In such a system, the currency is inconvertible.

Market integration across national boundaries has certainly increased in recent years (witness the European integration that took place on January 1, 1993) but, quite apart from the remaining barriers to trade, considerable evidence suggests that, at least for certain classes of commodities and financial assets, domestic and foreign counterparts are not regarded as perfect substitutes. This creates substantial deviations from the law of one price, at least in the short run.

Exchange-rate theory abstracts from the particular details of payment and instead examines the ways in which particular classes of arrangements (fixed exchange rates, flexible exchange rates, etc.) affect the economic system in general and the international economy in particular.

From a Keynesian (Traditional) perspective, under a fixed exchange-rate regime, a payments disequilibrium can be corrected, with the use of public policy, through price, income, and interest rate adjustments. A Monetary perspective concludes that the adjustment instead occurs through the money market. Under a true floating-rate regime, a payments correction will occur through changes in currency values. Today, the majority of economists prefer the floating-rate arrangement, contending that it is more acceptable than the often slow and ineffective mechanisms of changes in prices, nominal incomes, and interest rates.

Exchange-rate determination and the behavior of the foreign currency market are of importance to investors and multinational firms, to central banks and governments, and to academic researchers, whether they are interested in making speculative profits, protecting their investments, pursuing public objectives or improving social welfare. Exchange rates have been observed to follow certain empirical regularities, which have been formalized in economic relations and models that seek to explain and predict the behavior of the relative values of different currencies.

Various econometric techniques and tests have been used to determine the validity of different theories of exchange-rate determination. Empirical support exists for most of the models under the fixed and flexible exchange-rate systems discussed here, but the methods that have been built on these approaches have not produced very impressive results. Clearly, we have yet to generate models that will improve on the random walk theory. Overall, the evidence, from the extensive literature that exists on the subject is somewhat mixed, due either to ambiguous coefficients, data limitations, wrong assumptions (hypotheses), misspecified models, unanticipated interventions, or the high instability of the world today, which, unfortunately, we have created yet we do not correct.

Every nation must use domestic fiscal and monetary policies (as the Traditional approach believes) to reach its own objectives, but it must not ignore the need for cooperation and respect of the sovereignty for the others, especially the less wealthy and industrialized countries. The Group of Seven (G-7) and the other international organizations and institutions must increase the coordination of macroeconomic policies (stabilization of incomes, prices, exchange rates, etc.) among all nations. For an economy to be strong and stable, it must depend on, and give priorities to, first, the primary sector of the economy (agriculture, fishery, mining, etc.), while, of course, showing great respect for the environment; second, the secondary sector (manufacturing and high technology); and third, the tertiary sector (services). Economics is "not a body of concrete truth, but an engine for the discovery of concrete truth'' as Marshall (1925, p. 159) has said. Apparently we still have a long way to go with our theories, models, statistics, applications, and policy suggestions involving analysis, forecasting, and economics as a discipline.

NOTES

The authors are grateful to Karen Buholski for her valuable research assistance and to Nancy Gownley for the word processing.

1. See Krueger (1983) and Malindretos (1988).

2. The inequality is a necessary and sufficient condition for the stability of international equilibrium. See Samuelson (1947).

3. The rate of change of a variable is the same as percentage change, namely:

$$\dot{E} = \frac{\Delta E}{E} = \frac{E_t - E_{t-1}}{E_{t-1}} = e_t - e_{t-1}, \ \%\Delta E = \frac{E_t - E_{t-1}}{E_{t-1}} 100.$$

4. A similar simple-demand approach was used by Meade (1951) to illustrate possible country scenarios under a regime of fixed exchange rates.

5. Where $\varepsilon \sim N(0, \sigma^2)$ and $E(\varepsilon_i \ \varepsilon_j) = 0$ for $i \neq j$.

6. The variable representing lagged values of the effective exchange rate (E) can be used for testing a J-curve effect on the trade balance due to a devaluation of the currency. If a J-curve effect exists, the β_is must have positive values.

7. See Malindretos (1988), p. 52, and Goldstein and Khan (1978). Here, we assume an initial trade balance as depicted in equation (6).

8. The terms of trade are:

$$Q = \frac{S_{ij}P_{mj}^d}{P_{x_i}^s}$$

9. See Kallianiotis and Patel (1990).

10. Using equation (2), we can test the existence of the J-curve effect for different countries.

11. Efficiency requires perfect capital mobility and rational expectations.

12. However, if there is transaction cost, then, for example, a product that costs \$3 in the United States and 4.5 deutsche marks (DM) in Germany, the exchange rate is .6 \$/DM. Then, the parity condition requires that \$3 = .6 $(\frac{\$}{DM})$ *DM* 4.5 + \$.3. On the right-hand side, we have: *DM* 4.5 × .6 $(\frac{\$}{DM})$ = \$2.7.

There is \$.3 difference between United States and Germany. This is due to transaction cost (C_T). In practice there will be room for some divergence from the strict law of one price, so we have $P = S \ P^* + C_T$ as the open economy version of the law of one price.

13. Further investigation into the structural relationship may be necessary, which require a complete macro-asset model for exchange rate determination. See Kallianiotis (1988).

14. It should be noted that s is the natural logarithm of S, and that in general, lower case letters are logarithms of the capital counterparts.

15. See Samuelson (1966) and Fama and Farber (1979).

16. See Kallianiotis (1988).

17. On financial markets, see Dornbusch (1976).

18. See Dornbusch (1980a) and Frenkel (1980).

19. See Gilbert and Kravis (1954); Officer (1976); Rogalski and Vinso (1977); Magee (1978); Frenkel (1978); Officer, Altman, and Walter (1982); Darby (1983); Rush and Husted (1985); Manzur (1990); and Goodwin, Grennes, and Wohlgemant (1990).

20. It is impossible for anyone to perfectly forecast the future. Here the reasons are the unanticipated interventions by central banks and governments in the foreign exchange market and the high uncertainty and risk that exist—and are growing—in the world today.

21. The precise equilibrium condition was derived as

$$\frac{i_t - i_t^*}{1 + i_t^*} = fp;$$

where

$$fp = \frac{F_t - S_t}{S_t} \cdot \frac{12}{n} + 100$$

and n is the number of months in the contract.

22. See Grubel (1965), Poole (1967), Upson (1972), Aliber (1973), Frenkel and Levich (1975, 1977), and Glassman (1987).

23. There is a body of literature dealing with reasons why the interest-rate parity theorem might not hold. Aliber (1973) and Dooley and Isard (1980) argued that political risk—the probability that government and financial authorities will impose controls on foreign exchange fluctuations—is one of the factors.

24. See Mishkin (1984).

25. See Kallianiotis (1991, p. 22).

26. See Giddy and Dufey (1975); Fama (1976); Logue, Sweeney, and Willett (1978); and Kallianiotis (1985).

27. See Kallianiotis and Sum (1993).

28. See Kallianiotis and Sum (1993).

29. The sum of the current account (CA) plus the capital account (KA) and the official settlement account is zero: CA + KA = 0. Then, the balance of payments will always stay in balance.

30. See also Niehans (1965) and Sedjo (1971).

31. See, Dornbusch (1980b), p. 199.

32. The identity is $CA = -KA \equiv \Delta NFA \equiv \Delta B - \Delta DC$, where CA is the current account balance, KA is the capital account balance, ΔNFA is the change of net foreign assets, ΔB is the change of monetary base, and ΔDC is the change in domestic credit.

33. See Branson (1975).

34. Maintaining the stability of the exchange rate must also be one of the objectives of the central banks.

35. See Meese (1990).

36. Bandwagon expectations are market expectations of exchange rates formed in such a way that a depreciation in the current spot rate will generate an expectation of further depreciation over the next period.

REFERENCES

Alexander, Sidney S. "Effects of a Devaluation on a Trade Balance." *International Monetary Fund Staff Papers*, 2 (1952): 263–278.

Aliber, Robert Z. "The Interest Rate Parity Theorem: A Reinterpretation." *Journal of Political Economy*, 8, no. 6 (1973): 1451–1459.

Branson, William H., and Raymond D. Hill. *Capital Movements in the OECD Area: An Econometric Analysis*. Paris: Organization for Economic Cooperation and Development, 1971.

Cassel, Gustav. "The Present Situation of the Foreign Exchanges." *Economic Journal*, 26 (March 1916): 62–65.

Cassel, Gustav. "Abnormal Deviations in International Exchanges." *Economic Journal*, 28 (December 1918): 413–415.

Cassel, Gustav. *The World's Monetary Problems*. London: Constable, 1921.

Cumby, Robert, E., and Maurice Obstfeld. "A Note on Exchange Rate Expectations and Nominal Interest Differentials: A Test of the Fisher Hypothesis." *Journal of Finance* (June 1981): 697–703.

Darby, Michael R. "Movements in Purchasing Power Parity: The Short and Long Runs." In *The International Transmission of Inflation*, ed. Michael R. Darby and James R. Lothian. Chicago: University of Chicago Press, 1983.

Dooley, Michael P., and Peter Isard. "Capital Controls, Political Risk, and Deviations from Interest Parity Theory." *Journal of Political Economy*, 88, no. 2 (1980): 370–384.

Dornbusch, Rudiger. "Expectations and Exchange Rate Dynamics." *Journal of Political Economy*, 84 (1976): 1161–1176.

Dornbusch, Rudiger. "Exchange Rate Economics: Where Do We Stand?" *Brookings Papers on Economic Activity*, no. 1 (1980a): 195–202.

Dornbusch, Rudiger. *Open Economy Macroeconomics*. New York: Basic Books, 1980b.

Dornbusch, Rudiger, and Paul Krugman. "Flexible Exchange Rates in the Short Run." *Brookings Papers on Economic Activity*, no. 3 (1976): 537–575.

Fama, Eugene F. "Forward Rates as Predictors of Future Spot Rates." *Journal of Financial Economics*, 3, no. 4 (October 1976): 361–377.

Fama, Eugene F., and Andre Farber. "Money, Bonds and Foreign Exchange." *American Economic Review*, 69 (1979): 639–649.

Fleming, J. Marcus. "Domestic Financial Policies under Fixed and Floating Exchange Rates." *International Monetary Fund Staff Papers*, 9 (1962): 369–379.

Frenkel, Jacob. "Purchasing Power Parity: Doctrinal Perspective and Evidence from the 1920s." *Journal of International Economics* (May 1978): 169–191.

Frenkel, Jacob. "The Collapse of Purchasing Power Parities during the 1970s." NBER Working Paper no. 569. *European Economic Review*, 16, no. 1 (May 1981): 145–165.

Frenkel, Jacob, and R. M. Levich. "Covered Interest Arbitrage: Unexploited Profits?" *Journal of Political Economy*, 83, no. 2 (1975): 325–338.

Frenkel, Jacob, and R. M. Levich. "Transaction Costs and Interest Arbitrage: Tranquil versus Turbulent Periods." *Journal of Political Economy* (November–December 1977): 1209–1226.

Giddy, Ian H., and Gunter Dufey. "The Random Behavior of Flexible Exchange Rates." *Journal of International Business Studies*, 6 (Spring 1975): 1–32.

Gilbert, Milton, and Irving B. Kravis. *An International Comparison of National Products and the Purchasing Power of Currencies.* Paris: Organization for European Economic Cooperation, 1954.

Glassman, Debra. "Exchange Rate Risk and Transactions Costs: Evidence from Bid-Ask Spreads." *Journal of International Money and Finance*, 6, no. 4 (December 1987): 479–491.

Goldstein, Morris, and Mohsin Khan. "The Supply and Demand for Exports—A Simultaneous Approach." *Review of Economics and Statistics*, 60 (May 1978): 275–286.

Goodwin, Barry K., Thomas Grennes and Michael K. Wohlgemant. "Testing the Law of One Price When Trade Takes Time." *Journal of International Money and Finance*, 9, no. 1 (March 1990): 21–40.

Grubel, Herbert G. "Profits from Forward Exchange Speculation." *Quarterly Journal of Economics*, 79 (May 1965): 248–262.

Grubel, Herbert G. *Forward Exchange, Speculation and the International Flow of Capital.* Stanford, Calif.: Stanford University Press, 1966.

Houthakker, H. S., and S. P. Magee. "Income and Price Elasticities in World Trade." *Review of Economics and Statistics*, 51, no. 2 (May 1969): 111–125.

Houthakker, H. S., and Lester D. Taylor. *Consumer Demand in the U.S.: Analyses and Projections.* Cambridge, Mass.: Harvard University Press, 1970.

Kallianiotis, I. N. "Exchange Rates and Rational Expectations." Ph.D. dissertation, City University of New York, 1985.

Kallianiotis, I. N. "A Theoretical Monetary and Real Approach to the Balance of Payments." *Greek Economic Review*, 10, no. 2 (December 1988): 383–404.

Kallianiotis, I. N. "Is the U.S. Budget Deficit Harming the Financial Markets and the Overall Economy?" University of Scranton, SOM Research Report Series no. 9110, October 1991, pp. 1–49.

Kallianiotis, I. N., and Ashish Patel. "Income and Price Elasticities: U.S. Imports from and Exports to E.C. Countries." In *Northeast Decision Sciences Institute 1990 Proceedings*, ed. Paul Mangiameli. Saratoga Springs, N.Y., April 1990, pp. 115–117.

Kallianiotis, I. N., and Gisele Sum. "Real Exchange Rates and Real Interest Differentials under Uncertainty." Unpublished manuscript, University of Scranton, March 1993, pp. 1–28.

Kenen, Peter B. "Short Term Capital Movements and the U.S. Balance of Payments." In *The United States Balance of Payments.* Hearings before the Joint Economic Committee, 88th Cong., 1st Sess., 1963.

Krause, Lawrence B. "Comments and Discussion." *Brookings Papers on Economic Activity*, no 3 (1975): 546–548.

Krueger, Anne O. *Exchange Rate Determination*, Cambridge Surveys of Economic Literature. Cambridge: Cambridge University Press, 1983.

Logue, Dennis E., Richard J. Sweeney and Thomas D. Willett. "The Speculative Behavior of Foreign Exchange Rates during the Current Float." *Journal of Business Research*, 6, no. 2 (1978): 159–173.

Magee, Stephen P. "Currency Contracts, Pass-Through and Devaluation." *Brookings Papers on Economic Activity*, no 1 (1973): 303–325.

Magee, Stephen P. "Prices, Incomes, and Foreign Trade." In *International Trade and Finance*, ed. Peter Kenen. Cambridge: Cambridge University Press, 1975, p. 178.

Magee, Stephen P. "Contracting and Spurious Deviations from Purchasing Power Parity." In *The Economics of Exchange Rates*, ed. Jacob A. Frenkel and Harry G. Johnson. Reading, Mass.: Addison-Wesley, 1978, pp. 67–74.

Malindretos, John. "The Keynesian and the Monetary Approaches to International Finance: A Reexamination." *International Journal of Finance*, 1, no. 1 (Autumn 1988): 46–89.

Manzur, Meher. "An International Comparison of Prices and Exchange Rates: A New Test of Purchasing Power Parity." *Journal of International Money and Finance*, 9, no. 1 (March 1990): 75–91.

Marshall, Alfred. "The Present Position of Economics." 1885. Reprinted in *Memorials of Alfred Marshall*, ed. A. C. Pigou. London: Macmillan, 1925, pp. 152–174.

McKinnon, Ronald I. *Money in International Exchange*. New York: Oxford University Press, 1979.

Meade, James E. *The Balance of Payments*. New York: Oxford University Press, 1951.

Mishkin, Frederick S. "Are Real Interest Rates Equal across Countries? An Empirical Investigation of International Parity Conditions." *Journal of Finance*, 39, no. 5 (December 1984): 1345–1357.

Mundell, Robert A. "The Monetary Dynamics of International Adjustment under Fixed and Flexible Exchange Rates." *Quarterly Journal of Economics*, 74 (May 1960): 227–257.

Mundell, Robert A. "Capital Mobility and Stabilization Policy under Fixed and Flexible Exchange Rates." *Canadian Journal of Economics and Political Science*, 29 (1963): 475–485.

Murray, Tracy, and Peter J. Ginman. "An Empirical Examination of the Traditional Aggregate Import Demand Model." *Review of Economics and Statistics*, 58 (February 1976): 75–80.

Niehans, Jurg. "Interest Rates and the Balance of Payments: An Analysis of the Swiss Experience." In *Trade Growth and the Balance of Payments*, ed. R. E. Baldwin et al. Chicago: Rand McNally, 1965.

Officer, Lawrence H. "The Purchasing-Power-Parity Theory of Exchange Rates: A Review Article." *International Monetary Fund Staff Papers* (March 1976): 1–60.

Officer, Lawrence H., Edward I. Altman and Ingo Walter, eds. *Purchasing Power Parity and Exchange Rates: Theory, Evidence, and Relevance*. Vol. 35 of *Contemporary Studies in Economic and Financial Analysis*. London: JAI Press, 1982.

Polak, J. J. "Monetary Analysis of Income Formation and Payments Problems." *International Monetary Fund Staff Papers*, 6 (1977): 1–50.

Poole, William. "Speculative Prices as Random Walks: An Analysis of Ten Time Series of Flexible Exchange Rates." *Southern Journal of Economics*, 33 (April 1967): 468–478.

Rogalski, J., and Joseph D. Vinso. "Price Level Variations as Predictors of Flexible Exchange Rates." *Journal of International Business Studies*, 8, no. 1 (Spring/Summer 1977): 71–81.

Rush, Mark, and Steven Husted. "Purchasing Power Parity in the Long Run." *Canadian Journal of Economics*, 18, no. 1 (February 1985): 137–145.

Samuelson, Paul A. *Foundations of Economic Analysis*. Cambridge, Mass.: Harvard University Press, 1947.

Samuelson, Paul A. "Theoretical Notes on Trade Problems." In *The Collected Scientific Papers of Paul A. Samuelson*, ed. Joseph E. Stiglitz, Vol. 2. Cambridge, Mass.: MIT Press, 1966, pp. 821–830.

Sedjo, Rojer A. "Price Trends, Economic Growth and the Canadian Balance of Trade: A Three Country Model." *Journal of Political Economy*, 79 (May–June 1971): 596–613.

Tobin, James. "Liquidity Preference as Behavior towards Risk." *Review of Economic Studies* (February 1958).

Tobin, James. "Economic Progress and the International Monetary System." *Proceedings of the Academy of Political Science* (May 1963): 84–85.

Upson, Roger C. "Random Walk and Forward Exchange Rates: A Spectral Analysis." *Journal of Financial and Quantitative Analysis*, 7 (September 1972): 1897–1906.

Whitman, Marina V. N. "Global Monetarism and the Monetary Approach to the Balance of Payments." *Brookings Papers on Economic Activity*, no. 3 (1975): 491–555.

Chapter 14

Doctrinal Views on Exchange Rate Determination: An Eclectic Approach

Dilip K. Ghosh, Abraham Mulugetta and Asrat Tessema

INTRODUCTION

Foreign exchange is the transmission fluid for international transactions in global markets. Since our world has become a truly global village, these transactions and the exchange rates that underlie them have assumed a significance of paramount proportion. How are foreign exchange rates determined? This question has been raised and answered for a long time, and the discussions have formed the basis for several doctrines. From the early 1920s onward, several theoretical paradigms have been posited in attempts to explain what factors determine exchange rates or how exchange rates are determined. It is therefore essential for anyone interested in this issue that we bring out the theoretical determinants of the exchange rate as presented in the existing literature. However, since it is neither possible, nor desirable perhaps, to bring every aspect or every argument advanced in the past, we will present only the major works that attempt to answer the question: what determines the rate of foreign exchange?

Although it is very difficult to pinpoint where the issue was first discussed, it is easy to identify Cassel's (1925) *purchasing power parity* and Keynes's (1930) subsequent comments on the British exchange rate policy in the 1920s as the definitive endeavors to define the determinants of the exchange rate. Later, however, Robinson (1949), Machlup (1949), and Haberler (1949), among others, identified the exchange rate as the balancer of the flows of foreign currency demanded by domestic residents for the purchase of foreign goods and assets and the flows of foreign currency supplied by foreigners by their purchase of goods and assets created by the domestic residents. Demand and supply schedules of foreign exchange are thus derived from the corresponding demand and supply schedules for imports and exports. The equilibrium exchange rate is the

Figure 14.1
Market for British Pound: Demand and Supply Conditions

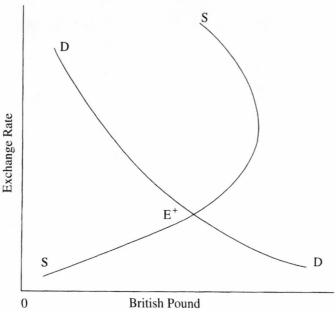

price that equates the demand for, and supply of, foreign currency. This traditional view has become the textbook approach to the determination of the foreign exchange rate. Figure 14.1 exhibits the determinants of foreign exchange and shows how foreign exchange is determined. Here the horizontal axis measures foreign exchange (say, British pounds demanded and supplied in the marketplace), and the vertical axis represents the price of foreign exchange (British pounds, in this instance), measured in terms of U.S. dollars (which is assumed to be the domestic currency for our purpose). The curves DD and SS represent, respectively, the demand for, and supply of, British pounds at each rate of exchange. The DD curve is normally negatively sloped and the SS curve is mostly positively sloped, although a backward bouncing situation is a distinct possibility. The intersection of these two schedules defines the equilibrium price of British pounds in terms of U.S. dollars and identifies the equilibrium exchange rate. Here E^+ is the equilibrium exchange rate.

THE BALANCE OF PAYMENTS APPROACH

If one looks back at this exposition, it is almost inescapable to accept the fact that the equilibrium exchange rate is the value of British pounds that brings about the balance of payments equilibrium (BP). The balance of payments equilibrium (BP = 0) of the United States is described as follows:

$$BP = 0 = X(EP^*/P, Y^*) - M(EP^*/P, Y) + K_I(r, r^*, s) - K_O(r, r^*, s) \quad (1)$$
$$+ \; UT + NFR + EO,$$

where X = export earnings, M = import expenditure, K_I = capital inflows, K_O = capital outflows, UT = unilateral transfers, NFR = net foreign reserves, and EO = errors and omissions, all expressed in U.S. dollar terms. The symbols inside the brackets are the arguments of these functions of export earnings (X), import expenditure (M), capital inflows (K_I) and capital outflows (K_O); E represents exchange rate ($\$/£$), P stands for domestic price, P^* is foreign price, Y is domestic national income, Y^* is foreign income, r is domestic interest rate, r^* is foreign interest rate, and s captures the speculative variable. EP^*/P measures competitiveness in trade transactions. It is expected that the following conditions normally hold:

$$\frac{\partial X}{\partial [EP^*/P]} > 0, \; \frac{\partial M}{\partial (EP^*/P)} < 0, \; \frac{\partial X}{\partial Y^*} > 0, \; \frac{\partial M}{\partial Y} > 0, \; \frac{\partial K_I}{\partial r} > 0,$$
$$\frac{\partial K_I}{\partial r^*} < 0, \; \frac{\partial K_O}{\partial r} < 0, \; \frac{\partial K_O}{\partial r^*} > 0.$$

Taking exports and imports together, on the one hand, and capital inflows and outflows on the other, one can rewrite the balance of payments equilibrium as follows:

$$BP = 0 = CUB(EP^*/P, Y, Y^*) + CAB(r, r^*, s), \quad (1')$$

treating errors and omissions as negligible. Here current account balance (CUB) is $X - M + UT$, and capital account balance (CAB) is $K_I - K_O + NFR$. In condition of equilibrium, $BP = O$, which implies that $CUB + CAB = O$. At a given exchange rate, say $E = E_0$ the CUB schedule is, as Ghosh (1987) noted, negatively sloped with respect to r (given r^*), as shown in Figure 14.2, owing to the normal Keynesian open-economy multiplier. The logic is as follows: as the domestic interest rate drops, domestic investment expenditure, *ceteris paribus*, goes up, which in terms raises the domestic national income higher via the investment multiplier; moreover, increased income increases the import expenditure alone, without affecting domestic exports. This sequence of events tends to create a deterioration in the current account balance, which is portrayed in Figure 14.2. Capital account balance is obviously a positively sloped function of (domestic) interest rate (see Figure 14.2). The intersection of these schedules determines the equilibrium interest rate, r_0^+ for $CUB(E_0)$. That is, the current account balance schedule (corresponding to exchange rate E_0), and the capital account balance schedule (denoted by CAB), yield the equilibrium interest rate, r_0^+. If the exchange rate were E_1 (where $E_1 > E_0$), the current account balance schedule would be defined by a further inward curve such as $CUB(E_1)$ and the equilibrium interest rate would be lower (as with r_1^+ in Figure 14.2). What tran-

Figure 14.2
Current Account and Capital Account Balance and the Shift Thereof

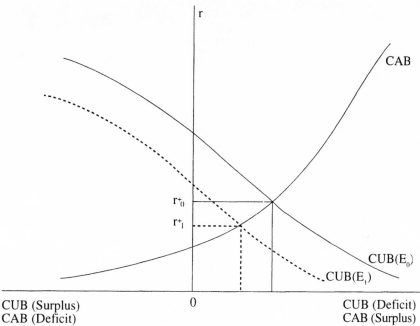

CUB (Surplus)   0   CUB (Deficit)
CAB (Deficit)   CAB (Surplus)

spires is a trade-off between the interest rate and exchange rate to maintain balance of payments equilibrium (this relationship is exhibited in Figure 14.3). In a different fashion, Dornbusch (1979) presented the same relationship; he furthermore showed that the long-run trade-off schedule is steeper (see the dotted curve in Figure 14.3).

THE FLEMING-MUNDELL APPROACH

Following further the Keynesian open-economy framework in terms of IS, LM, and BP (that is balance of payments equilibrium) within the quadrant with domestic interest rate and domestic income, Fleming (1962) and Mundell (1968) expositions under perfect capital mobility are described by Figure 14.4. As perfect mobility signifies a uniform interest rate across nations with the maintenance of balance of payments balance, the overall equilibrium is attained when the downward-sloping IS curve, upward-sloping LM curve, and horizontal BP curve intersect (at, say, point Z). If the interest rate had been lower, capital outflows would have occurred that would have tended to, as Dornbusch (1979) put it, "swamp any current account surplus," and in the opposite scenario, the opposite picture would appear. If, for some reasons, the interest rate happened to be lower to begin with, say, at r_1 (corresponding to the intersection of the IS_1 and LM

Figure 14.3
Exchange-Rate–Interest-Rate Tradeoff

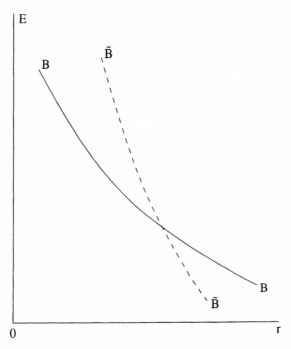

curves), the interest rate would have to go up to contain the demand for money to match the existing supply of money underlying the given LM schedule. Note here that since in this open economy, the IS_1 schedule is impacted by current account balance (which is influenced by income level and competitiveness), following an incipient currency depreciation, the IS_1 schedule will move upward to the right to the IS schedule, and thus the cycle of reactions and market adjustments will restore the equilibrium interest rate (consistent with Z).

Next, consider an exogenous increase in money supply in the economy. Obviously, as a consequence to such an increase, the LM curve will move to the right to, say, point LM^1, and the interest rate will move down to r_2. The drop in interest rate then will induce a depreciation, and thereby a shift to the top-right of the IS curve (to, say, IS^1), thus restoring the overall equilibrium interest rate, r^+_0.

THE PORTFOLIO BALANCE APPROACH

The Portfolio Balance Model, as enunciated and interpreted by Dornbusch (1979), Dornbusch and Fischer (1980), Boyer (1977), Kouri (1975, 1980), and others in the mid-1970s and later, is a step forward in modeling the exchange

Figure 14.4
Open Economy IS–LM Interaction

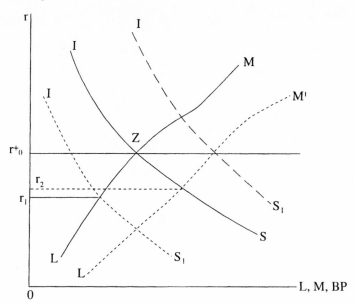

rate determination by postulating a limited substitution between domestic and foreign assets as opposed to a high degree of substitution between such assets as was envisioned in the Fleming-Mundell framework. In this portfolio balance model, the building blocks are as follows:

$$M = \alpha(r, r^*)W;\ \alpha_r < 0,\ \alpha_{r^*} < 0;\tag{2}$$
$$X = \beta(r, r^*)W;\ \beta_r > 0,\ \beta_{r^*} < 0;\tag{3}$$
$$W = M + EF + X\tag{4}$$

In other terms:

$$EF = (1 - \alpha - \beta)W \equiv \gamma(r, r^*)W;\ \gamma_r < 0,\ \gamma_t^* > 0\tag{5}$$

Equation (2) defines the condition of monetary equilibrium that states that the demand for domestic money (M) equals the fraction ($\alpha([r, r^*]$) of total nominal wealth (W). Equation (3) states that equilibrium in the market for domestic assets occurs when the existing supply (X) equals the demand. The notation $\beta(r, r^*)$ denotes the desired ratio of domestic assets to wealth. Equation (4) is the wealth constraint, where F is the value of the net holdings of foreign assets, and equation (5) then defines the equilibrium condition in the market for foreign assets.

Figure 14.5 portrays the equilibrium interest and exchange rates. The upward-

Figure 14.5
Internal and External Balances

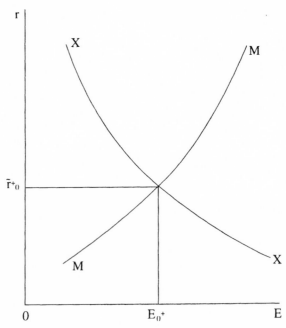

sloping schedule MM shows the constellation of interest and exchange rate pairs (r, E) for which the domestic money market is in equilibrium, and the downward sloping schedule XX shows the constellation of interest and exchange rate pairs (r, E) for which the domestic asset market is in equilibrium. The notations r^+_0 and E^+_0 are, obviously, the equilibrium interest and exchange rates in the environment described in this diagram. Here one can go a step further and assert that if the foreign interest rate rises for any reason, there will be an excess supply of domestic money and securities. This will trigger a rightward shift of both the MM and XX schedules, which then will inevitably cause a depreciation of the exchange rate. Consider next the effect of an increase in domestic money supply on the exchange rate. From equations (2) through (4) taken together, one can easily obtain the following:

$$\frac{dE}{dM} = \frac{\beta_r \gamma + \beta(\beta_r + \alpha_r)}{F(\alpha\beta_r - \beta\alpha_r)} > 0 \qquad (6)$$

Thus, it can be shown that an increase in domestic money supply causes a deterioration in the exchange rate.

It ought to be noted that this model is couched in a partial equilibrium framework, and thus it fails to bring out the interaction of the goods market and the financial markets. However, Dornbusch (1979) contends that "it extends the monetary model because we do not have to rely on shifts in money demand or supply as sole determinants of exchange rate movements" (p. 348). The question then is: what is the monetary model for exchange rate determination?

THE MONETARY APPROACH

Many works have surfaced in the decade of 1970s on the determination of exchange rates based on money as a major factor. Frenkel (1976), among others, provides a clear exposition of the doctrinal approach and empirical evidence on this issuee. The basic monetary model is the virtual extension of the Quantity Theory of Money in the open economic structure. The Fisherian Quantity Theory of Money states that $MV = PQ$, whence:

$$P = MV/Q, \tag{7a}$$

$$P^* = M^*V^*/Q^* \tag{7b}$$

where V and V^* are the measures of the velocity of circulation of money in domestic and foreign economies, respectively. The variable Q represents the aggregate domestic product (real domestic income), and Q^* is the aggregate foreign national product (real foreign income). Add to this structure the purchasing power parity, and the monetary model of exchange rate determination emerges. The purchasing power parity doctrine, brought out first by Cassel (1925), is one of the fundamental ingredients in the Monetary approach to exchange rate determination. Purchasing power parity means that in absolute terms, $P = EP^*$, where P and P^* denote the domestic and foreign price levels, respectively. In simple language, if £1 = \$2 is the exchange rate between the British pound and the U.S. dollar, and if £20,000 buys a certain model of automobile, then \$40,000 will buy the same model.

From $P = EP^*$, one gets, following logarithmic differentiation, $\hat{E} = \hat{P} - \hat{P}^*$, where $\hat{P} \equiv dP/P$, and $\hat{P}^* \equiv dP^*/P^*$. That is, the exchange rate change (in percentage) equals the inflation rate differential between the domestic and foreign economies. However, Frenkel (1981) observed that "during the 1970s short-run changes in exchange rates bore little relationship to short-run diffentials in national inflation rates, and frequently, divergencies from purchasing power parities have been cumulative" (p. 227). Many economists share the same view.

Note that from the purchasing power parity relation, one can get:

$$E = P/P^* \tag{8}$$

Substituting (7a) and (7b) into (8), we obtain the following expression:

$$E = \left(\frac{M}{M^*}\right)\left(\frac{Y^*}{Y}\right)\left(\frac{V}{V^*}\right)$$

(9)

The logarthmic differentiation of equation (9) yields the percentage change in the exchange rate as follows:

$$\hat{E} = (\hat{M} - \hat{M}^*) + (\hat{Y}^* - \hat{Y}) + (\hat{V} - \hat{V}^*)$$

(10)

where a "hat" (Λ) over a variable signifies the percentage change in that variable (that is, $\hat{E} \equiv \dfrac{dE}{E}$, etc.). Expression (10) then states that percentage change in the exchange rate is equal to the percentage change in the money supply of the domestic economy relative to that in the foreign economy ($\hat{M} - \hat{M}^*$) plus percentage change in aggregate foreign national product relative to that in the domestic economy ($\hat{Y} - \hat{Y}^*$) plus the relative percentage change in velocity of circulation in the home economy ($\hat{V} - \hat{V}^*$). If one assumes that velocity depends on income level and the cost of holding money, or more specifically,

$$V = Q^{\epsilon-1}e^{\eta r},$$

(11a)

$$V = Q^{*\epsilon-1}e^{\eta r^*}$$

(11b)

then expression (10) comes out as follows:

$$\hat{E} = (\hat{M} - \hat{M}^*) + \epsilon(\hat{Y}^* - \hat{Y}) + \eta(r - r^*)$$

(12)

Here ϵ and η are the elasticity parameters of incomes and interest rates. This is the monetary model of exchange determination.

Moving further beyond the portfolio balance model, which has been characterized as an extension of the monetary model, Dornbusch (1979) introduced dynamics and expectations in the synthetic analytical structure behind exchange rate. In the open Fisher parity,

$$r - r^* = (\frac{\tilde{E}}{E} - 1)$$

(13)

where $(\dfrac{\tilde{E}}{E} - 1)$ is the expected depreciation of the domestic currency. From equation (13) one easily gets the following:

$$E = \frac{\tilde{E}}{1 + r - r^*}$$

(14)

It thus brings out the fact that movement of the current rate of exchange is predicated on either changes in expectations over the future course of exchange rates and/or changes in interest rate differentials, given expectations. Now, if we can assume that the foreign interest rate is given, and we can postulate the following functional relation for the domestic interest rate:

$$r = r(M/P, Q) \tag{15}$$

The expected (future) exchange rate $(\tilde{E})$ is a function of the terms of trade (σ) and of the long-run price relative $(\dfrac{\tilde{P}}{\tilde{P}*})$:

$$\tilde{E} = \sigma( )\frac{\tilde{P}}{\tilde{P}*} = \sigma( )\frac{\kappa\tilde{M}}{\kappa^*\hat{M}*} \tag{16}$$

where $\tilde{M}$ and $\tilde{M}^*$ are the expected future stocks of money supply in home and foreign economies, and κ and κ^* are the factors of proportionality, respectively. Plugging in these functional relations in equation (14), one gets expression (17):

$$E = \frac{\sigma( )\dfrac{\kappa\tilde{M}}{\kappa^*\tilde{M}*}}{1 + r(\dfrac{M}{P},Q) - r^*} \equiv E(\sigma, M/P, Q; \kappa, \kappa^*, \tilde{M}, \tilde{M}*) \tag{17}$$

Figure 6 exhibits the equilibrium exchange rate, as defined by equation (16). Here the vertical axis measures P, and the horizontal axis measures E. The AA curve shows, *ceteris paribus*, the trade-off between domestic price level and exchange rate. Note that for every increase in P there will be a rise in r, and thus a differential in favor of the home economy. To offset this situation, E has to go down to the point where it equals $r - r^*$. If money supply increases in the long run and all prices remain flexible, prices will increase, as will the exchange rate in the same proportion. This will then cause a shift of the AA curve to the BB curve, as shown in Figure 14.6, and the long-run equilibrium constellation of (P, E) will be at A', with all the real variables remaining unchanged.

In the short run, however, price level may not respond to the change in the money supply, and hence, the nominal and real stocks of money will be virtually identical in size. Under this situation, an increase in nominal money supply will induce a drop in interest rate, which then will trigger a net capital outflow to the point where the exchange rate depreciates enough to create the expectation of appreciation to match the interest rate differential. In this scenario, the economy moves to the point A", which defines the true long-run exchange rate. This overshooting of exchange rate is the result of a permanent monetary expansion

Figure 14.6
Domestic Price and Exchange-Rate Tradeoffs over Time

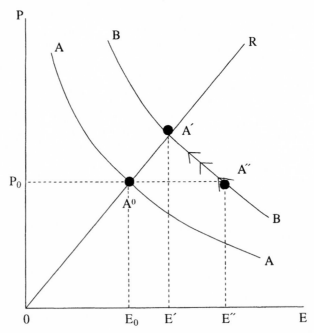

in a situation of price rigidity and capital mobility. If the short-run sticky price condition disappears over time, the equilibrium will move to A' (along BB schedule in Figure 14.6).

Exchange rate determination is a continuous search. Understanding what determines the exchange rate depends on all the theories and factors we have just enunciated. The relative strength of each factor or theory will vary in different situations, and speculation on such movement continually adds new forces to the dynamics driving its path over time.

REFERENCES

Boyer, R. "Devaluation and Portfolio Balance." *American Economic Review*, 67, no. 2 (March 1977): 54–63.

Cassel, G. "Rates of Exchange and Purchasing Power Parity." *Skandinaviska Kerditaktieholaget Quarterly Report*, 98 (1925): 325–336.

Dornbusch, R. "Monetary Policy under Exchange Rate Flexibility." Conference Series no. 20. Federal Reserve Bank of Boston, 1979, pp. 1–27.

Dornbusch, R., and S. Fisher. "Exchange Rate and the Current Account." *American Economic Review*, 70, no. 5 (1980): 960–971.

Fleming, J. M. "Domestic Financial Policies under Fixed and Floating Exchange Rates." *International Monetary Fund Staff Papers*, 9 (1962): 369–379.

Frenkel, J. A. "A Monetary Approach to the Exchange Rate: Doctrinal Aspects and Empirical Evidence." *Scandinavian Journal of Economics* (May 1976): 200–224.

Frenkel, J. A. "The Collapse of Purchasing Power Parities during the 1970s." NBER Working Paper no. 569. *European Economic Review*, 16, no. 1 (May 1981): 145–165.

Ghosh, D. K. "Some Comments on the Economics of Exchange Rate." In *Asia-Pacific Economies: Promises and Challenges: Research in International Business and Finance*, ed. M. Dutta. Greenwich, Conn.: JAI Press, 1987, pp. 303–307.

Haberler, G. "The Market for Foreign Exchange and the Stability of the Balance of Payments: A Theoretical Analysis." *Kyklos*, 115 (1949): 781–789.

Keynes, J. M. *A Treatise on Money*. Vol. 1. London, 1930.

Kouri, P. "The Theory of Exchange Rates." Ph.D. dissertation, Massachusetts Institute of Technology, 1975.

Kouri, P. "Monetary Policy, the Balance of Payments, and the Exchange Rate." In *The Functioning of Floating Exchange Rates: Theory, Evidence, and Policy Implications*, ed. D. Bigman and T. Taya. Cambridge, Mass.: Ballinger Publishing Company, 1980, pp. 168–181.

Machlup, F. "The Theory of Foreign Exchanges." In *Readings in the Theory of International Trade*, ed. H. S. Ellis and L. A. Metzler. Philadelphia: Blakiston, 1949, pp. 334–349.

Mundell, R. A. *International Economics*. New York, Macmillan, 1968.

Murphy, R. G., and C. Van Duyne. "Asset Market Approaches to Exchange Rate Determination: A Comparative Analysis." *Weltwirtschaftliches Archive*, 116, no. 4 (1980): 627–656.

Robinson, J. "The Foreign Exchanges." In *Essays in the Theory of Employment*. 2nd ed. Oxford, U.K.: Blackwell, 1947. Reprinted in *Readings in the Theory of International Trade*, ed. H. S. Ellis and L. A. Metzler. Philadelphia: Blakiston, 1949, pp. 129–143.

Part VII

Empirical Evidence on Exchange Rate Determination

Chapter 15

Recent Evidence on the Determinants of Foreign Exchange Rates

Demetrios Giannaros

INTRODUCTION

Foreign exchange-rate fluctuation has been an issue of discussion by economists for a very long time. It was not until the decision by the United States to move toward a flexible exchange-rate system in the 1970s that empirical investigations to determine the cause of variations in the exchange rate became a very prominent subject. Since then, exchange-rate determination has evolved to a stage characterized by many theoretical models specified and tested empirically in an attempt to explain exchange-rate behavior and develop appropriate forecasts. The task has been very difficult, given the complexities of the macroeconomic linkages both domestically and within the global economy context—variables that influence, directly and indirectly, the value of a currency relative to another. Many issues seem to be still unresolved. In this chapter, we present the basic ideas of two competing theoretical exchange-rate models and discuss empirical evidence of the most recent period.

Although numerous articles have been written on this subject with different perspectives, two basic theoretical views have dominated the discussion since the 1970s. One of the prominent exchange-rate determination theoretical models is the Monetary approach (MA), which emphasizes the impact of monetary-related variables. The other primary model developed is the Portfolio Balance approach (PBA), which emphasizes the impact of balance of payments related variables on foreign exchange rates. This model is also referred to as the Traditional or the Keynesian-type model in some of the literature examining the determination of exchange-rate variation.

THE BASIC EXCHANGE-RATE MODELS

The Monetary approach, as developed by Francisco Rivera-Batiz and Luis Rivera-Batiz (1994), states that the exchange rate is the price of a nation's currency relative to that of another currency, and thus, just as with any other relative price, its value should be determined by the supply-and-demand conditions for the two monies being exchanged. More specifically, the money supply and demand for both the domestic and foreign money markets must be at equilibrium. Moreover, exchange rates impact money market equilibrium through their linkage to the domestic and foreign prices. Therefore, assuming absolute purchasing power parity (PPP) and expressing the equation in terms of exchange rates, we get:

$$e = P/P^* \qquad (1)$$

where e is the exchange rate, P is the domestic prices variable, and P* is a measure for foreign prices. This expression implies that a higher domestic price relative to international prices will result in an increased exchange in order to maintain purchasing power parity between the two currencies in question. It is clear, then, that the Monetary approach assumes PPP and money market equilibrium in both the domestic and foreign markets. If these assumptions are incorporated into the exchange-rate equation (1) and we express the money equilibrium equation in terms of prices (P = M/L [i, Y] for the domestic market, and P* = M* /L*[i*, Y*] for the foreign market), we get the exchange-rate equation:

$$e = [M L^*(i^*, Y^*)/M^* L(i, Y)] \qquad (2)$$

The Monetary approach equation, shown as equation (2), expresses the exchange rate as a function of the relative money supplies and the demand for foreign money supply relative to demand for domestic supply. Therefore, equation (2) is used as the theoretical basis for various modified equations employed in a number of studies testing the validity of the MA. Simplistically speaking (for more details on derivation, see Rivera-Batiz and Rivera-Batiz, 1994, pp. 553–560), the basic equation used to test the MA approach to exchange-rate determination is a function of the changes in the relative money supplies (M − M*), in the relative income (Y − Y*), and in the relative interest rates (i − i*) between the domestic and foreign markets in question. Therefore, the standard Monetary approach equation examined is expressed as:

$$e = (M - M^*) + f(Y - Y^*) + z(i - i^*) \qquad (3)$$

Equation (3) and its variants have been tested extensively since the 1970s. However, this approach has been questioned by those who believe that the Monetary approach's assumption of perfect substitutability between domestic and foreign bonds is unrealistic and instead assume imperfect domestic and foreign bonds markets. Those who adhere to the portfolio balance approach (PBA) of foreign exchange-rate determination suggest that the short-run exchange rate is determined by the conditions of demand for, and supply of, financial assets in the domestic market relative to the foreign market. They contend that domestic and foreign bonds or other financial assets are not perfect substitutes because of different levels of risk (political, default, and currency exchange) and inter-country differences in liquidity, regulation, taxes, and so forth. Furthermore, if the exchange rate is affected by the relative demand for assets in the two economic environments, then changes in current accounts of the balance of payments will cause changes in exchange rates. As per MacDonald and Taylor (1992, pp. 8–9), "a surplus (deficit) of their current account represents a rise (fall) in net domestic holdings of foreign assets, which in turn affects the level of wealth, which in turn affects the level of asset demand, which again affects the exchange rate." Therefore, in the short run, the exchange rate is a function of the relative demand and supply of assets. In this model (MacDonald and Taylor, 1992), wealth (W), domestic demand, and its components are defined as:

$$W = M + B + SF \tag{4}$$

$$M = M(r, r^*)W \tag{5}$$

$$B = B(r, r^*)W \tag{6}$$

$$SF = F(r, r^*)W \tag{7}$$

where M is domestic money, B measures issues of domestic bonds, SF is a measure of foreign bonds denominated in foreign currency, and r and r* are the domestic and foreign interest rates, respectively. According to this theory, an increase in money supply increases nominal financial wealth, increases the demand for domestic and foreign bonds and, as foreign bonds are bought, causes the exchange rate to depreciate. A reduced-form exchange-rate equation, using the portfolio balance approach, may be derived from equations (4) through (7) and may be expressed as follows (see MacDonald and Taylor, 1992, p. 17; or Branson, Halttunen, and Masson, 1977):

$$e = g(M, M^*, B, B^*, fB, fB^*) \tag{8}$$

where fB and fB* measure foreign holdings of domestic and foreign bonds, respectively. Equation (8) can be considered the basic model for the PBA approach. The empirical studies testing both the theoretical propositions use variations of the basic models summarized in this section.

BRIEF REVIEW OF SOME RECENT EMPIRICAL STUDIES

Exchange-rate determination has attracted a plethora of studies over the last 25 years. It is probably one of the most studied areas since the floating exchange-rate system was reintroduced in the early 1970s. Among other things, exchange rates impact the flow of goods, investments, money, and relative prices between nations. Furthermore, the flexible exchange-rate system, relative to the fixed exchange-rate system, has introduced a new element of transaction risk in international trade among nations and individuals. Therefore, many empirical studies have been carried out to determine which model captures most accurately the behavior of exchange-rate fluctuations and/or which may be a better exchange-rate forecasting model.

John Malindretos (1988) and MacDonald and Taylor (1992) present in great detail the theoretical propositions of these two, competing balance-of-payment and exchange-rate theories. Malindretos reviewed extensively the theoretical underpinnings of the Monetary and Portfolio Balance (Traditional) approaches and empirical evidence, primarily from the 1960s and 1970s. Moreover, he carried out a substantial empirical analysis for the case of the Federal Republic of Germany (Malindretos, 1986). He used the basic theoretical equations reflecting the Monetary and Traditional approaches to exchange rate determination and the exchange rate's influence on the trade balance to examine the validity of the models. In this study, Malindretos found that "in terms of signs of the parameters test both theories have merit." He concluded that the two theories are "complements not substitutes to each other. . . . no one can claim superiority. . . . there is merit for both . . . in explaining movements of goods, securities, and money across nations" (Malindretos, 1986, pp. 87–88). However, the emphasis of his study was on the effects of exchange rates on the balance of payments accounts.

In a more recent survey article on exchange-rate economics, Ronald MacDonald and Mark Taylor (1992) thoroughly reviewed the exchange-rate determination literature. In this article, they analyzed different exchange-rate models of the Monetary and Portfolio Balance approaches. They also examined a number of empirical studies (spanning from the 1970s through 1992) which applied either the Monetary and/or the Portfolio Balance approaches to exchange-rate determination. After elaborately reviewing many empirical studies, MacDonald and Taylor concluded that the asset-approach models may have performed well during certain sample periods but not others. They attribute this weakness to econometric and economic misspecification and state that the "breakdown in performance of the *monetary approach* could be due to omission of important variables such as the current account, wealth, and risk factors" (1992, p. 24). This, of course, implies that a synthesis of the two basic theories of exchange-rate determination may be necessary to capture all the endogenous and exogenous macroeconomic effects. This view is also presented, although in somewhat different context, by Malindretos (1996), who suggested that both the predominant theories have something to offer in analyzing exchange-rate behavior. After an evaluation of more recent propositions, MacDonald and Taylor (1992, p. 2) concluded that "despite extensive research, a large number of unresolved issues still remain, and exchange rate economics continues to be an extremely challenging area."

In 1995, a number of articles again addressed issues pertaining to exchange-rate determination for the two basic, competing models—the Monetary and the Portfolio Balance approaches. The empirical results continue to show mixed performance for the two theories.

Recently, Moazzami and Gupta (1995) examined the basic theoretical propositions of the *quantity theory of money*. They tested empirically the validity of the neutrality hypothesis, the Fisher hypothesis, and the Monetary approach to exchange-rate determination. The study was applied to six developed countries (United States, Canada, France, Germany, Italy, and Great Britain). They tested the three propositions independently and jointly. The latter approach was carried out to determine whether all three propositions can be satisfied simultaneously. They used a "dynamic framework which incorporates the long-run proposition as its steady-state solution while allowing for short-run deviation from the hypothesized long-run relationships to take place" (I, p. 1). The empirical results in this study indicate some support for the Monetary model of exchange rates. Their finding "supports the neutrality proposition in three countries, the Fisher hypothesis for all six countries and the *monetary approach* to exchange rate determination for five countries" (I, p. 680). They also found, in two countries, evidence for the joint hypothesis—that all three variants of the quantity theory of money existed simultaneously. It is obvious that this study's empirical analysis supports the MA approach in explaining variations in exchange rates.

In another recent study, Karfakis and Kim (1995) examined the impact of current account news announcements on exchange rates for Australia. More specifically, they used a Portfolio Balance approach model to test the impact of current account news announcements on a number of Australian exchange rates. Their portfolio balance model seems to perform well in explaining the effect of current account news on the exchange rates. They concluded that "these results infer that market participants had the *portfolio balance* model of exchange rate determination in mind when they responded to news" (I, p. 593).

Sarantis and Stewart (1993) and Sarantis (1994) also tested the validity of alternative Monetary approach, Portfolio Balance and Modified Uncovered Interest Parity models. Their studies conclude that the Monetary approach exchange-rate models lacked significantly in performance and are not appropriate for exchange-rate forecasting. However, cointegration tests revealed that the Portfolio Balance model and a Modified Uncovered Interest Parity model relationship observed long-run equilibrium. In a recent study by Sarantis and Stewart (1995), the authors compared the out-of-sample forecasting capability of structural, BVAR and VAR models for different sterling exchange rates. Their forecasting model validation uses the Portfolio Balance and the Modified

Uncovered Interest Parity models. The latter approach synthesizes some of the characteristics of both of the other two models. Sarantis and Stewart concluded that these structural equations perform better than the BVAR and VAR models in the medium term. The Modified Uncovered Interest Parity model outperformed the Portfolio Balance model. However, the BVAR models performed better in forecasting short-term sterling exchange-rate fluctuations. Moreover, "the ranking performance of the models differs for different forecast horizons" (1995, p. 212).

CONCLUSION

This chapter reviewed briefly the theoretical underpinnings of the two exchange-rate models used most frequently to study and/or forecast foreign exchange rates. The Monetary approach and Portfolio Balance approach models of exchange-rate determination have been studied extensively. The former explains changes in exchange rates as a monetary phenomenon, whereas the latter expresses them as a function of variables related to changes in the balance of payments and financial assets held between two nations.

Although this review of the literature regarding empirical studies testing these propositions was not exhaustive, the results indicate that neither exchange theory has consistently performed well. The empirical findings differ, depending on time frame (time-series sample) studied, short term versus long term, specific foreign exchange rate studied, use of single equation versus simultaneous equations and similar factors. Two decades after the completion of extensive research on this subject, it is clear that there is no acceptable unified theory of exchange-rate determination. The simultaneity effects, globalization of markets, domestic and external economy linkage effects, market shocks, inefficiency and continuous transformation of markets and technological advancements affecting markets create more exchange-rate uncertainty and volatility. Therefore, different models of one approach, another approach, or a synthesis of the two major competing theories of exchange-rate determination may be appropriate for different exchange rates and different time horizons. Undoubtedly, research and evaluation will continue for as long as empirical results continue to present different conclusions on the various exchange-rate models being tested.

REFERENCES

Branson, William H., Hannu Halttunen and Paul Mason. "Exchange Rates in the Short Run: The Dollar-Deutschenmark Rate." *European Economic Review*, 10 (December 1977): 303–324.

Karfakis, Costas, and Suk-Joong Kim. "Exchange Rates, Interest Rates and Current Account News: Some Evidence from Australia." *Journal of International Money and Finance*, 14, no. 4 (1995): 575–595.

MacDonald, Ronald, and Mark P. Taylor. "Exchange Rate Economics: A Survey." *International Monetary Fund Staff Papers*, 39, no. 1 (March 1992): 1–57.

Malindretos, John. "A Theoretical and Empirical Comparison of the Two Theories of International Finance: The Case of the Federal Republic of Germany." Ph.D. dissertation, Rutgers University, 1986.

Malindretos, John. "The Keynesian and the Monetary Approaches to International Finance: A Reexamination." *International Journal of Finance*, 1, no. 1 (Autumn 1988): 46–89.

Moazzami, Bakhtiar, and Kanhaya L. Gupta. "The Quantity Theory of Money and Its Long-Run Implications." *Journal of Macroeconomics*, 17, no. 4 (Fall 1995): 667–681.

Rivera-Batiz, Francisco L., and Luis A. Rivera-Batiz. *International Finance and Open Economy Macroeconomics*. 2nd ed. New York: Macmillan, 1994.

Sarantis, Nicholas. "The Monetary Exchange Rate Model in the Long-Run: An Empirical Investigation." *Weltwirtschaftliches Archiv*, 130, no. 4 (1994): 698–711.

Sarantis, Nicholas, and Chris Stewart. "Monetary and Asset Models for Sterling Exchange Rates: A Cointegration Approach." Economics Discussion Paper 93/1. United Kingdom: Kingston University, 1993.

Sarantis, Nicholas, and Chris Stewart. "Structural, VAR and BVAR Models of Exchange Rate Determination: A Comparison of Their Forecasting Performance." *Journal of Forecasting*, 14 (1995): 201–215.

Wolff, Christian C. P. "Exchange Rates, Innovations and Forecasting." *Journal of International Money and Finance*, 7 (1988): 49–61.

Chapter 16

A Re-examination of the Monetary Approach to the Exchange Rate: A Long-Run Approach

Bill Francis, Iftekhar Hasan and James R. Lothian

INTRODUCTION

As the 1980s drew to a close, the consensus view in international finance was that purchasing power parity (PPP) was of little use empirically and, moreover, that models of exchange-rate behavior that used it as a building block were also of little practical relevance.[1] In the past five years, however, such assessments have had to be tempered as studies have increasingly shown that as a long-run equilibrium condition, PPP has, in fact, been a useful first approximation, both historically and, according to several quite recent articles, under the current float.[2]

The purpose of this chapter is to see whether the more favorable findings with regard to purchasing power parity carry over to the Monetary approach to exchange rates (MAER). Evidence to date on this subject has been rather scanty and somewhat mixed.[3] The results that we report here for the Canadian-U.S. dollar rate do, however, support the MAER, particularly as a long-run equilibrium relation. We present these results in the third section of the chapter, after deriving the basic MAER model and reviewing the existing empirical work both on the MAER and, because it is closely related, on PPP. The last section of the chapter contains our conclusions along with several suggestions with regard to future work in this area.

THEORY AND PREVIOUS EVIDENCE

At the heart of the Monetary approach to exchange rates (MAER) are two essential elements, the quantity theory of money and the purchasing power parity theorem.

A three-equation system that gives rise to the MAER can therefore be written as:

$$s_t = p_t - p, \tag{1}$$

$$p_t = m_t - a(y_t) + \lambda i_t, \tag{2}$$

$$p = m - a(y_t)\lambda_i, \tag{3}$$

where s is the nominal exchange rate, p and p* are the domestic and foreign price levels, m and m* are the domestic and foreign money supplies, y and y* are domestic and foreign real income, i_t and i are domestic and foreign nominal interest rates, a and λ are parameters of the money demand functions (assumed to be the same in both countries), and where all variables other than the interest rates are in logarithmic form. Combining equations (1), (2) and (3) results in the basic version of the MAER:

$$s_t = [m_t - a(y_t) + i_t] - [m - a(y) + i], \tag{4}$$

in which the nominal exchange rate is seen as solely a function of the excess supplies of money in the two countries.

Equation (4) thus embodies the commonsense notion that countries that follow relatively expansive monetary policies will see their exchange rates depreciate, while countries that follow relatively restrictive policies will see their exchange rates appreciate. As such, it is best viewed as a longer-term equilibrium relationship, though in early empirical applications it was, at times, applied to higher-frequency (quarterly, or even monthly) data. In our tests of the model, we exploit this equilibrium property.

Because all of the variables in equation (4) have generally been found to be nonstationary in levels but stationary in first differences—that is, I(1), the equilibrium posited by equation (4) can only occur if s_t and the right-hand variables in (4), the "fundamentals" influencing nominal exchange rates, form a cointegrating relationship. Only then will their linear combination be stationary, or I(0), short-run deviations of s_t from the value consistent with the values of the fundamentals become zero in the long run. To test the long-run implications of the model, we therefore test for cointegration between s_t and the fundamentals.

Previous Results

The initial empirical versions of the MAER that were based on equation (4) worked well (e.g., Bilson, 1978; Frenkel, 1976). In the early 1980s, however, the performance of even the less-restrictive versions of the MAER began to suffer. They produced parameter estimates that were inconsistent with theory and, at times, even had the wrong sign, and they explained little of the actual variation in nominal exchange rates (Frankel, 1984). In forecasting, they proved inferior to simple random-walk models in ex post dynamic simulations (Meese and Rogoff, 1983). By the close of the decade, the models had been largely, though not unanimously, written off as failures.[4] In this regard, and not surprisingly given the link between the two, their fate was similar to that of the concept of purchasing power parity.

Since then, however, purchasing power parity has found increasing empirical support. Studies of long-term historical data indicate that deviations from PPP, though persistent and often substantial, dissipate almost completely in the end.[5] Real exchange rates, therefore, can be characterized as mean reverting, rather than, as had been argued a scant half-decade previously, as random walks. A series of very recent studies using data for the current float exclusively reached much the same conclusions.[6]

At the same time, some evidence of the improved performance of MAER models has begun to surface. Using cointegration tests and error correction models, MacDonald and Taylor (1993, 1994) have presented evidence supportive of the MAER for both the dollar-mark and the dollar-pound exchange rates. Other researchers, however, have reported more mixed results. Ballie and Pecchenino (1991) conducted separate cointegration tests for the money-demand and PPP relations for the United Kingdom and the United States and, although they were able to reject the hypothesis of no cointegration for money demand, they were unable to do so for PPP. DeJong and Husted (1993), using data for five major currencies relative to the U.S. dollar, also presented evidence inconsistent with the MAER.

The reversal of views with regard to PPP that has taken place over the past half-decade stems, we suspect, from two sets of developments. One is the use of a more careful research design than previously. Earlier studies, for the most part, used whatever monthly or quarterly data existed up until that point and estimated relatively simple regression models. More recent studies, in contrast, have used substantially expanded data sets—either very long-term time series or panel data—more powerful statistical techniques, or both. The other factor that we believe is important concerns changes in the floating-rate data themselves. For one thing the span of the data relative to a decade ago has doubled. Perhaps more important, however, is the fact that the volatility that characterized real and nominal exchange rate behavior in the early 1980s (particularly U.S. dollar rates), the causes of which are still being debated, has largely dissipated. The signal in the data has, therefore, very likely increased both in absolute terms and as a ratio to the "noise."

DATA AND METHODOLOGY

The Data

The data utilized in this study were hand-collected from the *International Financial Statistics*. They are quarterly and cover the period 1974 through 1993. The exchange rate used is U.S. dollar per Canadian dollar (line ag is in monthly IFS data type). For both countries, the monetary aggregate is M1 (line 34); the income measure is industrial production (line 66C); and the interest-rate measure is the long-term government bond yields (line 61).

Methodology

The cointegration technique—which was pioneered by Engle and Granger (1987) and extended by Johansen (1988), Johansen and Juselius (1990), and Stock and Watson (1988), among others—allows us to estimate both long- and short-run relationships without having to difference the data. In testing for the presence of these relationships among the variables included in our data set, we employed the Johansen procedure. This procedure was chosen because work by Gonzalo (1994) demonstrated that the Johansen procedure has superior properties to the other methods of testing for cointegration. A brief outline of the procedure follows.

The Johansen procedure requires specifying a kth-order vector autoregression (VAR) model for an n $\times$ 1 vector of I(d) variables, X_t:

$$X_t = \mu + A_1 X_{t-1} + ... + A_k X_{t-k} + \varepsilon_t, \tag{5}$$

where each of the A_i matrices is an (n $\times$ n) matrix of parameters, μ is a deterministic term and ε_{et} is a vector of residuals, which is assumed to be an i.i.d. Gaussian process. This system of equations can be re-parameterized in the following error correction form:

$$\Delta X_t = \mu + \Gamma_1 \Delta X_{t-1} + ... + \Gamma_{k-i} \Delta X_{t-k+i} + \Pi X_{t-k} + \varepsilon_t, \tag{6}$$

where, $\Pi = -I + A_1 + ... + A_k$, and $\Gamma_i = -I + A_1 + ... + A_i$, i $= 1, ..., k - 1$. The symbol Γ_i represents the matrix of traditional first-difference coefficients, which captures the short-run dynamics. More important, however, is Π, which represents the long-run impact matrix. That is, it contains information about the long-run relationships between variables comprising the data set. As such, it is the rank (r) of Π, which indicates the number of cointegrating vectors. If Π is of full rank, no cointegration is present as all series are themselves stationary, and thus we confront a conventional regression problem. On the other hand, if Π has a rank of zero, no stationary, long-run relationships are present, and equation (2) is reduced to a VAR in differences. However, if Π has rank r, such that $0 < r < n$, it can be factored as $\Pi = \alpha \beta N$ where α and β are n $\times$ r matrices. The r columns of β are the cointegrating vectors, such that $\beta N X_t$ is stationary although X_t is not, while n $-$ r represents the number of common stochastic trends. The ith row of α tells us the importance of each of these cointegrating vectors to the dynamics of the ith equation. The individual values α_{ir} represent the speed with which the ith series adjusts to the rth cointegrating vector; larger values indicate a more rapid speed of adjustment. Thus, not only can we determine the existence of equilibrium relationships, we can also deter-

Table 16.1
ADF(4) Statistics

	Without Trend*	With Trend**
IND*	-3.222	-3.205
IND	-0.455	-3.022
M*	0.131	-2.354
M	1.209	-1.692
INT*	-1.609	-1.796
INT	-1.340	-1.907
S*	-2.374	-2.190

*95 percent critical value $= -2.901$.
**95 percent critical value $= -3.470$.

mine the relative speed of adjustment to disequilibrium shocks of each cointegrating vector.

The Johansen procedure uses two likelihood ratio (LR) statistics that test for cointegrating vectors—the "trace statistic" and the λ_{max} statistic. The former tests the hypothesis that there are, at most, r distinct cointegrating vectors, while the latter tests the hypothesis of $r + 1$ cointegrating vectors given r cointegrating vector. These statistics follow nonstandard distributions. The asymptotic distributions for both LR statistics were tabulated and are presented in Johansen and Juselius (1990) and Osterwald-Lenum (1992).

Johansen and Juselius (1992) pointed out that some ambiguity exists in determining the appropriate number of significant eigenvalues. The distributions of the test statistics depend only on the number of nonstationary components, but because of differences in the specification of the alternative hypothesis, the critical values associated with the λ_{max} and trace statistics often lead to different conclusions. This dilemma is usually the result of the low power of the test in cases where the cointegrating relationship is quite close to the nonstationary boundary. In the empirical analysis, however, we find that our results are consistent across both test statistics at the 95 percent confidence level.

COINTEGRATION RESULTS

The initial step in testing for cointegration is to test for the presence of unit roots in each of the series. Two tests we performed using the Augmented Dickey-Fuller test. The first tests the series for a unit root with zero trend, while the second tests for a unit root with a nonzero, linear trend. The results are reported in Table 16.1. In neither case could the null hypothesis be rejected, which indicates the presence of a unit root with a trend in each of the series included in our data set.

Given the presence of a unit root in each series, we proceeded with Johansen's

Table 16.2
Johansen Test for Cointegration among S, IND, IND*, M, M*, INT and INT*[a, b]

			Panel A			
			Eigenvalues in Descending Order			
0.663	0.473	0.401	0.342	0.173	0.0928	0.003

Panel B

			Critical Values			
			λ_{max}		Trace	
	k = 4					
Null	λ_{max}	Trace	95%	90%	95%	90%
r = 0	76.06	206.38	44.06	42.06	124.25	118.99
r < = 1	44.79	130.33	39.43	36.35	95.18	90.39
r < = 2	35.88	85.54	33.32	30.84	70.60	66.49
r < = 3	29.33	49.65	27.14	24.78	48.28	45.23
r < = 4	13.32	20.32	21.07	18.90	31.53	28.71
r < = 5	6.82	7.00	14.90	12.91	17.95	15.66
r < = 6	0.19	0.19	8.18	6.50	8.18	6.50

[a] Trend maintained.
[b] k refers to the number of lags.

method in testing for the presence of cointegration among the exchange rate and our set of macroeconomic variables. The results are presented in Table 16.2. Evidence from both the "λmax" and "trace" statistics indicates that there are four cointegrating vectors.[7]

The finding of four cointegrating vectors indicates that there are three common stochastic trends. These results are consistent with an equilibrium subspace between the exchange rate and domestic and foreign industrial levels of outputs, money supplies, and long-term interest rates. Thus, strong support was found for the Monetary model of exchange rates. Except for the study of MacDonald and Taylor (1994), this finding contrasts with those of earlier studies of the Monetary model of exchange rates and the more recent studies, which used the cointegration methodology to test this model. We are inclined to attribute the difference in results to two factors. First, as argued by MacDonald and Taylor (1994), previous studies used the cointegration approach with single equation methodology, as proposed by Engle and Granger (1987). As is well documented in the literature, this regression-based approach is inefficient in that it fails to fully capture the dynamics of the data. Additionally, the cointegration results

Table 16.3
**Estimated Cointegrated Vectors Partitioned into the Stationary Components (β_i)
and Their Weights (α_i)**

	Eigenvectors			
	β_1	β_2	β_3	β_4
S	-1.000	-1.000	-1.000	-1.000
INT	0.423	-0.169	-0.067	0.026
INT*	-0.877	0.229	0.042	0.006
IND	0.258	0.001	0.001	-0.029
IND*	0.123	0.023	-0.002	0.009
M	0.008	0.001	0.001	-0.001
M*	-0.165	-0.010	-0.007	0.014

are sensitive to the specific normalization used. Second, since the completion of those earlier studies, the substantial depreciation in real U.S. dollar exchange rates in the mid-1980s, which occurred following the Plaza and Louvre accords—and that more or less offset its earlier appreciation—has had sufficient time to be fully reflected in our set of variables. Thus our finding may be reflecting the impact of the Plaza and Louvre accords.

The eigenvectors and weights are presented in Tables 16.3 and 16.4, respectively. The weights are the estimated α coefficients and can be interpreted as the average speed of adjustment of each series toward the equilibrium subspace. As such, a large (small) coefficient reflects a high speed of adjustment, while a small coefficient reflects a slow speed. The important factor to note about Table 15.4 is the difference in the speeds of adjustment of the two countries' variables. Specifically, in all cases the Canadian variables are substantially larger than those of the United States, indicating that the former variables responded much faster to disequilibrium shocks than the latter.

MacDonald and Taylor (1994) pointed out that if the flexible-price Monetary approach is correct, then the coefficient on IND and IND* should be negative and positive, respectively, with numerical values equal to income elasticities from the domestic (IND) and foreign (IND*) demand functions; the coefficients on I and I* should be positive and negative, respectively, with the size of the coefficients similar to interest rate semielasticities obtained from money-demand functions. Finally, the coefficients on M and M* should be positive one and negative one, respectively. The results displayed in Table 16.3 are, in general, consistent with these expectations. The first cointegrating vector appears to support the interest-rate relationship, with the industrial-output relationship supported by the fourth cointegrating vector. Note, however, that although the second and third cointegrating vectors possess the hypothesized sign for the money-supply relationship, their sizes are significantly different from one.[8]

Table 16.4
Cointegrating Weights

	α_1	α_2	α_3	α_4
S	-0.003	-0.012	0.205	0.221
INT	0.327	1.278	-4.275	-0.072
INT*	0.452	-0.380	-10.956	3.467
IND	0.013	-2.587	-1.969	0.699
IND*	0.427	-5.599	22.847	-7.316
M	0.008	0.001	0.001	-0.001
M*	1.466	-16.909	0.844	-8.314

Johansen and Juselius (1992) point out that the eigenvalues can be used as a measure of the relative strength of the long-run relationships, with larger values indicating that the corresponding cointegrating vector(s) are more correlated with the stationary part of the process. Table 16.2 contains estimates of the eigenvalues in descending order of magnitude; the corresponding cointegrating vectors are displayed in Table 16.3. These results indicate that the exchange-rate relationship is most correlated with the stationary part of the process, the industrial-output relationship is the least correlated, and the monetary-policy relationship is the intermediate case. The finding that the interest-rate relationship is most correlated with the equilibrium subspace may reflect the fact that the financial markets between these countries are relatively well integrated.

CONCLUSIONS

In summary, the results indicate that there are four cointegrating relationships that indicate an equilibrium subspace between the exchange rate and the set of macroeconomic variables characterizing the system of equations. The discovery of four cointegrating vectors provides strong support for the long-run Monetary model of exchange rates. Additionally, the presence of cointegration among the set of variables included in the system provides indirect evidence in favor of long-run purchasing power parity (PPP). This is informative given that the existence of PPP is still debated.

The results that we have reported are, impressive in one, rather important respect. They suggest, in contrast to widespread belief, that the Monetary approach to exchange rates, like the PPP relation, which is one of its underpinnings, continues to be of use empirically as a long-run predictive tool. It provides an anchor, so to speak, to the nominal exchange rate—a value from which the nominal exchange rate cannot wander indefinitely, and therefore a guide for judging long-run exchange-rate behavior.

As such, these results accord well with those presented by MacDonald and

Taylor (1993, 1994) in similar studies of the dollar-mark and dollar-pound exchange rates, respectively. Future work should extend such analysis to other industrial-country exchange rates and also to investigate further the short-run behavior of these exchange rates.

NOTES

1. See, for example, the survey articles written near the start of this decade by Dornbusch (1987), Frankel and Meese (1987), and Meese (1990).

2. For historical evidence on the performance of PPP over the past two centuries, see Lothian and Taylor (1996). Recent studies of the current float include Flood, Frankel and Rose (1995), Lothian (1995) and Mark (1995).

3. MacDonald and Taylor (1993, 1994) presented results favorable to the MAER for the dollar-mark and dollar-pound exchange rates, but Ballie and Pecchenino (1991) also investigated the behavior of the dollar-pound rate and reached somewhat different conclusions.

4. See Boughton (1988) for a comprehensive review of these models. Note, however, that some studies did continue to lend support to the MAER. These include Finn (1996), Somanath (1985), and for Canada, LaFrance and Racette (1985) and Marquez and Schinasi (1988). Also on Canada, see Backus (1984) and Boothe and Poloz (1988).

5. The list of such studies is now voluminous. Examples include Abuaf and Jorion (1990), Diebold, Husted, and Rush (1991) and Lothian and Taylor (1996).

6. See Flood, Frankel, and Rose (1995) and Lothian (1995), for evidence derived from multicountry panel data for this period. Evans and Lothian (1993) and Mark (1995) investigated the time series for a number of the major currencies separately.

7. This result is consistent across multiple VAR lag structures. However, four lags produce an error series that was white noise and minimized the AIC criterion.

8. Although not reported here, hypothesis tests that the coefficients are equal to $+1$ and -1 were not supported.

REFERENCES

Abuaf, Niso, and Phillipe Jorion. "Purchasing Power Parity in the Long Run." *Journal of Finance*, 45 (March 1990): 157–174.

Backus, David. "Empirical Models of the Exchange Rate: Separating the Wheat from the Chaff." *Canadian Journal of Economics*, 17 (1984): 824–846.

Ballie, Richard T., and Rowena Pecchenino. "The Search for Equilibrium in Relationships in International Finance: The Case of the Monetary Model." *Journal of International Money and Finance*, 10 (December 1991): 582–593.

Bilson, John F. O. "Rational Expectations and the Exchange Rate." In *The Economics of Exchange Rates*, ed. Jacob Frenkel and Harry G. Johnson. Reading, Mass.: Addison-Wesley, 1978.

Boothe, Paul M., and Stephen S. Poloz. "Unstable Money Demand and the Monetary Model of the Exchange Rate." *Canadian Journal of Economics*, 21 (November 1988): 785–798.

Boughton, James. *The Monetary Approach to Exchange Rates: What Now Remains?*

Princeton Studies in International Finance no. 171. Princeton, N.J.: Princeton University Press, 1988.

DeJong, David, and Steven Husted. "Towards a Reconciliation of the Empirical Evidence on the Monetary Approach to Exchange Rate Determination." *Review of Economics and Statistics*, 75 (1993): 123–128.

Diebold, Francis X., Stephen Husted and Mark Rush. "Real Exchange Rates under the Gold Standard." *Journal of Political Economy*, 99 (December 1991): 1252–1271.

Dornbusch, Rudiger. "Purchasing Power Parity." In *The New Palgrave: A Dictionary of Economics*, ed. John Eatwell, Murray Milgate and Peter Newman. New York: Stockton, 1987, pp. 1075–1085.

Engle, Robert F., and Clive W. J. Granger. "Cointegration and Error Correction: Representation, Estimation, and Testing." *Econometrica*, 55 (March 1987): 251–277.

Evans, Martin D. D., and James R. Lothian. "The Response of Exchange Rates to Permanent and Transitory Shocks under Floating Exchange Rates." *Journal of International Money and Finance*, 11 (December 1993): 563–586.

Finn, Mary. "Forecasting Exchange Rate: A Monetary or Random Walk Phenomenon." *Journal of International Money and Finance*, 5 (June 1996): 181–194.

Flood, Robert, Jeffrey A. Frankel and Andrew Rose. "Mean Reversion within and between Countries: A Panel Project on Purchasing Power Parity." Unpublished manuscript, 1995.

Frankel, Jeffrey A. "On the Mark: A Theory of Floating Exchange Rates Based on Real Interest Rate Differentials." *American Economic Review*, 64 (May 1979): 610–622.

Frankel, Jeffrey A. "A Test of Monetary and Portfolio Balance Models." In *The Theory of Exchange Rate Determination*, ed. John F. O. Bilson and Richard C. Marston. Chicago: University of Chicago Press for the NBER, 1984.

Frankel, Jeffrey A., and Richard Meese. "Are Exchange Rates Excessively Variable?" In *NBER Macroeconomics Annual*, ed. Stanley Fischer. Cambridge, Mass.: MIT Press, 1987.

Frenkel, Jacob. "A Monetary Approach to the Exchange Rate: Doctrinal Aspects and Empirical Evidence." *Scandinavian Journal of Economics*, 78 (May 1976): 200–224.

Gonzalo, J. "Five Alternative Methods of Estimating Long-Run Equilibrium Relationships." *Journal of Econometrics*, 60 (1994): 203–234.

International Monetary Fund. *International Financial Statistics*, various issues.

Johansen, S., and K. Juselius. "Maximum Likelihood Estimation and Interference on Cointegration—With Applications to the Demand for Money." *Oxford Bulletin of Economics and Statistics*, 52 (1990): 169–210.

Johansen, S., and K. Juselius. "Testing Structural Hypotheses in a Multivariate Cointegration Analysis of the PPP and UIP for the UK." *Journal of Econometrics*, 53 (1992): 211–244.

Johansen, Søren. "Statistical Analysis of Cointegration Vectors." *Journal of Economic Dynamics and Control*, 12 (1988): 231–254.

LaFrance, R., and D. Racette. "The Canadian-U.S. Dollar Exchange Rate: A Test of Alternative Models for the Seventies." *Journal of International Money and Finance*, 4 (1985): 237–252.

Lothian, James R. "Multi-Country Evidence on the Behavior of Purchasing Power Parity under the Current Float." *Journal of International Money and Finance*, 16 (1997): 19–35.

Lothian, James R., and Mark P. Taylor. "The Recent Float from the Perspective of the Past Two Centuries." *Journal of Political Economy*, 104 (1996): 488–509.

MacDonald, Ronald, and Mark P. Taylor. "The Monetary Approach to the Exchange Rate: Rational Expectations, Long-Run Equilibrium, and Forecasting Short-Run Dynamics and How to Beat a Random Walk." *International Monetary Fund Staff Papers*, 40 (March 1993): 89–107.

MacDonald, Ronald, and Mark P. Taylor. "The Monetary Model of the Exchange Rate: Long-Run Relationships, Short-Run Dynamics and How to Beat a Random Walk." *Journal of International Money and Finance*, 13 (June 1994): 276–290.

Mark, Nelson. "Exchange Rates and Fundamental Evidence on Long-Horizon Predictability." *American Economic Review*, 85 (March 1995): 201–218.

Marquez, Jaimé, and Gary J. Schinasi. "Measures of Money and the Monetary Model of the Canadian-U.S. Dollar Exchange Rate." *Economic Letters*, 26 (1988): 183–188.

Meese, Richard. "Currency Fluctuations in the Post–Bretton Woods Period." *Journal of Economic Perspectives*, 4 (Winter 1990): 117–134.

Meese, Richard A., and Kenneth Rogoff. "Empirical Exchange Rate Models of the Seventies: Do They Fit Out of Sample?" *International Economic Review*, 14 (February 1983): 3–24.

Osterwald-Lenum, M. "Recalculated and Extended Tables of the Asymptotic Distribution of Some Important Maximum Likelihood Cointegrating Test Statistics." Working Paper, University of Copenhagen, 1992.

Somanath, V. S. "Efficient Exchange Rate Forecasts: Lagged Models Better Than the Random Walk." *Journal of International Money and Finance*, 5 (June 1986): 195–220.

Stock, J., and M. Watson. "Testing for Common Trends." *Journal of the American Statistical Association*, 85 (1988): 1097–1107.

Conclusion

We have given a detailed account of each of the two theories of international finance, both theoretically and empirically. Additionally, we have criticized both theories on the points where they contain drawbacks. We have also compared the two theories and indicated what conditions are necessary in order to combine them into a comprehensive theory of explanation of international accounts adjustment and exchange rate determination. The reason for this goal is that neither approach individually is sufficient to explain either exchange rates or the adjustment of international accounts.

The authors in this book share the premise that each of the competing theories has merit. Each of the approaches, though, either emphasizes or addresses different issues. The Traditional approach assumes that there is unemployment in the economy, while the Monetary approach contradicts it by stating that there is full employment, perhaps at the natural level of unemployment. Second, the Traditional approach argues that there are sufficient discontinuities in the world to have different prices at different locations, which are not due only to transportation costs. The Monetary approach, however, asserts that the law of one price holds supreme. Third, the Traditional approach gives preeminence to the real goods and services market while accepting money and financial assets as somewhat important. The Monetary approach asserts that the real goods and services market is extremely important; it also gives most of its weight to the financial assets market and even more weight to the money market. Fourth, the Traditional approach assumes the disequilibrium of markets, while the Monetary approach asserts a general equilibrium framework where all markets clear. Finally, the Traditional approach is set in a short-term environment where there are political realities and where politicians undertake policy to influence the economy on their behalf. The Monetary approach, in contrast, emphasizes the long term.

To conclude, in this volume we have argued, implicitly and explicitly, that both views have merit and that both should be used in an all-encompassing approach of adjustment to international accounts and exchange rate determination.

Selected Bibliography

Abuaf, Niso, and Phillipe Jorion. "Purchasing Power Parity in the Long Run." *Journal of Finance*, 45 (March 1990): 157–174.

Adams, Gerard F., and Helen B. Junz. "The Effects of the Business Cycle on Trade Flows of Industrial Countries." *Journal of Finance*, 26 (May 1971): 251–268.

Aghevli, Bijan B., and Mohsin S. Khan. "The Monetary Approach to Balance of Payments Determination: An Empirical Test." In *The Monetary Approach to the Balance of Payments: A Collection of Research Papers by Members of the Staff of the International Monetary Fund*. Washington, D.C.: International Monetary Fund, 1977, pp. 275–290.

Alexander, Sidney S. "Effects of a Devaluation on a Trade Balance." *International Monetary Fund Staff Papers*, 2 (1952): 263–278.

Aliber, Robert Z. "The Interest Rate Parity Theorem: A Reinterpretation." *Journal of Political Economy*, 8, no. 6 (1973): 1451–1459.

Almon, Shirley. "The Distributed Lag between Capital Appropriations and Expenditures." *Econometrica*, 33, no. 1 (January 1965): 178–196.

Artus, Jacques R. "The Behavior of Export Prices for Manufactures." In *The Effects of Exchange Rate Adjustment*, ed. Peter B. Clark, Dennis E. Logue, and Richard J. Sweeney. Proceedings of a conference sponsored by OASIA Research, Department of the Treasury, 1974. Washington, D.C.: U.S. Department of the Treasury, 1977, pp. 319–338.

Backus, David. "Empirical Models of the Exchange Rate: Separating the Wheat from the Chaff." *Canadian Journal of Economics*, 17 (1984): 824–846.

Balassa, Bela. "Export Composition and Export Performance in the Industrial Countries, 1953–71." *Review of Economics and Statistics*, 61, no. 4 (1979): 604–607.

Ball, R. J., and K. Marwah. "The U.S. Demand for Imports, 1948–1952." *Review of Economics and Statistics*, 44 (November 1962): 395.

Ballie, Richard T., and Rowena Pecchenino. "The Search for Equilibrium in Relationships in International Finance: The Case of the Monetary Model." *Journal of International Money and Finance*, 10 (December 1991): 582–593.

Barro, R. *Macroeconomics*. New York: John Wiley and Sons, 1993.

Bean, Donna L. "International Reserve Flows and Money Market Equilibrium." In *The Monetary Approach to the Balance of Payments*, ed. Jacob A. Frenkel and Harry G. Johnson. Toronto: University of Toronto Press, 1976, pp. 326–337.

Behrman, Jack N. "World Investment Report, 1993: Transnational Corporations and Integrated International Production." *Transnational Corporation*, 2 (December 1993): 149–162.

Bilson, John F. O. "Rational Expectations and the Exchange Rate." In *The Economics of Exchange Rates*, ed. Jacob Frenkel and Harry G. Johnson. Reading, Mass: Addison-Wesley, 1978.

Blejer, Mario. "The Short-Run Dynamics of Price and the Balance of Payments." *American Economic Review*, 67 (June 1977): 419–428.

Bonitsis, Theologos Homer. "Dollar Exchange Rate Indices and U.S. Exports: Is There an Intertemporal Linkage?" *Journal of Business and Economic Studies*, 1, no. 2 (Fall/Winter 1991): 1–10.

Bonitsis, Theologos Homer, and Raj Aggarwal. "U.S. Direct Foreign Investment and Economic Growth in Brazil: An Econometric Causal Analysis." *International Journal of Finance*, 2, no. 2 (Spring 1990): 12–19.

Bonitsis, Theologos Homer, Krishna M. Kasibhatla and John Malindretos. "A Comparison of the Monetary and Traditional Approaches to International Competitive Adjustment: The Case of South Korea." *Journal of International Economic Studies*, no. 9 (1995): 123–138.

Bonitsis, Theologos Homer, and Demetri Tsanacas. "Yen Appreciation, Hysteretic Effects, and Japanese Micro-Adjustments." *Detroit Business Journal*, 3, no. 1 (Spring 1990): 1–10.

Boothe, Paul M., and Stephen S. Poloz. "Unstable Money Demand and the Monetary Model of the Exchange Rate." *Canadian Journal of Economics*, 21 (November 1988): 785–798.

Boughton, James. *The Monetary Approach to Exchange Rates: What Now Remains?* Princeton Studies in International Finance no. 171. Princeton, N.J.: Princeton University Press, 1988.

Boyer, R. "Devaluation and Portfolio Balance." *American Economic Review*, 67, no. 2 (March 1977): 54–63.

Boyer, Russel S. "Sterilization and the Monetary Approach to Balance of Payments Analysis." *Journal of Monetary Economics*, 5 (April 1979): 295–300.

Branson, William H. *Financial Capital Flows in the U.S. Balance of Payments*. Amsterdam: North Holland Publishing Company, 1968.

Branson, William H. "The Trade Effects of the 1971 Currency Realignments." *Brookings Papers on Economic Activity*, no. 1 (1972): 15–69.

Branson William H., and Raymond D. Hill. *Capital Movements in the OECD Area: An Econometric Analysis*. Paris: OECD, 1971.

Bronfenbrenner, J. "Sources and Size of Least-Squares Bias in a Two-Equation Model." In *Studies in Econometric Method*, ed. W. C. Hood and T. C. Koopmans. Cowles Foundation Monographs no. 14. New York: Wiley, 1953.

Bryant, Ralph C., and Patrick H. Hendershott. "Empirical Analysis of Capital Flows: Some Consequences of Alternative Specifications." In *International Mobility and Movement of Capital*, ed. Fritz Machlup et al. New York: Columbia University Press, 1972, pp. 211–213.

Buckler, M., and C. Almon. "Imports and Exports in an Input-Output Model." Research Memorandum no. 38. Baltimore, Md.: Maryland Interindustry Forecasting Project, 1972.

Cassel, Gustav. "The Present Situation of the Foreign Exchanges." *Economic Journal*, 26 (March 1916): 62–65.

Cassel, Gustav. "Abnormal Deviations in International Exchanges." *Economic Journal*, 28 (December 1918): 413–415.

Cassel, Gustav. "Rates of Exchange and Purchasing Power Parity." *Skandinaviska Kerditaktieholaget Quarterly Report*, 98 (1925): 325–336.

Cassel, Gustav. *Post War Monetary Stabilization*. New York: Columbia University Press, 1928.

Caves, Richard. "International Corporations: The Industrial Economics of Foreign Investment." *Economica*, 38, no. 149 (February 1971): 1–27.

Cooper, Richard N. "The Balance of Payments in Review." *Journal of Political Economy*, 74, no. 4 (August 1966): 379–395.

Cumby, Robert E., and Maurice Obstfeld. "A Note on Exchange Rate Expectations and Nominal Interest Differentials: A Test of the Fisher Hypothesis." *Journal of Finance*, 36 (June 1981): 697–703.

Darby, Michael R. "Movements in Purchasing Power Parity: The Short and Long Runs." In *The International Transmission of Inflation*, ed. Michael R. Darby and James R. Lothian. Chicago: University of Chicago Press, 1983.

Davidson, P. "A Keynesian View of Friedman's Theoretical Framework for Monetary Analysis." In *Milton Friedman's Monetary Framework: A Debate with His Critics*, ed. R. J. Gordon. Chicago: University of Chicago Press, 1974, pp. 100–101.

Davidson, P. "Money and General Equilibrium." *Economie Appliqué*, 30, no. 4 (1977): 541–563.

Davidson, P. *Money and the Real World*. 2nd ed. London: Macmillan, 1978.

Davidson, P. *International Money and the Real World*. London: Macmillan, 1982.

De Grauwe, Paul. "International Capital Flows and Portfolio Equilibrium: Comment." *Journal of Political Economy*, 83 (October 1975): 1077–1080.

De Grauwe, Paul. *Monetary Interdependence and International Monetary Reform*. Lexington, Mass.: Heath, 1976.

DeJong, David, and Steven Husted. "Towards a Reconciliation of the Empirical Evidence on the Monetary Approach to Exchange Rate Determination." *Review of Economics and Statistics*, 75 (1993): 123–128.

Diebold, Francis X., Stephen Husted and Mark Rush. "Real Exchange Rates under the Gold Standard." *Journal of Political Economy*, 99 (December 1991): 1252–1271.

Dooley, Michael P., and Peter Isard. "Capital Controls, Political Risk, and Deviations from Interest Parity Theory." *Journal of Political Economy*, 88, no. 2 (1980): 370–384.

Dornbush, Rudiger. "Currency Depreciation, Hoarding and Relative Prices." *Journal of Political Economy*, 4 (July/August 1973): 893–915.

Dornbush, Rudiger. "Devaluation, Money and and Nontraded Goods." *American Economic Review*, 62, no. 5 (December 1973): 871–883.

Dornbush, Rudiger. "Expectations and Exchange Rate Dynamics." *Journal of Political Economy*, 84 (1976): 1161–1176.

Dornbush, Rudiger. "Monetary Policy under Exchange Rate Flexibility." Conference Series no. 20. Federal Reserve Bank of Boston, 1979.

Dornbush, Rudiger. "Exchange Rate Economics: Where Do We Stand?" *Brookings Papers on Economic Activity*, no. 1 (1980): 195–202.

Dornbush, Rudiger. "Purchasing Power Parity." In *The New Palgrave: A Dictionary of Economics*, ed. John Eatwell, Murray Milgate and Peter Newman. New York: Stockton, 1987, pp. 1075–1085.

Dornbush, Rudiger, and S. Fisher. "Exchange Rate and the Current Account." *American Economic Review*, 70, no. 5 (1980): 960–971.

Dornbush, Rudiger, and Paul Krugman. "Flexible Exchange Rates in the Short Run." *Brookings Papers on Economic Activity*, no. 3 (1976): 537–575.

Eichengreen, Barry, James Tobin and Charles Wyplosz. "Two Cases for Sand in the Wheels of International Finance." *Economic Journal*, 105 (January 1995): 162–172.

Eiteman, David K., Arthur I. Stonehill and Michael H. Moffett. *Multinational Business Finance*. 6th ed. Reading, Mass.: Addison-Wesley, 1992.

Engle, Robert F., and Clive W. J. Granger. "Cointegration and Error Correction: Representation, Estimation, and Testing." *Econometrica*, 55 (March 1987): 251–277.

Evans, Martin D. D., and James R. Lothian. "The Response of Exchange Rates to Permanent and Transitory Shocks under Floating Exchange Rates." *Journal of International Money and Finance*, 11 (December 1993): 563–586.

Fama, Eugene F. "Forward Rates as Predictors of Future Spot Rates." *Journal of Financial Economics*, 3, no. 4 (October 1976): 361–377.

Fama, Eugene F., and Andre Farber. "Money, Bonds and Foreign Exchange." *American Economic Review*, 69 (1979): 639–649.

Finn, Mary. "Forecasting Exchange Rate: A Monetary or Random Walk Phenomenon." *Journal of International Money and Finance*, 5 (June 1996): 181–194.

Fleming, J. Marcus. "Domestic Financial Policies under Fixed and Floating Exchange Rates." *International Monetary Fund Staff Papers*, 9 (1962): 369–379.

Flood, Robert, Jeffrey A. Frankel and Andrew Rose. "Mean Reversion within and between Countries: A Panel Project on Purchasing Power Parity." Unpublished manuscript, 1995.

Frankel, Jeffrey A. "On the Mark: A Theory of Floating Exchange Rates Based on Real Interest Rate Differentials." *American Economic Review*, 64 (May 1979): 610–622.

Frankel, Jeffrey A. "A Test of Monetary and Portfolio Balance Models." In *The Theory of Exchange Rate Determination*, ed. John F. O. Bilson and Richard C. Marston. Chicago: University of Chicago Press for the NBER, 1978.

Frenkel, Jacob A. "A Dynamic Analysis of the Balance of Payments in a Model of Accumulation." In *The Monetary Approach to the Balance of Payments*, ed. J. A. Frenkel and H. G. Johnson. Toronto: University of Toronto Press, 1976, pp. 109–146.

Frenkel, Jacob A. "A Monetary Approach to the Exchange Rate: Doctrinal Aspects and Empirical Evidence." *Scandinavian Journal of Economics*, 78 (May 1976): 200–224.

Frenkel, Jacob A. "Purchasing Power Parity: Doctrinal Perspective and Evidence from the 1920s." *Journal of International Economics* (May 1978): 169–191.

Frenkel, Jacob A. "The Collapse of Purchasing Power Parities during the 1970s." In *International Volatility and Economic Growth*, ed. G. de Menil and R. J. Gordon. New York: Elsevier Science, 1991, pp. 217–237.

Frenkel, Jacob A., Thorvaldur Gylfason and John F. Helliwell. "A Synthesis of Monetary and Keynesian Approaches to Short-Run Balance of Payments Theory." *Economic Journal*, 96 (September 1980): 582–592.

Frenkel, Jacob A., and Harry G. Johnson, eds. *The Monetary Approach to the Balance of Payments*. Toronto: University of Toronto Press, 1976.

Frenkel, Jacob A., and R. M. Levich. "Covered Interest Arbitrage: Unexploited Profits?" *Journal of Political Economy*, 83, no. 2 (1975): 325–338.

Frenkel, Jacob A., and R. M. Levich. "Transaction Costs and Interest Arbitrage: Tranquil versus Turbulent Periods." *Journal of Political Economy*, 85, no. 6 (December 1977): 1209–1226.

Frenkel, Jacob A., and Assaf Razin. "The Mundell-Fleming Model, a Quarter Century Later." *International Monetary Fund Staff Papers*, 34 (December 1987): 567–620.

Friedman, Benjamin. "Lessons of Monetary Policy from the 1980s." *Journal of Economic Perspectives*, 2 (Summer 1988): 51–72.

Friedman, M. "The Role of Monetary Policy." *American Economic Review*, 58, no. 1 (March 1958): 1–17.

Genberg, Hans A. "Aspects of the Monetary Approach to Balance of Payments Theory: An Empirical Study of Sweden." In *The Monetary Approach to the Balance of Payments*, ed. Jacob A. Frenkel and Harry G. Johnson. Toronto: University of Toronto Press, 1976, pp. 298–325.

Ghosh, Dilip K. "Some Comments on the Economics of Exchange Rate." In *Asia-Pacific Economies: Promises and Challenge: Research in International Business and Finance*, ed. M. Dutta. Greenwich, Conn.: JAI Press, 1987, pp. 303–307.

Giddy, Ian H., and Gunter Dufey. "The Random Behavior of Flexible Exchange Rates." *Journal of International Business Studies*, 6 (Spring 1975): 1–32.

Gilbert, Milton, and Irving B. Kravis. *An International Comparison of National Products and the Purchasing Power of Currencies*. Paris: Organization for European Economic Cooperation, 1954.

Glassman, Debra. "Exchange Rate Risk and Transactions Costs: Evidence from Bid-Ask Spreads." *Journal of International Money and Finance*, 6, no. 4 (December 1987): 479–491.

Godley, Wynne, and William S. Milberg. "U.S. Trade Deficits: The Recovery's Dark Side?" *Challenge* (November/December 1994): 40–47.

Goldstein, Morris, and Mohsin Kahn. "The Supply and Demand for Exports—A Simultaneous Approach." *Review of Economics and Statistics*, 60 (May 1978): 275–286.

Goldstein, Morris, Mohsin Kahn, and Lawrence H. Officer. "Prices of Tradable and Nontradable Goods in Demand for Total Imports." *Review of Economics and Statistics*, 62, no. 2: 190–199.

Gomez-Oliver, Antonio. "La Demando de Dinero en Mexico." In *Cincuenta Anos de Banca Central*, ed. E. Fernandez. Mexico: Fondo de Cultura Económica, 1976, pp. 275–327.

Gonzalo, J. "Five Alternative Methods of Estimating Long-Run Equilibrium Relationships." *Journal of Econometrics*, 60 (1994): 203–234.

Goodwin, Barry K., Thomas Grennes and Michael K. Wohlgemant. "Testing the Law of One Price When Trade Takes Time." *Journal of International Money and Finance*, 9, no. 1 (March 1990): 21–40.

Gray, H. Peter. *An Aggregate Theory of International Payments Adjustment*. London: Macmillan, 1974.

Gray, H. Peter. *A Generalized Theory of International Trade*. London: Macmillan, 1976.

Gray, H. Peter. "The Monetary Approach to International Payments Theory: A Critique." Mimeo, Rutgers University, March 1976.

Gray, H. Peter. "Dangers in the Reduction in U.S. International Net Worth," *International Trade Journal*, 6 (Summer 1992): 427–442.

Gray, H. Peter. "Hicksian Instability in Asset Markets and Financial Fragility." *Eastern Economic Journal*, 18 (Summer 1992): 249–258.

Gray, H. Peter. "The Burdens of Global Leadership." In *International Trade in the 21st Century*, ed. Khosrow Fatemi. London: Pergamon, 1996.

Gray, H. Peter, and Jean M. Gray. "International Payments in a Flow-of-Funds Format." *Journal of Post Keynesian Economics*, 7 (Winter 1988–1989): 241–260.

Gray, Jean M., and H. Peter Gray. "The Multinational Bank: A Financial MNC?" *Journal of Banking and Finance*, 5 (March 1981): 33–63.

Grenfeld, Yehuda, and Zvi Griliches. "Is Aggregation Necessarily Bad?" *Review of Economics and Statistics*, 42 (February 1960): 1–13.

Grubel, Herbert G. "Profits from Forward Exchange Speculation." *Quarterly Journal of Economics*, 79 (May 1965): 248–262.

Grubel, Herbert G. *Forward Exchange, Speculation and the International Flow of Capital*. Stanford, Calif.: Stanford University Press, 1966.

Grubel, Herbert G. "Internationally Diversified Portfolios: Welfare Gains and Capital Flows." *American Economic Review*, 58, part 1 (December 1968): 1299–1314.

Guitian, Manuel. "The Balance of Payments as a Monetary Phenomenon: Empirical Evidence, Spain 1955–71." In *The Monetary Approach to the Balance of Payments*, ed. Jacob A. Frenkel and Harry G. Johnson. Toronto: University of Toronto Press, 1976, pp. 338–356.

Gujarati, Damodar. *Basic Econometrics*. New York: McGraw-Hill, 1978, pp. 272–279.

Haberler, G. "The Market for Foreign Exchange and the Stability of the Balance of Payments: A Theoretical Analysis." In *Selected Essays of Gottfried Haberler*, ed. Anthony Y. C. Koo. Cambridge, Mass.: MIT Press, 1985, pp. 143–165.

Hasan, Aynul S., Ghulam Kadir, and S. Fakhre Mahmud. "Substitutability of Pakistan's Monetary Assets under Alternative Monetary Aggregates." *Pakistan Development Review*, 27, no. 3 (Autumn 1988): 317–326.

Hooper, Peter. "The Construction of Trade Sector for the Michigan Quarterly Forecasting Model of the U.S. Economy, DHL-III." Unpublished paper, University of Michigan. Presented at the Winter Meetings of the Econometric Society, Toronto, December 28–30, 1972.

Houthakker, Hendrik S., and Stephen P. Magee. "Income and Price Elasticities in World Trade." *Review of Economics and Statistics*, 51, no. 2 (May 1969): 111–125.

Houthakker, Hendrik S., and Lester D. Taylor. *Consumer Demand in the U.S.: Analyses and Projections*. Cambridge, Mass.: Harvard University Press, 1970.

Humphrey, T. M., and T. A. Lawler. "Factors Determining Exchange Rates: A Simple Model and Empirical Tests." In *The Monetary Approach to International Adjustment*, ed. B. H. Putnam and D. S. Wilford (rev. ed.) New York: Praeger Publishers, 1978, pp. 134–146.

International Monetary Fund. *International Financial Statistics*, various issues.

International Monetary Fund. *The Monetary Approach to the Balance of Payments*. Washington, D.C.: International Monetary Fund, 1977.

Johannes, James M. "Testing the Exogeneity Specification Underlying the Monetary Approach to the Balance of Payments." *Review of Economics and Statistics*, 62, no. 1 (February 1981): 29–34.

Johansen, S., and K. Juselius. "Testing Structural Hypotheses in a Multivariate Cointegration Analysis of the PPP and UIP for the UK." *Journal of Econometrics*, 53 (1992): 211–244.

Johansen, S., and K. Juselius. "Maximum Likelihood Estimation and Interference on Cointegration—With Applications to the Demand for Money." *Oxford Bulletin of Economics and Statistics*, 52 (1990): 169–210.

Johansen, Søren. "Statistical Analysis of Cointegration Vectors." *Journal of Economic Dynamics and Control*, 12 (June–September 1988): 231–254.

Johnson, Harry G. "Equilibrium under Fixed Exchange Rates." *American Economic Review*, 53 (May 1963): 112–119.

Johnson, Harry G. "The Objectives of Economic Policy and the Mix of Fiscal and Monetary Policy under Fixed Exchange Rates." In *Maintaining and Restoring Balance in International Payments*, ed. Fritz Machlup et al. Princeton, N.J.: Princeton University Press, 1966, pp. 1–198.

Johnson, Harry G. "Some Aspects of the Theory of Economic Policy in a World of Capital Mobility." In *Essays in Honor of Macro Fanno*, ed. T. Bagiotti. Padua, Italy: Cadam, 1966, pp. 228–245.

Johnson, Harry G. *Money, Trade and Economic Growth*. Cambridge, Mass.: Harvard University Press, 1967.

Johnson, Harry G. "The Monetary Approach to Balance of Payments Theory." In *Further Essays in Monetary Theory*, ed. H. G. Johnson. London: George Allen and Unwin, 1972.

Johnson, Harry G. "Why Devaluations Often Appear to Fail." *Eastern Economic Journal*, 1 (October 1974): 231–238.

Johnson, Harry G. "Money, Balance of Payments Theory, and the International Monetary System." Essays in International Finance no. 14. Princeton University, Department of Economics, International Finance Section, 1977.

Johnson, Harry G. "Towards a General Theory of the Balance of Payments." In *International Trade and Economic Growth*. London: George Allen and Unwin, 1958, pp. 153–168.

Johnston, J. *Econometric Methods*. New York: McGraw-Hill, 1972.

Jones, Ronald W. "Monetary and Fiscal Policy for an Economy with Fixed Exchange Rates." *Journal of Political Economy*, 76, no. 4 (July–August 1968): 921–943.

Kahn, Mohsin S. "Macroeconomic Policies and the Balance of Payments in Pakistan: 1972–1986." International Monetary Fund Working Paper 90/78. International Monetary Fund, Research Department, Washington, D.C., September 1990.

Kallianiotis, I. N. "Exchange Rates and Rational Expectations." Ph.D. dissertation, City University of New York, 1985.

Kallianiotis, I. N. "A Theoretical Monetary and Real Approach to the Balance of Payments." *Greek Economic Review*, 10, no. 2 (December 1988): 383–404.

Kallaniotis, I. N. "Is the U.S. Budget Deficit Harming the Financial Markets and the Overall Economy?" University of Scranton, SOM Research Report Series no. 9110, October 1991.

Kallianiotis, I. N., and Gisele Sum. "Real Exchange Rates and Real Interest Differentials under Uncertainty." Unpublished manuscript, University of Scranton, March 1993.

Kamas, Linda. "External Disturbances and the Independence of Monetary Policy under the Crawling Peg in Columbia." *Journal of International Economics*, 19 (November 1985): 313–327.

Kamas, Linda. "The Balance of Payments Offset to Monetary Policy: Monetarist, Portfolio Balance, and the Keynesian Estimates for Mexico and Venezuela." *Journal of Money, Credit, and Banking*, 18, no. 4 (November 1986): 467–481.

Karfakis, Costas, and Suk-Joong Kim. "Exchange Rates, Interest Rates and Current Account News: Some Evidence from Australia." *Journal of International Money and Finance*, 14, no. 4 (1995): 575–595.

Kemp, Donald S. "A Monetary View of the Balance of Payments." *Federal Reserve Bank of St. Louis Review*, 57, no. 4 (April 1975): 14–22.

Kemp, Murray C. *The Demand for Canadian Imports: 1926–55*. Toronto: University of Toronto Press, 1962.

Kemp, Murray C. "Errors of Measurement and Bias in Estimates of Import Demand Parameters." *Economic Record*, 38 (September 1962): 369–372.

Kemp, Murray C. "A Monetary View of the Balance of Payments." In *The Monetary Approach to International Adjustment*, ed. B. H. Putnam and D. S. Wilford. New York: Praeger, 1978, p. 52.

Kenen, Peter B. "Short Term Capital Movements and the U.S. Balance of Payments." In *The United States Balance of Payments*. Hearings before the Joint Economic Committee, 88th Cong., 1st Sess., 1963.

Keynes, J. M. "The German Transfer Problem." *Economic Journal*, 39 (March 1929): 1–7.

Keynes, J. M. *A Treatise on Money*. Vol. 1. New York: Harcourt, Brace and Company, 1930.

Keynes, J. M. *The General Theory of Employment, Interest, and Money*. London: Macmillan, 1936.

Khan, Mohsin. "Imports and Export Demand in Developing Countries." *International Monetary Fund Staff Papers*, 21, no. 3 (November 1974): 678–694.

Kindleberger, Charles P. "Measuring Equilibrium in the Balance of Payments." *Journal of Political Economy*, 77 (November–December 1969): 873–891.

Kindleberger, Charles P. "The Case for Fixed Exchange Rates." In *International Adjustment Mechanism*. Conference Series no. 2. Proceedings of a Conference held in October 1969. Boston: Mass.: Federal Reserve Bank of Boston, March 1970, pp. 93–108.

Kouri, Pentti. "The Theory of Exchange Rates." Ph.D. dissertation, Massachusetts Institute of Technology, 1975.

Kouri, Pentti. "Monetary Policy, the Balance of Payments, and the Exchange Rates." In *The Functioning of Floating Exchange Rates: Theory, Evidence, and Policy Implications*, ed. D. Bigman and T. Taya. Cambridge, Mass.: Ballinger Publishing Company, 1980, pp. 168–181.

Kouri, Pentti J. K., and Michael G. Porter. "International Capital Flows and Porfolio Equilibrium." *Journal of Political Economy*, 82 (May–June 1974): 46–89.

Krause, Lawrence B. "Comments and Discussion." *Brookings Papers on Economic Activity*, no. 3 (1975): 546–548.

Kreinin, Mordechai E., and Lawrence H. Officer. "The Monetary Approach to the Balance of Payments: A Survey." Princeton Studies in International Finance no. 43.

Princeton University, Department of Economics, International Finance Section, 1978.

Krueger, Anne. *Exchange Rate Determination*. Cambridge Surveys of Economic Literature. Cambridge: Cambridge University Press, 1983.

Krueger, Anne O. "The Balance-of-Payments Theory." *Journal of Economic Literature*, 7, no. 1 (March 1969): 1–26.

Kyle, John F. *The Balance of Payments in a Monetary Economy*. Princeton, N.J.: Princeton University Press, 1976.

Laffer, Arthur B. "Monetary Policy and the Balance of Payments." *Journal of Money, Credit and Banking*, 4, no. 1 (February 1972): 13–22.

Laffer, Arthur B., "Exchange Rates, the Terms of Trade, and the Trade Balance." In *The Effects of Exchange Rate Adjustments*, ed. Peter B. Clark, Dennis E. Logue and Richard J. Sweeney. Proceedings of a conference sponsored by OASIA Research, Department of Treasury, 1974. Washington, D.C.: Department of the Treasury, 1977.

Laffer, Arthur B., and Marc A. Miles. *International Economics in an Integrated World*. Glenview, Ill.: Scott, Foresman, 1982.

LaFrance, R., and D. Racette. "The Canadian-U.S. Dollar Exchange Rate: A Test of Alternative Models for the Seventies." *Journal of International Money and Finance*, 4 (1985): 237–252.

Leamer, Edward, and Robert M. Stern. *Quantitative International Economics*. Chicago: Aldine Pubishing Company, 1970.

Logue, Dennis E., Richard J. Sweeney and Thomas D. Willett. "The Speculative Behavior of Foreign Exchange Rates during the Current Float." *Journal of Business Research*, 6, no. 2 (1975): 159–173.

Lothian, James R. "Multi-Country Evidence on the Behavior of Purchasing Power Parity under the Current Float." Unpublished working paper, Fordham University, Graduate School of Business Administration, 1995.

Lothian, James R., and Mark P. Taylor. "The Recent Float from the Perspective of the Past Two Centuries." *Journal of Political Economy*, 104 (1996): 488–509.

MacDonald, Ronald, and Mark P. Taylor. "Exchange Rate Economics: A Survey." *International Monetary Fund Staff Papers*, 39, no. 1 (March 1992): 1–57.

MacDonald, Ronald, and Mark P. Taylor. "The Monetary Approach to the Exchange Rate." *International Monetary Fund Staff Papers*, 40 (March 1993): 89–107.

MacDonald, Ronald, and Mark P. Taylor. "The Monetary Model of the Exchange Rate: Long-Run Relationships, Short-Run Dynamics and How to Beat a Random Walk." *Journal of International Money and Finance*, 13 (June 1994): 276–290.

MacDougall, G. B. A. "British and American Exports: A Study Suggested by the Theory of Comparative Costs, Part II." *Economic Journal*, 62 (September 1952): 493.

Machlup, F. *International Trade and the National Income Multiplier*. Philadelphia: Blakiston, 1943.

Machlup, F. "The Theory of Foreign Exchanges." In *Readings in the Theory of International Trade*, ed. H. S. Ellis and L. A. Metzler. Philadelphia: Blakiston, 1949, pp. 344–349.

Machlup, F. "Three Concepts of the Balance of Payments and the So-called Dollar Shortage." *Economic Journal*, 60, no. 1 (March 1950): 46–68.

Machlup, F. "The Terms of Trade Effects of Devaluation upon Real Income and the Balance of Trade." *Kyklos*, 4 (Fasc.) (1956): 417–452.

Machlup, F. "Adjustment, Compensatory Correction, and Financing of Imbalances in International Payments." In *Trade, Growth and the Balance of Payments: Essays in Honor of Gotfried Haberler*, ed. Richard E. Caves, Harry G. Johnson, and Peter B. Kenen. Chicago: Rand McNally, 1964.

Magee, Stephen P. "A Traditional and Empirical Examination of Supply and Demand Relationships in the U.S. International Trade." Unpublished study for the Council of Economic Advisors, 1970.

Magee, Stephen P. "Currency Contracts, Pass-Through and Devaluation." *Brookings Papere on Economic Activity*, no. 1 (1973): 303–325.

Magee, Stephen P. "Prices, Incomes, and Foreign Trade." In *International Trade and Finance*, ed. Peter Kenen. Cambridge: Cambridge University Press, 1975, p. 178.

Magee, Stephen P. "The Empirical Evidence on the Monetary Approach to the Balance of Payments and Exchange Rates," *American Economic Review Papers and Proceedings*, 66 (May 1976): 163–170.

Magee, Stephen P. "Contracting and Spurious Deviations from Purchasing Power Parity." In *The Economics of Exchange Rates*, ed. Jacob A. Frenkel and Harry G. Johnson. Reading, Mass.: Addison-Wesley, 1978, pp. 67–74.

Malindretos, John. "The Traditional and Monetary Approaches to the Balance of Payments: A Theoretical Comparison." *American Business Review*, 2 (June 1984): 31–42.

Malindretos, John. "A Theoretical and Empirical Comparison of the Two Theories of International Finance: The Case of the Federal Republic of Germany." Ph.D dissertation, Rutgers University, 1986.

Malindretos, John. "The Keynesian and the Monetary Approaches to International Finance: A Reexamination." *International Journal of Finance*, 1, no. 1 (Autumn 1988): 46–89.

Malindretos, John. "An Examination of the Two Views of International Finance for an Advanced, Medium Sized, Reserve Currency Country." In *Advances in Quantitative Analysis of Finance and Accounting*, vol. 1, part B, ed. Chen-Few Lee. Greenwich, Conn.: JAI Press, 1991, pp. 183–214.

Malindretos, John, and Demetri Tsanacas. "A Policy Orientation of the Criticisms of the Traditional Theory of International Finance in the Context of Fixed Exchange Rates." In *Quantity and Quality in Economic Research: Studies in Applied Business Research*, vol. 4, ed. T. H. Bonitsis and Roy C. Brown, Hampshire, U.K.: Ashate Publishing, 1997.

Manzur, Meher. "An International Comparison of Prices and Exchange Rates: A New Test of Purchasing Power Parity." *Journal of International Money and Finance*, 9, no. 1 (March 1990): 75–91.

Mark, Nelson. "Exchange Rates and Fundamental Evidence on Long-Horizon Predictability." *American Economic Review*, 85 (March 1995): 201–218.

Marquez, Jaimé, and Gary J. Schinasi. "Measures of Money and the Monetary Model of the Canadian-U.S. Dollar Exchange Rate." *Economic Letters*, 26 (1988): 183–188.

Marshall, Alfred. "The Present Position of Economics." 1885. Reprinted in *Memorials of Alfred Marshall*, ed. A. C. Pigou. London: Macmillan, 1925, pp. 152–174.

McKinnon, Ronald I. *Money in International Exchange*. New York: Oxford University Press, 1979.

Meade, James E. *The Theory of International Economic Policy. Volume 1: The Balance of Payments.* London: Oxford University Press, 1951, rpt. 1970.

Meese, Richard. "Currency Fluctuations in the Post–Bretton Woods Era." *Journal of Economic Perspectives,* 4 (Winter 1990): 117–134.

Meese, Richard A., and Kenneth Rogoff. "Empirical Exchange Rate Models of the Seventies: Do they Fit Out of Sample?" *International Economic Review,* 14 (February 1983): 3–24.

Meiselman D. I. "Worldwide Inflation: A Monetarist View." In *The Phenomenon of Worldwide Inflation,* ed. D. I. Meiselman and A. B. Laffer. Washington, D.C.: American Enterprise Institute for Public Policy Research, 1975, pp. 69–112.

Metzler, Allan H. "The Demand for Money: The Evidence from the Times Series." *Journal of Political Economy,* 71 (June 1963): 287–297.

Milberg, William S., and H. Peter Gray. "International Competitiveness and Policy in Dynamic Industries." *Banca Nazionale del Lavoro Quarterly Review* (March 1992): 59–80.

Miles, Marc A. "Currency Substitution, Flexible Exchange Rates, and Monetary Independence." *American Economic Review,* 68 (June 1978): 428–436.

Miles, Marc A. *Devaluation, the Trade Balance and the Balance of Payments.* New York: Marcel Dekker, 1978.

Miles, Marc A. "The Effects of Devaluation on the Trade Balance and the Balance of Payments: Some New Results." *Journal of Political Economy,* 87 (June 1979): 600–620.

Mishkin, Frederick S. "Are Real Interest Rates Equal across Countries? An Empirical Investigation of International Parity Conditions." *Journal of Finance,* 39, no. 5 (December 1984): 1345–1357.

Moazzami, Bakhtiar, and Kanhaya L. Gupta. "The Quantity Theory of Money and Its Long-Run Implications." *Journal of Macroeconomics,* 17, no. 4 (Fall 1995): 667–681.

Mundell, Robert A. "The Monetary Dynamics of International Adjustment under Fixed and Flexible Exchange Rates." *Quarterly Journal of Economics,* 74 (May 1960): 227–257.

Mundell, Robert A. "The Appropriate Use of Monetary and Fiscal Policy for Internal and External Stability." *International Monetary Fund Staff Papers,* 9, no. 1 (March 1962): 532–548.

Mundell, Robert A. "Capital Mobility and Stabilization Policy under Fixed and Flexible Exchange Rates." *Canadian Journal of Economics and Political Science,* 29 (1963): 475–485.

Mundell, Robert A. "Inflation and Real Interest." *Journal of Political Economy,* 71 (June 1963): 280–283.

Mundell, Robert A. *International Economics.* New York: Macmillan, 1968, pp. 111–133.

Mundell, Robert A. "Barter Theory and the Monetary Mechanism of Adjustment." In *Monetary Theory, Inflation, Interest Rates and Growth in the World Economy.* Pacific Palisades, Calif.: Goodyear Publishing, 1971, pp. 147–169.

Mundell, Robert A. "Inflation from an International Viewpoint." In *The Phenomenon of Worldwide Inflation,* ed. D. I. Meiselmann and A. B. Laffer. Washington, D.C.: American Enterprise Institute for Public Policy Research, 1975, pp. 141–152.

Murphy, R. G., and C. Van Duyne. "Asset Market Approaches to Exchange Rate Determinations: A Comparison Analysis.'' *Weltwirtschaftliches Archive*, 116, no. 4 (1980): 627–656.

Murray, Tracy, and Peter J. Ginman. ''An Empirical Examination of the Traditional Aggregate Import Demand Model.'' *Review of Economics and Statistics*, 58 (February 1976): 75–80.

Mussa, Michael. ''A Monetary Approach to Balance of Payments Analysis.'' *Journal of Money, Credit and Banking*, 6 (August 1974): 99.

Mussa, Michael. ''Tariffs and the Balance of Payments: A Monetary Approach.'' In *The Monetary Approach to the Balance of Payments*, ed. J. A. Frenkel and H. G. Johnson. Toronto: University of Toronto Press, 1976, pp. 187–221.

Niehans, Jurg. ''Interest Rates and the Balance of Payments: An Analysis of the Swiss Experience.'' In *Trade Growth and the Balance of Payments*, ed. R. E. Baldwin et al. Chicago: Rand McNally, 1965.

Niehans, Jurg. ''Monetary and Fiscal Policies in Open Economies under Fixed Exchange Rates: An Optimizing Approach.'' *Journal of Political Economy*, 76 (1968): 281–297.

Officer, Lawrence H. ''The Purchasing-Power-Parity Theory of Exchange Rates: A Review Article.'' *International Monetary Fund Staff Papers* (March 1976): 1–60.

Officer, Lawrence H., Edward I. Altman and Ingo Walter, eds. *Purchasing Power Parity and Exchange Rates: Theory, Evidence, and Relevance*. Vol. 35 of *Contemporary Studies in Economic and Financial Analysis*. London: JAI Press, 1982.

Ohlin, B. *Interregional and International Trade*. Cambridge, Mass.: Harvard University Press, 1933.

Orcutt, Guy H. ''Measurements of Price Elasticities in International Trade.'' *Review of Economics and Statistics*, 32 (May 1975): 117–132.

Osterwald-Lenum, M. ''Recalculated and Extended Tables of the Asymptotic Distribution of Some Important Maximum Likelihood Cointegrating Test Statistics.'' Working Paper, University of Copenhagen, 1992.

Polak, J. J. ''Monetary Analysis of Income Formation and Payment Problems.'' *International Monetary Fund Staff Papers*, 6 (1977): 1–50.

Poole, William. ''Speculative Prices as Random Walks: An Analysis of Ten Time Series of Flexible Exchange Rates.'' *Southern Journal of Economics*, 33 (April 1967): 468–478.

Putnam, Bluford H., and D. Sykes Wilford. ''International Reserve Flows: Seemingly Unrelated Regressions.'' In *The Monetary Approach to International Adjustment*, ed. B. H. Putnam and D. S. Wilford. New York: Praeger Publishers, 1978, pp. 71–84.

Putnam, Bluford H., and D. Sykes Wilford. ''Money, Income and Causality in the United States and the United Kingdom.'' *American Economic Review*, 68, no. 3 (June 1978): 423–427.

Rasulo, James A., and D. Sykes Wilford. ''Estimating Monetary Models of the Balance of Payments and Exchange Rates: A Bias.'' *Southern Economic Journal*, 47, no. 1 (July 1980): 136–146.

Rhomberg, Rudolf F., and Lorette Boisonneault. ''The Foreign Sector.'' In *The Brookings Quarterly Economic Model of the United States*. Chicago: Rand McNally, 1965, pp. 375–406.

Rivera-Batiz, Francisco L., and Luis A. Rivera-Batiz. *International Finance and Open Economy Macroeconomics*. New York: Macmillan, 1985.

Robinson, Joan. "The Foreign Exchanges." In *Essays in the Theory of Employment*. 2nd ed. Oxford: Blackwell, 1947. Reprinted in *Collected Economic Papers IV*. Cambridge, Mass.: MIT Press, 1973.

Rogalski, J., and Joseph D. Vinso. "Price Level Variations as Predictors of Flexible Exchange Rates." *Journal of International Business Studies*, 8, no. 1 (Spring/Summer 1977): 71–81.

Roosa, Robert V. "Capital Movements and Balance-of-Payments Adjustment." In *Money, and Policy Essays in Honor of Karl R. Bopp*, ed. David P. Eastburn. Philadelphia: Federal Reserve Bank of Philadelphia, 1970, pp. 171–194.

Rush, Mark, and Steven Husted. "Purchasing Power Parity in the Long Run." *Canadian Journal of Economics*, 18, no. 1 (February 1985): 137–145.

Salvatore, Dominick. "European and International Monetary Systems: Problems and Prospects." *The International Trade Journal*, 9 (Winter 1995): 453–474.

Samuelson, Paul A. *Foundations of Economic Analysis*. Cambridge, Mass.: Harvard University Press, 1947.

Samuelson, Paul A. "Theoretical Notes on Trade Problems." In *The Collected Scientific Papers of Paul A. Samuelson*, ed. Joseph E. Stiglitz. Vol. 2. Cambridge, Mass.: MIT Press, 1966, pp. 821–830.

Sarantis, Nicholas. "The Monetary Exchange Rate Model in the Long-Run: An Empirical Investigation." *Weltwirtschaftlisches Archiv*, 130, no. 4 (1994): 698–711.

Sarantis, Nicholas, and Chris Stewart. "Monetary and Asset Models for Sterling Exchange Rates: A Cointegration Approach." Economics Discussion Paper 93/1. United Kingdom: Kingston University, 1993.

Sarantis, Nicholas, and Chris Stewart. "Structural, VAR and BVAR Models of Exchange Rate Determination: A Comparison of Their Forecasting Performance." *Journal of Forecasting*, 14 (1995): 210–215.

Sedjo, Rojer A. "Price Trends, Economic Growth and the Canadian Balance of Trade: A Three Country Model." *Journal of Political Economy*, 79 (May–June 1971): 596–613.

Sohmen, Egon. "Fiscal and Monetary Policies under Alternative Exchange-Rate Systems." *Quarterly Journal of Economics*, 81, no. 3 (August 1967): 515–523.

Sohmen, Egon. "The Assignment Problem." In *Monetary Problems of the International Economy*, ed. R. A. Mundell and A. Swoboda. Chicago: University of Chicago Press, 1968.

Somanath, V. S. "Efficient Exchange Rate Forecasts: Lagged Models Better Than the Random Walk." *Journal of International Money and Finance*, 5 (June 1986): 195–220.

Sommariva, Andrea, and Giuseppe Tullio. "International Gold Flows in Gold Standard Germany: A Test of the Monetary Approach to the Balance of Payments 1880–1911." *Journal of Money, Credit and Banking*, 20 (February 1988): 132–140.

Swoboda, A. K. "Monetary Policy under Fixed Exchange Rates: Effectiveness, the Speed of Adjustment, and Proper Use." *Economica*, 40 (May 1973): 136–154.

Swoboda, A. K. "Gold, Dollars, Euro-Dollars, and the World Money Stock under Fixed Exchange Rates." *American Economic Review*, 68, no. 4 (September 1978): 625–642.

Tinbergen, Jan. *Economic Policy: Principles and Design*. Amsterdam: North Holland Publishing Company, 1964.

Tobin, James. "Liquidity Preference as Behavior towards Risk." *Review of Economic Studies*, 25, no. 1 (February 1958): 65–86.

Tobin, James. "Economic Progress and the International Monetary System." *Proceedings of the Academy of Political Science* (May 1963): 84–85.

Upson, Roger C. "Random Walk and Forward Exchange Rates: A Spectral Analysis." *Journal of Financial and Quantitative Analysis*, 7 (September 1972): 1897–1906.

Vernon, Raymond. "International Investment and International Trade in the Product Cycle." *Quarterly Journal of Economics*, 80 (May 1966): 190–207.

White, William H. "Bias in Export Substitution Elasticities Derived through Use of Cross-Section (Sub-Market) Data." Mimeographed manuscript, International Monetary Fund, 1970.

Whitman, Marina V. N. "Global Monetarism and the Monetary Approach to the Balance of Payments." *Brookings Papers on Economic Activity*, no. 3 (1975): 491–555.

Wilford, D. Sykes, and J. Richard Zecher. "Monetary Policy and the Balance of Payments in Mexico, 1955–75." *Journal of Money, Credit and Banking*, 11, no. 3 (August 1979): 340–348.

Wilson, William. "J-Curve Effect and Exchange Rate Pass-Through: An Empirical Investigation of the United States." *International Trade Journal*, 7, no. 4 (Summer 1993): 463–483.

Wolff, Christian C. P. "Exchange Rates, Innovations and Forecasting." *Journal of International Money and Finance*, 7 (1988): 49–61.

Zecher, Richard. "Monetary Equilibrium and International Reserve Flows in Australia." In *The Monetary Approach to the Balance of Payments*, ed. Jacob A. Frenkel and Harry G. Johnson. Toronto: University of Toronto Press, 1976, pp. 287–297.

Zellner, Arnold, and Claude Montmarquette. "A Study of Some Aspects of Temporal Aggregation Problems in Econometric Analyses." *Review of Economics and Statistics*, 53 (November 1971): 335–342.

Index

Absorption theory, 113, 174; versus Monetary theory, 98–102

Adjustment size and pace, of Keynesian versus Monetarist parameters, 146–47

Alexander, S. S., 83, 113

Almon polynomial distributed lag model, 128–29, 130

Analysis of variance test, 59

Arize, Augustine C., 35, 39, 153, 171

Armington world trade model, 44–45

Augmented Dickey-Fuller test, 226

Balance of payments: monetary nature of, 20–22, 62–64, 118–19; speed of adjustments to, 9, 25, 77. *See also* Monetary approach; Traditional approach

Balance of payments view (BPV) of exchange rate determination, 184–85, 201–3

Bickerdike, C. F., 113

Bonitsis, Theologos Homer, 83, 140

Capital account: empiricists and, 35; long-term (illiquid), 89–90, 99; models, 187–88; in Monetary approach, 27, 113; money market disturbances and, 117; short-term (liquid), 90–91; trade flows and, 35–38; in Traditional approach, empirical analysis of, 35–38, 116

Capital flows: capital-flow equations and, 56–57; as claims, 36; and money supply, under fixed exchange regime, 56–57; portfolio distribution model and, 35–36, 187; trade balance and, 35–38

Cassel, Gustav, 178

Central banking: automatic adjustment process, 115; problems, Monetary versus Absorption approach to, 102–5

Commercial policy, and monetary equilibrium, 18–20

Comparative statics framework, in Traditional model, 4–9

Competitiveness: international, and trade balance, 40, 45–50; market imperfections and, 84; in Traditional model, 137–38

Constant-market share (CIA) model, 43

Country size, 24–25, 85–86

Covered interest arbitrage, 183

Currency(ies): appreciation, and monetary equilibrium, 18; foreign and interest rates, 127; inconvertibility, in monetary theory, 30; international reserve status, 86–87; movements, threat of, 103–4

Currency devaluation: country size and, 24–25; currency substitution and, 29; deficit reduction and, 99, 101–2; monetary equilibrium and, 17, 18; official

Tariffs, 19, 92
Technological improvements, 26–27, 85
Terms of trade: disturbance in, 27; exchange rate changes and, 18; single equation model and, 174
Tessema, Asrat, 200
Tobin, James, 187, 190
Trade account, in Keynesian approach, 118–19
Trade balance: capital account flows and, 35–38; currency devaluation and, 18, 101–2; deficits, in Absorption theory versus Monetary theory, 99–102; fundamental determination of, 40, 45; income effects and, 50–52; international competitiveness and, 40, 45–50; Monetary model of, 125–26, 135–36; real income increases and, 21; in Traditional model, 127–28, 137, 141–42; world trade models and, 44–45
Trade transactions, international, exchange-rate volatility and, 155
Trade value elasticities of demand, 44–45

Traditional (Keynesian) theory, 15, 114–21, 142–43; assumption of market perfection in, 84; critique of, 83–95; current account in, 39–52; exchange rate changes in, 17, 18; flow perspective in, 22, 25; goods ands services as focus of, 114; money demand in, 21–22; nonrelevance of monetary factors in, 92; reserve currency status in, 87–88; as static equilibrium model, 4–9, 94; trade balance model in, 127–28, 141–42
Transfer account, and external adjustment, 88, 89
Tsanacas, Demetri, 15

Unbiased forward rate hypothesis (UFRH), in exchange-rate determination, 185–86
Unified equity market hypothesis, 59
U.S. dollar, possible flight from, 105–6

Walras's law, 23, 114, 115
World equilibrium, 58–60
World trade models, 44–45

About the Editors and Contributors

AUGUSTINE C. ARIZE is Professor of Statistics at the Department of General Business and Systems Management at Texas A&M University–Commerce. His research has appeared in several journals, including the *Journal of Business and Economic Statistics, International Advances in Economic Research, Review of Financial Economics*, the *Journal of Post-Keynesian Economics* and the *Southern Economic Journal*.

THEOLOGOS HOMER BONITSIS is Associate Professor of Finance at the School of Management at New Jersey Institute of Technology as well as a member of The Graduate Faculty of Rutgers University. He has been a Visiting Scholar at Columbia University in New York City. His research interests are in the areas of international finance and economic competitiveness. His research has been published in *The Journal of Applied Business Research, The International Journal of Finance* and *The International Journal of Economic Studies*. He is the editor of the ongoing research volume of the International Society of Statistical Science in Economics titled *Quantity and Quality in Economic Research, Studies in Applied Business Research*. Dr. Bonitsis is a reviewer for several professional journals and is listed in *Marquis Who's Who in Finance and Industry*.

IOANNIS N. KALLIANIOTIS is Associate Professor of Finance at the Arthur J. Kania School of Management at the University of Scranton, Pennsylvania. He has also held teaching and research appointments at the City University of New York, Rutgers University, and at financial institutions in Greece. His research interests are in the areas of international finance and financial institutions.

His research has appeared in many journals, including *Quarterly Economic Review, Greek Economic Review, International Journal of Commerce and Management* and *International Research in the Business Disciplines.*

KRISHNA M. KASIBHATLA is Associate Professor of Economics and Chair of the Department of Business and Economics at Bennett College, Greensboro, North Carolina. Dr. Kasibhatla's research interests are in the areas of monetary economics and international finance. His research has been published in various publications such as *New Advances in Finance and Economics, International Journal of Finance, Rivissta Internazionale, International Business and Economics* and *Detroit Business Journal.*

JOHN MALINDRETOS is currently employed at Global Financial Management and Consulting, Inc. Previously he held academic professional appointments as an Associate Professor of Finance at St. John's University in New York and New Jersey Institute of Technology. He has numerous publications in professional journals and research volumes, such as *Advances in Quantitative Analysis of Finance and Accounting, Applied Economic Letters, Business Journal, International Journal of Finance* and the *Journal of Business and Society.*

GILLES DUTEIL is Professor of Finance at CETFI–University d' Aix-Marseille III, Aix en Provence, France and Director of the Trading Room at CESIB–Groupe ESC Marseille, France.

VALERIE ENGLANDER is Professor of Economics at St. John's University. Her research interests are in the areas of public finance and program evaluation. Dr. Englander's research has been published in *The American Economist, The Journal of Behavioral Economics* and the *Journal of Business Ethics.*

BILL FRANCIS is Assistant Professor of Finance at the University of South Florida. His research interest centers on international finance, macro-finance and capital markets. His research has been published in *Applied Financial Economics, Global Finance Journal* and *European Financial Management.*

DILIP K. GHOSH, Professor of Finance at St. John's University in New York, is the editor of *The International Journal of Finance* and the associate editor of three other academic journals. He is Director of The Institute of Policy Analysis and one of the founding members of the International Trade and Finance Association. In addition, he has reviewed grant proposals for the National Science Foundation and advised financial firms. Dr. Ghosh's research has appeared in numerous academic journals.

DEMETRIOS GIANNAROS is Professor of Economics at the University of Hartford and is a Connecticut State Representative. He has taught at Boston University, Suffolk University and Jagiellonian University in Krakow, Poland.

Dr. Giannaros has been a Yale Visiting Faculty Fellow and an American Council on Education Fellow. He has served as Director of the U.S. Consortium for Management Education in Central and Eastern Europe. His research has been published in the *Journal of Macroeconomics, International Economic Journal* and the *Journal of Economic Development.*

H. PETER GRAY is Professor Emeritus of Economics and Finance, Rutgers University and Rensselaer Polytechnic Institute. He is past president of the Eastern Economic Association and the International Trade and Finance Association. He is the author of *Global Economic Involvement: A Synthesis of Modern International Economics* (1999) and is currently concerned with the contribution of globalization to the erosion of the resilience of the international financial system.

ELIAS C. GRIVOYANNIS is an Associate Professor in the Economics Department at Yeshiva University in New York City. His prior academic experience includes positions at New York University and the University of North Carolina. He has published numerous journal articles, two monographs and textbooks and several books of readings. His most recent research monograph is titled *Current Issues of Monetary Policy in the U.S. and Japan: Predictability of Money Demand.*

IFTEKHAR HASAN is Professor of Finance at New Jersey Institute of Technology. He is also a member of The Graduate Faculty of Rutgers University. Professor Hasan's research interests include financial institutions and their profit efficiency. His research has been published in several journals, including the *Journal of Money, Credit, and Banking, Financial Review* and *International Review of Economics and Finance.*

MELVIN JOHNSON is Associate Vice Chancellor for Academic Affairs for Technology and Telecommunications at North Carolina A&T State University, Greensboro, North Carolina. He has been a Nissan Fellow and an American Banking Association Ayres Fellow. Dr. Johnson's research has been published in the *Journal of Social Behavior and Personality, The International Journal of Finance* and *Finance in the New World Order.*

PAUL R. KUTASOVIC is Associate Professor of Finance and Economics at the New York Institute of Technology and is Director of Economic Analysis at Thomas Conoscenti & Associates, a firm specializing in regional economic analysis and municipal financing. Dr. Kutasovic's research has been published in *Managerial Finance in the Corporate Economy, Journal of Business Economics,* and the *Journal of State and Local Finance.*

STANLEY J. LAWSON is Professor of Economics and Finance at St. John's University and is a former International Civil Servant of the United Nations.

His field of specialization is international trade and investment. He has written six books and numerous book chapters.

JAMES R. LOTHIAN is University Distinguished Professor of Finance in the School of Business Administration of Fordham University and editor of the *Journal of International Money and Finance*. He has been a Visiting Professor of Economics at the Stern School of Business at New York University. He has published on domestic and foreign economic and financial topics. His research has appeared in the *American Economic Review, Journal of Political Economy*, and the *Journal of Monetary Economics*. In addition, Dr. Lothian has been a Research Associate at the National Bureau of Economic Research, a Visiting Scholar at the International Monetary Fund and a consultant to the Board of Governors of the Federal Reserve System.

ABRAHAM MULUGETTA is Professor of Finance and International Business and Founder and Director of the Center for Trading and Analysis of Financial Instruments, Ithaca College, Ithaca, New York. He is the author of numerous publications and is a frequent participant at national and international conferences on international trade, finance and foreign exchange.

LUIS EDUARDO RIVERA-SOLIS is Associate Professor of Finance and Division Coordinator at the School of Business at Dowling College, Oakdale, New York. Dr. Rivera has written extensively on the Spanish banking system. His articles have appeared in *The Journal of Applied Business Research, International Journal of Finance*, and *The Journal of Business and Society*. He has served as a board member of the Northeast Business and Economics Association and the Northeast Decision Sciences Institute.

ASRAT TESSEMA is Professor and Chairperson of the Department of Finance at Eastern Michigan University. His areas of research are corporate finance, international finance, and mergers and acquisitions.

DEMETRI TSANACAS is Professor of Business and Chair of the Division of Business and Economics at Ferrum College, Ferrum, Virginia. He is the author of numerous research papers published in the *Detroit Journal of Business, The Journal of Business Issues*, and the *Banca Nazionale Del Lavoro Quarterly Review*. His areas of expertise are international trade and finance and money and banking. Dr. Tsanacas was honored as the outstanding faculty member of the year and is the recipient of numerous grants from the Ford Foundation, the Mellon Foundation, and the Wal-Mart Foundation. He is founder and mentor of the award winning Students in Free Enterprise–SIFE Chapter at Ferrum College.